Chinese Cuisine from the Master Chefs of China

Little, Brown and Company

Boston   Toronto

The original idea of creating a book of authentic Chinese recipes for Western readers was first worked out with the editors of *China Pictorial* by John Mack Carter, Editor-in-Chief of *Good Housekeeping* magazine. The material in this work was gathered and photographed specifically for this purpose in the People's Republic of China by the editors of *China Pictorial* magazine, a division of the Foreign Languages Publications Bureau of the Chinese government. The Chinese material was edited for Western readers, and the book was planned, designed, and produced by Allen D. Bragdon Publishers Inc., 153 West 82nd Street, New York, New York 10024, which is responsible for licensing outside of China.

The following individuals joined in our work:

China Pictorial, Beijing, China

Editor-in-Chief: Sun Yifu (member of *China Pictorial* editorial board)

Editors: Xin Jiguang, Xiao Shiling

Photographers: He Shiyao, Wang Deying, Sha Renwen, Zhang Xiusheng, Sun Yifu

Contributing Photographers: Qian Hao (member of *China Pictorial* editorial board), Huang Lukui, Huang Taopeng, Zhao Mingqing, Gao Mingyi, Wang De, Chen Heyi, Zeng Xiangmin, Li Zhenting, Li Changjie

Illustrator: Cai Rong

Translators: Deng Xin (member of *China Pictorial* editorial board), Cui Sigan, Zhang Zongzhi, Bian Youfen, Huang Shang

Allen D. Bragdon Publishers Inc., New York, USA

Editor-in-Chief: Allen D. Bragdon

Designer: John B. Miller

Testing: David Dembo, with assistance from Dorothea Li, Grace Young

Text Editor: Susan Rhodes, The Asia Society

Contributing Editors: Chris Foley, Dorothea Li, Bernd Metz (index), Margaret Spader, Dee Wang

The American editors acknowledge with thanks the assistance by Edward Tripp of the Yale University Press and his permission to excerpt brief quotations from *Food in Chinese Culture*, edited by K.C. Chang, Yale Univ. Press, 1977; and the assistance of Richard Bush of The Asia Society's China Council and his permission to reprint "A Note on Romanization" from *The People's Republic of China: A Basic Handbook*, 3rd edition. We are grateful for the timely assistance of Jim Hinkley, Helen Kessler, Charles Byrne, Pan American Airways, and Yvonne Wong.

LITTLE, BROWN AND COMPANY
Boston • Toronto

Copyright © 1983 by *China Pictorial* and Allen D. Bragdon Publishers Inc.

Published simultaneously in Canada by Little, Brown & Company (Canada) Limited

Library of Congress Catalog Card No. 83-81-564

ISBN 0 316 54994 0

Printed in The Netherlands

from the Eastern editors

Chinese cuisine has a long history. It is a precious cultural legacy, and must be carried on and developed. Eventually it will enrich people's lives and promote cultural exchanges with other countries.

Mao Dun

from the Western editors

It's the skill of the chef, not the origin of the ingredients that counts.

Chinese Proverb

Contents

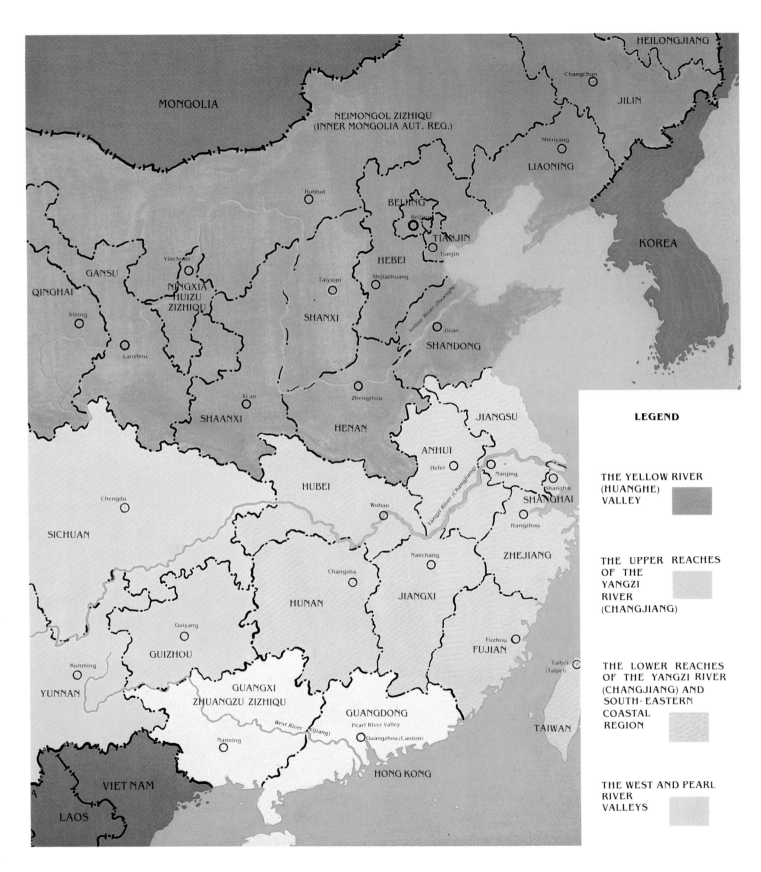

LEGEND

THE YELLOW RIVER (HUANGHE) VALLEY

THE UPPER REACHES OF THE YANGZI RIVER (CHANGJIANG)

THE LOWER REACHES OF THE YANGZI RIVER (CHANGJIANG) AND SOUTH-EASTERN COASTAL REGION

THE WEST AND PEARL RIVER VALLEYS

The Land

土　地

Be born in Soochow (known for the beauty of its women);
Eat in Kwangchow (known for its superb cooking);
Dress in Hangchow (where the finest silk brocades are woven);
Die in Liuchow (where the best wood for making coffins grows).

Old Saying

The People's Republic of China is such a vast country, with such diversity of climate, agricultural products, customs, and traditions that in order to understand its cuisine one must first understand how it differs from region to region.

Chinese cuisine is divided into four large geographic regions. Each of these encompasses a number of political provinces with distinctive cuisines; sometimes even cities within a province (seacoast vs. inland, for example) will be known for distinct techniques of cooking or flavorings.

The Yellow River (Huanghe) Valley to the North.
Shandong cuisine dominates this area. Shandong restaurants are famous in Hebei and Henan provinces and northwestern China. Their dishes are rich, but light in taste, because they are stir-fried quickly at high temperatures. The most frequently used flavorings are garlic and scallions, though in the north, leeks are sometimes used in place of scallions. In this region, there are also Henan, Shanxi (Shansi), Shaanxi (Shensi), Gansu, and Beijing cuisines. *Henan* Province, a major wheat producer, lies in the middle of the Yellow River Valley. Carp are plentiful and many peasant families raise chickens. As a result, Henan is famous for its fish, chicken, and egg dishes. "Sweet and Sour Fish Squares with Baked Noodles," "Daokou Fried Chicken," and "Skillet Baked Eggs," are examples included in this book. *Shanxi* is known for salty dishes and for sweet and sour specialties. Vinegar is a common condiment. *Gansu* and *Shaanxi* provinces are situated in the upper reaches of the Yellow River. Their cooks tend to preserve the original form, color, taste, and juices of the raw ingredients while they are cooking, rather than first mincing, disguising, and reforming them with spectacular culinary sleight-of-hand.

One day an especially irascible ruler of Shaanxi ordered that a chicken be prepared for him. He liked his meat cooked thoroughly but insisted that it retain the shape that nature bestowed upon it. Two of his chefs failed and were beheaded. The third chef, who was both highly motivated and clever, stuffed the chicken and bound it all around with fine thread, like a cocoon. When the bird was cooked and the thread removed it was crispy, fragrant, cooked all the way through and, like the chef, remained intact. Today it is called "Gourd Chicken."

The Shaanxi cuisine, originated in Xi'an, has carried on these Han and Tang Dynasty styles.

THE IMPERIAL PALACE

The construction of a suitable palace for the emperor of China in Beijing spanned two centuries. Its present configuration of 9000 halls and chambers was completed in 1420 during the 18th year of the Yong Le reign, that of the third emperor of the Ming Dynasty. This complex, which covered 178 acres (720,000 sq. m) was begun during the 13th century Yuan Dynasty. When the Yong Le emperor seized the throne, the Ming forces had their capital in Nanjing, Jiangsu Province. The new emperor, who had been Prince of Yan (in the north), naturally relocated the seat of government to the center of his native city (modern-day Beijing). Apparently, it was an effective move, for the Imperial Palace served as office and residence for the next 24 Ming and Qing emperors for a total of 490 years, and Beijing remains the capital of modern China.

THE TEMPLE OF HEAVEN

In 1420, the Yong Le emperor of the Ming Dynasty had the Temple of Heaven built in the southern section of Beijing. Generations of Ming and Qing emperors visited its main structure, the Hall of Prayer of Good Harvests, on the winter solstice, in the hopes of ensuring a fruitful year. Although this temple towers at 125 feet (38 m) and is 99 feet (30 m) in diameter, it was built without the use of a single beam.

THE GREAT WALL

From the shore of Bohai Bay in the east to the desert of Gansu Province in the west, the Great Wall of China spans the country. It is known among the Chinese as the "10,000 li Wall." This is not an exaggeration, for the actual measure of the wall is 12,000 li, or about 3750 miles (6000 km).

The Great Wall had humble beginnings. From 476 to 221 B.C. (the Warring States Period) rulers of independent kingdoms put up separate walls in strategic areas to ward off invasions. The first emperor of the Qin Dynasty (221 to 207 B.C.) unified China by force and began the gargantuan task of connecting each existing section, taking the wall up hill and down dale with the changing terrain. Indeed, the project was not completed until the Ming Dynasty, some 1500 years later.

Far from being just a long, solid wall, passes were constructed at various points; and in one section, between Juyong Pass and Badaling Outpost, it is complete with parapets, watch towers, and shooting slots. The shooting slots face only one way, north, where the invasions came from. The average height of this section is 22 feet (6.6 m) and is wide enough for five horses to gallop abreast over huge stone slabs that pave its top. To build that wall, workers moved 138 million cubic yards (124.2 million cu. m) of earth and another third that much of stone—all by hand.

STONE CAVES AT YUNGANG

At the base of the Wuzhou Hills in the western outskirts of Datong in the province of Shanxi, are sandy-colored stone caves filled with images of Buddha, bodhisattvas (potential Buddhas), and flying fairies. There are 51,000 figures in all, ranging in size from a few inches to over 55 feet (17 m). This vast treasure house of man's art is all the more awesome displayed within the random arts of nature.

THE PAGODA FOREST AT SHAOLIN TEMPLE

In Henan Province, in the western shadow of the sacred mountain Songshan, the Zen sect of Buddhism and the martial art of Shaolin wushu were born. Each time a Shaolin monk died, a pagoda was built on the spot where his ashes had been laid to rest. Thus in the years between 618 and 911 was created a forest of pagodas 275 yards (247.5 m) west of their monastery.

It was said that the number of pagodas was so great that no one could successfully count them. The Qian Long emperor of the Qing Dynasty took up the challenge and sent 500 of his soldiers into the graveyard, telling each one to stand by one of the pagodas. The soldiers appeared to be outnumbered! In fact the 220 pagodas stood in such dense foliage and their bulk was so large that two or three soldiers could have been standing on different sides of the same one without seeing each other. The Qian Long emperor was fooled.

Beijing (once spelled Peking) was, for much of China's imperial history, the national capital. The emperors' tastes and standards mixed with Mongol and Muslim meat-eaters' from the rugged, feisty northern cultures, and the bureaucrats, most of whom came from Shandong, made a market for their native cuisine. Thus, a conglomerate of cooking styles evolved in Beijing which attracted the best chefs from the provinces.

The Imperial Palace dominates Beijing architecturally even now. The imperial or court *genre* of cuisine is distinguished by exotic ingredients, by the high degree of technical skill required to prepare it, and by the auspicious names given its dishes. Bear's paw, camel's hump, dried caribou nose, and the testicles of tigers were obtainable—but only by command of the emperor who had limitless resources. In the imperial court a peasant's life was cheap. An incompetent cook in the royal kitchen was no exception. Conversely, favors were given to those who pleased. This atmosphere stimulated competition among the capital's chefs to perfect techniques of food preparation, presentation, and decoration. As is the practice of cosmopolitan cooks worldwide, the chefs in Beijing bestowed such flowery and auspicious titles upon their works as: "Royal Family Happiness" or "Dragon and Phoenix Offer Prosperity" (the dragon is a symbol for emperors; the phoenix for empresses).

An imperial dinner usually included dozens of dishes. Court records show that on the 11th day of the second month of 1762, the Qian Long emperor had 19 dishes for breakfast, and 37 dishes for supper. In the 19th century the Empress Dowager Ci Xi demanded 100 dishes for each meal. Of course, she could only have found time to glance at most of them. Today, on a more modest scale, court cuisine is still served in Beijing at the *Fangshan* and *Tingliguan* restaurants.

THE INNER MONGOLIAN GRASSLAND

There are 55 minority nationalities. Of these groups in China that make up a little over five percent of the population, 3.4 million are Mongolians who mostly inhabit the Inner Mongolian Autonomous Region in the cold, northeastern plains. Pictured here is a summer settlement of Mongolian herdsmen in the Hulun Buir League.

INNER MONGOLIAN SHEEP

The tasty, tender beef and mutton (lamb) served in the Beijing restaurants come from the pastures of Inner Mongolia. Mongol sheep herders raise an especially tender and mild-flavored breed of short-tailed sheep used for meat in the famous Mongolian hot-pot dishes.

STONE LIONS AT PAGODA GATE

These somewhat comic, yet ferocious looking lions guard the pagoda gate of the North Tomb. The elaborate workmanship places them among China's most highly valued works of art.

Mongolian cooking features lamb—thin, raw slices dipped at table by the diner in a "hot pot's" boiling broth, or shredded and grilled with fresh coriander on a hot griddle. A Muslim lamb feast held on the rugged plains to the north of the Great Wall could easily have 128 courses, punctuated by entertainment and feats of competitive horsemanship.

CHENGDU'S LANTERN FESTIVAL

The fifteenth day of the first month of the Lunar Calendar is China's national lantern festival. Chengdu, capital of Sichuan Province, started this festival in the Tang Dynasty (618–907). Houses and streets were beautifully decked with lanterns of colored paper for the holiday-makers. Today, in Chengdu, the festival is celebrated in the Cultural Park. Floral lamps are hung everywhere. Strings of lights blink amidst pine and cypress trees. The halls and pavilions are silhouetted by colored bulbs, and the floating lamps make spectacular reflections in the water.

MOUNT EMEI

The song of a bird, the gibbering of a monkey, and the soft murmuring of a creek greet the ear. The ancient monasteries and temples that dot the wooded slope suggest the peace of a Buddhist shrine. Worshippers and tourists come to Sichuan Province to climb almost 37 miles (60 km) of mountain path to the apex of Mount Emei. The other three Buddhist Mountains in China are Mount Puto in Zhejiang Province, Mount Jiuhua in Anhui Province, and Mount Wutai in Shanxi Province.

The Upper Reaches of the Yangzi River (Changjiang).

The *Sichuan* cuisine predominates in this region (southwestern China). The vast and fertile Sichuan Province has plenty of rainfall and is known as "the land of abundance." Inhabitants developed a full quiver of food preparation techniques including steaming, frying, stir-frying, and deep-frying ingredients, many of which they also had dried, salted, pickled, and otherwise preserved. Since Sichuan weather is damp, hot pepper, black pepper, prickly ash (a cooking mixture of salt and ground pepper), and ginger root are traditionally used as both flavoring and pharmacopoeia to "drive off humidity inside the body." A special emphasis is placed on diversity of flavors. The Chinese character for a typical Sichuan flavor means "odd" (sometimes translated as "ridiculous") and it is a term of praise. That flavor, at once hot, salty, sour, and sweet, comes from a mixture of soy sauce, vinegar, sesame, peanuts, preserved egg juice, prickly ash powder, and broad bean sauce. Two dishes with this flavoring are "'Odd Taste' Chicken Threads," and "'Odd Taste' Rabbit." A small number of Sichuan dishes, however, are not spicy. The best known among these are "Crisp and Fragrant Chicken," "Camphor-Tea Duck," "Bamboo and Chicken," "Bean Dreg Duck," and "Beancurd with Mushrooms."

THE YANGZI RIVER (CHANGJIANG)

One of the four longest rivers in the world, 3900 miles (6300 km), the Yangzi (Changjiang) rises in the Tanggula Mountains on the Qinghai-Tibet Plateau, and empties into the East China Sea near Shanghai. It collects water from 700 tributaries, in a basin 695,000 square miles (1.03 million km), supporting a river valley population of 300 million. The Three Gorges, the Wu, Xiling, and Qutang run between Fengjie County in Sichuan Province and Yichang in Hubei Province for 128 miles (204 km). Sheer rocks rise dramatically from the banks only a little over 100 yards (90 m) apart as the river twists and turns at its narrowest point.

The Middle and Lower Reaches of the Yangzi River (Changjiang) and Southeastern Coastal Regions

This region of many lakes and rivers includes Jiangsu, Zhejiang, Anhui, and Fujian Provinces. Jiangsu and Zhejiang cuisines are typical. They use only a few ingredients, small quantities of oil, and their taste is slightly sweet. Dishes are stewed, simmered, or steamed, and care is taken to retain the original juices. The best-known dishes of these provinces are made from fresh-water eel, turtle, and crab. Wild rice stems, winter bamboo, mushrooms, edible fungi, and beans are the most common vegetables. In the Jiangsu region, Huaiyang cuisine is considered superior, and in the Zhejiang region, Hangzhou cuisine is most popular. Hangzhou is set on beautiful, bountiful West Lake, which was created by the emperor to enhance the beauty of the city he chose for his summer residence. Favorites are "Sour West Lake Fish," "Dragon Tea Shrimps" (a tiny fresh water variety), and "West Lake Water-Shield Soup" (water shield, a watercress-like vegetable, grows *only* in Hangzhou).

Anhui cuisine, also famous, is represented by 100 restaurants in Shanghai. This cuisine of the mountains and sea is renowned for its game and fish dishes: "Steamed Chukar" (Partridge), "Stewed Shark's Fin," "Stewed Ham and Bamboo," and "Chicken Stewed with Rock Mushroom."

Anhui cuisine derives its character from large amounts of oil, the dark color given the food by a dark, uniquely flavored local soy sauce, and long cooking on a low fire. Southern Anhui is a tea-growing area and its people like their tea strong. They also believe that oil helps digestion. The hilly, heavily wooded land of the southern area provides the luxury of ample charcoal for long, low-heat cooking times. The local clay makes excellent earthen pots inside which the food can cook, almost sealed, so its liquids do not escape in steam.

SICHUAN FRUITS

Packing oranges and tangerines in the province of Sichuan for shipment through China.

MOUNT HUANG (HUANGSHAN)

Mount Huang's 72 main peaks hide in seas of clouds over a mile (1585 m) above sea level. It is 222 miles (330 km) south of Hefei, capital of Anhui Province. The regal beauty of its oddly shaped rock pinnacles, grotesque, wind-twisted pines, and hot springs prompted Xu Xiake, the great traveler of the Ming Dynasty, to call it the King of Mountains. The King's crown, its highest peak, is fittingly shaped like a lotus flower.

THE OU RIVER (OUJIANG)

Meandering in southern Zheijiang Province, the Ou River passes through Lishui and Qingtian counties and empties into the East China Sea near the city of Wenzhou. The river abounds in fish and shrimp. Green mountains stand on both sides in the shade of tallow trees.

The cuisine of *Fujian* Province, which is bordered by the Taiwan Strait, is predominantly seafood, including two widely used local condiments, shrimp sauce and shrimp paste. Fujian dishes are colorful, and slightly sweet, utilizing granulated sugar to cut the grease. Fermented grain mash and five spices powder (prickly ash, star anise, cinnamon, clove, and fennel) are used for seasoning. The famous dish "Buddha Leaps the Wall" consists of abalone, sea cucumber, shark's fin, dried scallop, chicken, and duck. (It has such a tempting fragrance that, it is said, a monk leaped over the temple wall in his determination to taste it.)

WEST LAKE

The exquisitely elegant West Lake borders the 2100-year-old city of Hangzhou, capital of Zhejiang Province. This historic city was made the capital of the State of Wuyue (907–947) and later, of the Southern Song Dynasty (1127–1279), because the emperor considered it the most beautiful city in all China. During the Northern Song Dynasty (960–1127), poet Su Dongpo was the magistrate of Hangzhou. He often compared the beauty of West Lake to the beauty of Lady Xi Shi in his Spring and Autumn period (B.C. 770–476). The lake, also known as Xi Shi Lake, is nested among lush green mountains on three sides. It is dotted with small islands, with vermilion pavilions connected by zigzag walkways through pools glittering with golden carp.

SHANGHAI

Shanghai, located at the mouth of the Yangzi River, has been one of the world's most famous ports since the 17th century. Its name has long been synonymous with adventure and intrigue. Many consider it still to be the most westernized, sophisticated city in modern China, partly because for centuries it was China's international commercial and banking center, partly for its famous university, and partly for its rank as the most populous city in the largest nation on earth.

SIKA DEER

Large herds of Sika deer are raised like cattle on a farm on Hainan Island, off the southeastern coast of Guangdong Province.

LUNAN STONE FORESTS

At Lunan, Yunnan Province, grotesque stony peaks burst out from the ground. Many legends have collected around these wonders of nature. One runs that when Immortal Zhang Guolao came to the place where the stone forests of Lunan now stand, he saw boys and girls courting each other on a piece of flat land. There was no privacy at all. Zhang immediately moved mountains of rocks from afar to give shelter to their gentle feelings. In fact, 200 million years ago, Lunan was part of a vast ocean with a limestone sea bottom that was thrust up above the surface, then etched by the weather into spectacular forms. The Stone Forest covers an area of some 103 square miles (266 sq. km) of land. It is 75 miles (110 km) from Kunming, capital of Yunnan Province.

THE LI RIVER (LIJIANG)

"The river is a blue ribbon; the hills jade hairpins." This is how Han Yu (768–824), writer of the Tang Dynasty, saw the Li River of Guangxi. The Li rises at Miao'er Mountain, Xingan County of Guangxi, flowing 62 miles (92 km) between Guilin and Yangshuo. The landscape is like a picture scroll: green water, mysterious caves, and elegant rocks. Tourists are of the same opinion, "Guilin's scenery is the best on earth; but Yangshuo's is even better than Guilin's." The land along the Li River belongs to the typical karst formation. The peaks and caves are masterpieces of nature.

SEVEN STAR CRAGS

In Zhao County, Guangdong Province, seven stony peaks rise from Star Lake, in the shape of the Big Dipper. Bridges and pathways connect these seven wonders of nature, so that man may walk the way of the stars.

The Pearl River Valley in the South

The cuisine of *Guangdong* Province (the capital of which is Guangzhou (Canton)) is the most famous in this region. This province's sub-tropical climate, its customs and traditions differ greatly from those of the Yellow River and Yangzi River Valleys. Traditionally Guangdong cuisine has been characterized as requiring a bizarre variety of ingredients, among them snake, cat, raccoon, dog, monkey, wild goose, sparrow, rice worm, and mouse. This is more myth than truth in contemporary cuisine.

Dishes made from cobra and the flesh of other poisonous reptiles, braised, stewed, stir-fried, and deep-fried, have been served in China for 2000 years. Snake meat, sometimes combined with other ingredients, has long been considered a tonic especially good for arthritis and anemia.

Frequently, the main ingredient of a dish is cooked whole, rather than cut into pieces. Roast suckling pig, considered a delicacy, is seasoned inside and out, then roasted over a charcoal fire until the skin turns a crispy golden brown and the tender flesh can be sliced very thin. The best known local condiments are oyster sauce and curry-in-oil, both widely exported. The chefs of Guangdong even tint their cornstarch mixtures to match the color of the dish they have created.

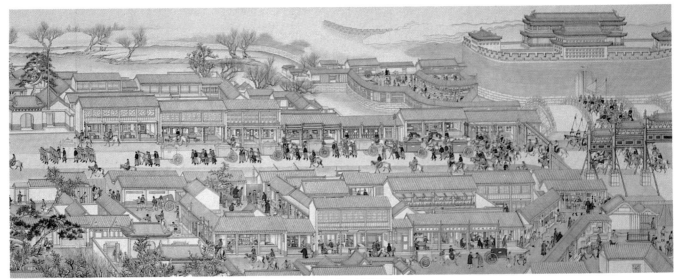

THE IMPERIAL CAPITAL

This detail section of a full city plan that measures 1½ feet high (32 cm) depicts a portion of Beijing during the Ming Dynasty (1368-1644). The original map from which this detail comes is in the collection of the Museum of Chinese History in Beijing.

Beijing PICTURE PORTFOLIO

China's current capital city, now called Beijing, has existed for almost 3000 years, although it wasn't always the capital. It started as a farming settlement called Ji, in the early Zhou Dynasty, about 1100 B.C. It is located at the northern edge of a great plain, near one of two passes in the mountains that formed the northern border of China. Because of the rugged surrounding terrain, it was able to hold at bay the constant threat of invasion by tribes from the north. For most of its early history it was little more than a garrison town. During its first two thousand years, it was destroyed and rebuilt several times under a variety of different names.

Most Chinese cities built during the imperial period followed the ideal plan for a city described in one chapter of an ancient text, "The Rites of Zhou," written in the early, semi-mythological years of the Zhou Dynasty (1122–221 B.C.). According to this ancient text, the walls of a new town or city should be built in a square shape around tramped earth or laid stones; it should be oriented on a north-south axis; the important buildings should be erected, facing south, on raised earthwork platforms; the palace area should be placed in the center of the city's walls.

In 1215 A.D. Genghis Khan invaded the city and totally destroyed it. During the Khan's Mongol rule, it was rebuilt, again according to the traditional Zhou Dynasty model, and named Dadu, capital of the Mongol Yuan Dynasty, which Marco Polo visited and described with wonder when he returned. Nearly 200 years passed before the Ming armies captured the city from the Mongol Yuan. The Ming ruler moved his capital from Nanjing (in the south) up to Dadu (in the north) and in 1406, plans were begun to transform the city into the new capital of the Ming Dynasty, the remnants of which can still be found in modern Beijing. It was to consist of an Inner City surrounded by an Outer City, totaling 24 square miles (62 sq. km). The walls of the Outer City were immense; the southern side measured five miles long when construction was abandoned. The outer wall was to serve as fortification, but, as with most of the imperial structures, its design was also dictated by religious and cultural beliefs. The outer wall protected the Temple of Heaven to which the emperor journeyed twice a year from the Inner City. The relationship of the walls to both the Imperial Inner City and the Temple of Heaven in the Outer City can be seen in the accompanying map.

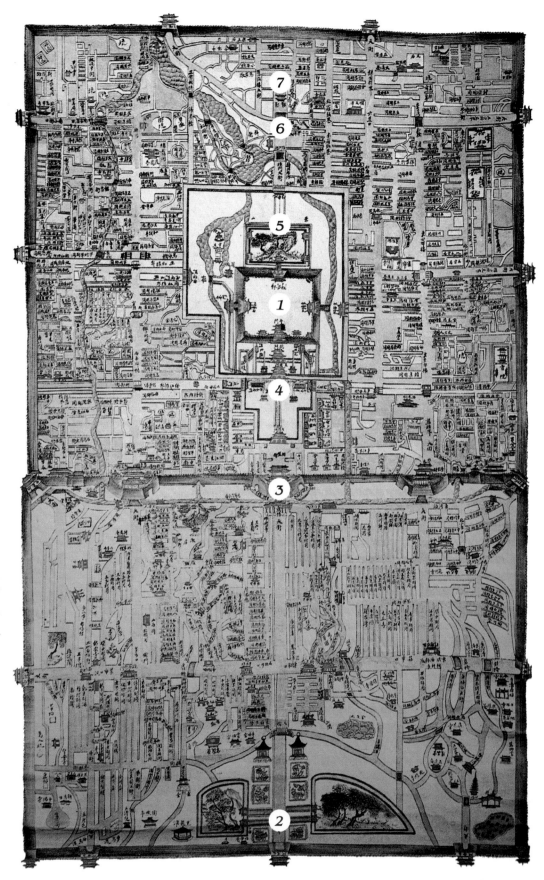

A MAP OF 18TH CENTURY BEIJING

One of the salient points of the city plan for old Beijing is the dominating north-south axial line that runs through the center of the Forbidden City (1). It starts at the Yongding Gate (2) in the center of the Outer City, passes through the Zheng-yang Gate (or Front Gate(Qianmen))(3), of the Inner City, the Gate of Heavenly Peace (4) of the Forbidden City, Coal Hill's (Jingshan) central peak (5), and stops at the Drum Tower (6) and the Bell Tower (7) in the north district. The entire length is about five miles (8 km). The Three Front Halls (symbols of imperial power) and the Three Back Halls (the emperor's office and residence) are located, facing south, directly on the axis. The other halls and palaces are symmetrically placed on both sides of the line. In recent years most of the old walls have been removed and used to construct perimeter roads. Major east-west arterial roads have also been built so that the city would be able to expand more evenly as it grew in size rather than spreading out only north and south.

When feasting with a man of superior rank and character, the guest first tasted the dishes and then stopt. He should not bolt the food, nor swill down the liquor. He should take small and frequent mouthfuls. While chewing quickly, he did not make faces with his mouth.
Li chi

Places of historic and scenic interest in modern Beijing.

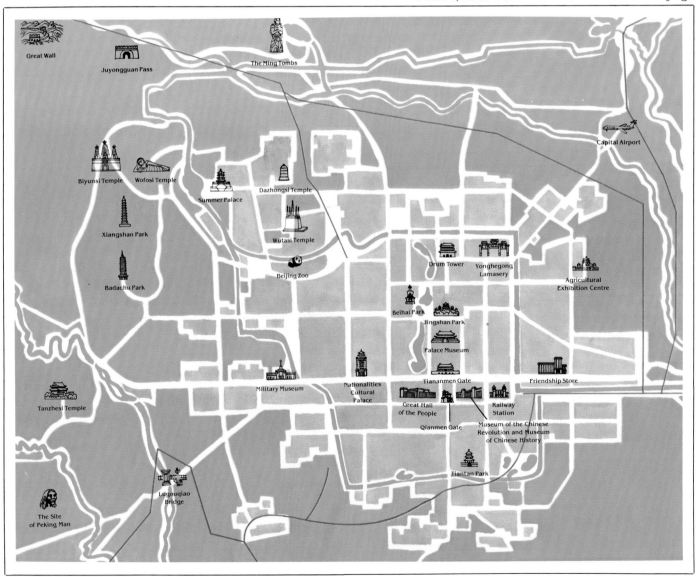

THE QIAN LONG EMPEROR VISITS THE SOUTH

This partial reproduction of an original scroll painting, measuring 2 feet by 62 feet (68 cm x 1988 cm), portrays business transactions around the Front Gate (Qianmen) during a visit by the Qian Long *Emperor of the Qing Dynasty to the southern area of the city. The original, in the Museum of Chinese History in Beijing, has never before been reproduced.*

When eating bamboo shoots, remember the men who planted them. Proverb

The plan of the Inner City can only be understood within the cultural context of the Chinese empire. The emperor, as Son of Heaven, and the capital, as the focal point of the only civilized society on earth, required a special structure. This is the north-south processional roadway, bordered by the imperial buildings. This road leads directly to the palace in which the emperors held their audiences.

Everything in the city centered around the emperor and his administration, and the entire structure of both the Inner and Outer Cities was to reflect and facilitate this. Except for the addition in 1860 of the Legation Quarter for foreigners, the essential plan of Beijing remained the same until the end of the imperial days and the revolution of 1911.

Peking street scene in 1717, showing food shops and restaurants.

Poet Tu Fu: stone engraving.
Ching period.

The Chinese also assured us that this City hath an hundred and three score Butchers shambles, and in each of them an hundred stalls, full of all kinds of flesh that the earth produceth, as veal, mutton, pork, goat, the flesh of horses, buffalo, rhinoceros, tygers, lions, dogs, mules, asses, otters, shamois, badgers, and finally of all other beasts whatever—There are withal many Taverns, where excellent fare is always to be had, and cellars full of gammons of bacon, dried tongues, poudered geese and other savoury viands, for to relish ones drink, all in so great abundance that it would be very superfluous to say more of it.
Peking by Pinto

DYNASTIES

B.C.

2205 to 1766 (approx.)	*Xia Dynasty*	
1766 to 1122	*Shang Dynasty*	*Three Dynasties*
1122 to 256	*Zhou Dynasty*	
255 to 207	*Qin Dynasty*	
206 to 220 A.D.	*Han Dynasty*	

A.D.

220 to 265	*The Three Kingdoms Period*
265 to 420	*Jin Dynasty*
386 to 589	*Northern and Southern Dynasties*
590 to 618	*Sui Dynasty*
618 to 907	*Tang Dynasty*
907 to 960	*Five Dynasties*
960 to 1279	*Song Dynasty*
1271 to 1368	*Yuan (Mongol) Dynasty*
1368 to 1644	*Ming Dynasty*
1644 to 1911	*Qing (Manchu) Dynasty*

A good cook cannot with the utmost application produce more than four successful dishes in one day, and even then it is hard for him to give proper attention to every detail; and he certainly won't get through unless everything is in its right place and he is on his feet the whole time. It is no use to give him a lot of assistants; each of them will have his own ideas, and there will be no proper discipline.

Yüan Mei

Chen Aiwu, of the Fengzeyuan Restaurant, is now in his late twenties and is already both a master chef and an artist. He came to the Fengzeyuan Restaurant in 1972. In addition to mastering the four elements of Chinese cuisine—color, fragrance, flavor, and shape—he has developed a special talent for carving techniques used for garnishes. Flowers, birds, and animals animate his dishes. He acquired the skill in seven years by visiting carving studios, the zoo, and the botanical gardens. In competition in 1978, he won a first prize by carving cranes with a pocket knife. In a 1980 contest, he again won top honors with his carving of a calla lily.

Lotus Flower and Cranes *by Chen Aiwu.*
The cooks are skilled at carving birds, flowers, and landscapes out of melons, fruits, green vegetables, *carrots, and potatoes. The crane here, created by one of the master chefs of Fengzeyuan for a banquet, is a symbol of wisdom.*

The Masters
北京的厨房師傅

The men and women profiled in this section are sixteen of the most honored master chefs in the People's Republic of China. They have made or enriched the reputations of the famous restaurants over which they preside. They started their careers young, at 12 or 14, and many have been perfecting the techniques and inventing new dishes in their regional idioms for four decades or more.

Some came young from provincial cities and towns to the capital city at Beijing in order to apprentice themselves to men who had been Master Chefs in the kitchens of the Empress Dowager of the Qing Dynasty. Some struggled and practiced to perfect the exacting techniques of preparing and presenting imperial court cuisine using exotic ingredients, elaborate visual effects, and incredible repertoires. Others came to work in the active, bustling northern capital and developed dishes using the techniques and flavors they had learned in provincial capitals all over China.

These are the most skilled chefs and the most famous restaurants in the capital city of the world's oldest continuing civilization.

Corridors and "Moon Gates" connect all of the dining and banquet rooms.

Fangshan Restaurant 仿膳饭庄

Fangshan literally translates into "cooking in the style of the (Qing Dynasty) imperial kitchens." The chefs who worked in the kitchens of the Imperial Courts had access to hundreds of recipes drawn from many centuries. Only a chef with superb skills could master the 39 steps necessary to present the famous "Lotus Prawn," for example, or to use the webs of duck's feet, a delicacy, added to minced fish and candied fruit to form an imperial dish called "Golden Fish Duck Webs"—so sinuously realistic that it seems to be swimming off the plate.

Under the direction of Dong Shiguo, Fangshan's chefs have a combined repertoire of 182 Manchu and Han recipes (134 hot dishes and 48 cold meat dishes), as well as over 200 Qing "court" dishes. Among the recipes in this collection, six were praised by the Empress Dowager Ci Xi of the Qing Dynasty: "Buddhist Prawns," "Deep-Fried Citron Rolls," "Sauteed Chicken Breasts in White Sauce," "Stuffed Mandarin Fish," and "Pigeon Eggs in White Sauce."

Dong Shiguo, now 47, has long been a master of his art. He started his apprenticeship at 14. In 1956, he studied the extremely exacting techniques of the imperial "court" cuisine under the master Wang Jingchun. After many years of practice and study, Dong recently succeeded in preparing the famous, 100-course "Manchu-Han Feast," which few contemporary chefs have ever mastered.

Tingliguan Restaurant 听鹂馆

In Chinese, *Tingliguan* means "The Pavilion for Listening to the Orioles." The buildings now occupied by this Beijing restaurant were first constructed during the reign of the Qian Long emperor (1736–1795) in the garden of the Qing Dynasty Summer Palace on Lake Kunming. The Anglo-French invaders burned it down in 1860 during the Second Opium War, but it was rebuilt in 1892. When the Empress Dowager Ci Xi started attending operas there, it acquired its name in order to exalt the court performers by comparing their musical skills to the lyrical voice of the oriole.

In the early 1950s the buildings were converted into the current restaurant, which, appropriate to its location in a royal palace, sought out chefs skilled in the preparation of "court" cuisine. It is famous for its carp, plucked so fresh from Lake Kunming that its gills are said to be still quivering when it is cooked. "Palace Gate Fish" is an honored specialty, for which the recipe is given here for the first time.

Private dinners are sometimes served on Chinese "Pleasure Boats," where customers can feast on the lake surrounded by imperial gardens. Nearby, the Empress Dowager Ci Xi had a mammoth, canopied barge constructed of solid marble and connected to the shore of the lake so that she could enjoy its beauties the year round. Occasionally, the restaurant holds special dinners on the "Marble Barge," with lyrical court music playing as dusk falls and colored lanterns dot the shores of the surrounding lake.

The house where the orioles sing.

Huang Enshun of the Tingliguan Restaurant is a cook of more than 30 years' standing. He learned to make Sichuan and Fujian dishes when he was 16 and developed an interest in the Imperial Cuisine. He was apprenticed to Tang Keming, chef of the last emperor of the Qing dynasty, and spent much of his time in the State museum, studying menus of imperial dinners. He has mastered 100 imperial dishes and has served 10 visiting heads of state. In 1982, the Japanese government invited him to Japan to demonstrate his technique.

Donglaishun Restaurant 东来顺饭庄

One of the largest Muslim restaurants in China, the eighty-year-old restaurant in the capital city offers more than 200 dishes and 30 appetizers and pastry dishes. The best of all is their "Mongolian Hot Pot" in which the diner dips thin slices of raw lamb into a boiling broth kept bubbling in the middle of the table. After a minute he lifts it out, dips it into one or more of the many sauces on the table, and eats it hot. This dish has been prepared by the nomadic peoples of Northern China for over 400 years. By the 18th century it had become the winter favorite in the Qing Dynasty court. In the 18th century a prince in the court of the Qian Long emperor gave a feast for the civilian and military officials of the court, along with some noted public figures, that required the simultaneous preparation of no fewer than 1,500 Mongolian hot pots.

The meat used for this dish is taken from short-tailed, male sheep raised near the city of Jining in Inner Mongolia. Their flesh is tender and lacks the strong odor of common mutton. For consumption in the spring and summer, the sheep weigh about 17 kilos (35–42 pounds). For autumn and winter, it should tip the scales at 24 kilos (50 to 60 pounds). Only the loin and rack, the most tender cuts, are used for this specialty. The meat is boned and frozen, which is easy in the climate of Mongolia, then sliced by hand into almost translucently thin strips while still frozen. At least a dozen condiments are specially prepared and laid out in separate bowls to complement the meat. The hot pot used for an outdoor banquet of lamb is somewhat different from the ordinary ones for home use. It has a larger charcoal chamber and a taller chimney, which prevent the ash from flying out and igniting a robe or a tent of skins. The bars of the charcoal grate are thick and farther apart, allowing in more air to maintain a brisk fire and thus keep the broth at a constant boil, even in the cold.

He Fengqing (front) has been working in the Donglaishun Restaurant since coming there as an apprentice in 1943. Often, after his duties were over in the evening, he would stay to practice his cutting technique before light faded. After 15 years of training he entered and won the championship in a meat-cutting competition for master chefs. Wielding a long cleaver weighing 3½ pounds (1.5 kg), it took him 180 seconds to cut a half-pound (250 g) piece of frozen lamb into 60 wafer-thin slices measuring exactly 6¼ inches by 1¼ inch (16 cm x 3 cm). His best record to date is 84 slices in the same period of time.

Fengzeyuan Restaurant 丰泽园饭庄

In Chinese, *Fengzeyuan* means "Garden of Abundance and Color." Beijing's Fengzeyuan Restaurant specializes in techniques and ingredients used in the cities and towns of the fertile province of Shandong, which is located on China's east coast on the Yellow Sea.

The cuisine, from its provincial capital of Jinan, is clear, delicious, crisp, and tender; while the dishes from Jiaodong, the coastal area of the province, are, not surprisingly, chiefly seafood specialties.

For more than fifty years this restaurant has been serving traditional Shandong dishes and has made the following ones famous: "Swallow's Nest Soup," "Shark's Fin Casserole," "Scallops and Egg White," "Stir-Fried Abalone," and "Fish Hot-Pot."

It is an unassuming three-story building, located just outside the Front Gate (Qianmen), with twelve dining rooms that can accommodate 320 diners at one seating.

Wang Yijun, of the Fengzeyuan Restaurant, is a famous Shandong chef. He is now 50, and has 34 years of experience. He can prepare 400 dishes of fish, shrimp, and sea food. Some of them, such as "Stir-Fried Abalone," are his own invention.

Tongchunyuan Restaurant 同春园饭庄

The repertoires of the master chefs of the Tongchunyuan Restaurant come from the southeastern province of Jiangsu. Within that province, the Yangzhou area (where the most popular dishes originated) is known as the land of fish and rice. Since ancient times, this transportation center has been noted for its strategic location. Consequently it attracted nobles and rich merchants. These upper-class individuals became the patrons of chefs who developed unusual skills and inventiveness to please their demanding, well-traveled masters. Their superb art—with seafood as their specialty—has been handed down from generation to generation. This accumulated experience equips them to prepare black carp in twenty different ways, all of which differ in color, flavor, and appearance.

Although the most famous Jiangsu-style dishes are from the Yangzhou area, recipes from Nanjing, Zhenjiang, and Suzhou are also very popular. Each place has its unique masterpieces—for instance, Nanjing's Eight Treasure Duck, Zhenjiang's Duck Meat with Dried Bean Curd, Yangzhou's Steamed Shad (hilsa herring) and eel dishes, and Suzhou's Crab and Pork Balls and "Squirrel-Like Mandarin Fish" (included in the recipe section).

The main chefs have been here for nearly forty years. One of the original masters is now the manager and teaches part-time at the Beijing Service Trade School. Among them they can offer close to 300 varieties of Jiangsu-style dishes. They are especially skilled at fixing eel and fried fish with sauce.

Gao Guolu is a cooking technician first grade, and manager of the Tongchunyuan Restaurant where he started to work in the kitchen at the age of 13. Over the past 40 years, he has learned to prepare over 600 varieties of Jiangsu and Sichuan dishes. He is especially skilled at quick frying with blinding speed—finishing with heating, flavoring, and thickening in seconds. His dishes retain the original fresh colors and gain an especially crisp tenderness. He trained himself to prepare fish by making research trips to Shanghai, Nanjing, Yangzhou, Suzhou, and Hangzhou. He also teaches in the Beijing Service Trade School.

Sichuan Restaurant 四川饭店

The Sichuan Restaurant is located on a quiet street (Rongxian Hutong), near North Xidan Street in the western part of Beijing. Its architecture is Beijing-style, with a courtyard in the middle. Originally, it was the mansion of a Qing Dynasty prince, so the red gate, bamboo trees, and corridors that link the dining rooms together give it a touch of elegance.

For more than a thousand years, Sichuan cooks have been known for their strict selection of ingredients, superb cooking skills, and their deft use of spices, making their style extremely popular throughout China. One *tour de force* is called simply "Fish-Flavored Shredded Pork." It contains no seafood, but by using a special combination of ingredients, cooked with a certain amount of oil under a controlled temperature, it is made to taste unmistakably like fish.

Sichuan food is not only known for its rare, imperial banquet delicacies (such as red-cooked bear paw and braised shark's fin), but also its easily prepared and inexpensive home-style dishes (such as "Mrs. Pockmark's Bean Curd," "Home-Style Beef Tendon," and "Fried Bamboo Shoots"). Step-by-step procedures for producing their dramatic sizzling dishes are described in this book. The sizzle comes when hot soup containing slices of meat, chicken, or squid is poured over fried rice crusts. The meat is delicious, the rice crusts stay crisp, and the soup is sweet and sour. Incidentally, if you go to the Sichuan Restaurant in Beijing, ask for a famous snack called the Dandan Noodle.

The Sichuan Restaurant Gate.

Chen Songru is the chef of the Sichuan Restaurant. He was apprenticed to a Sichuan master chef when he was 12 years old in the city of Chengdu, capital of Sichuan Province. Over the last 50 years he has often supervised the preparation of major state banquets. Chen Songru has trained many young cooks. Among the many now-famous cooks he has trained is his own son, now working in Switzerland. He often contributes articles to culinary magazines about his creative work in refining the Sichuan style.

"Site of the Yuewei Cottage" inscribed by the famous calligrapher Qi Gong.

The Beijing Jinyang Restaurant 晋阳饭庄

The Jinyang Restaurant in Taiyuan, Shanxi Province, has been famous for more than a century for its excellent Shanxi cuisine. To expand their business and meet the needs of the people in Beijing, they set up another restaurant bearing the same name in the capital in 1959.

Located on the northern side of Hufangqiao Road, outside the Gate of Heavenly Peace in Beijing, it is housed in a typical Beijing courtyard with red gates, richly ornamented buildings, and winding corridors. Originally called the "Yuewei Cottage," these peaceful surroundings were where Ji Xiaolan, chief editor of the voluminous Chinese encyclopedia *Siku Quanshu* (compiled in the 18th century), used to read and write.

The Beijing Jinyang Restaurant has more than 20 famous chefs brought to Beijing from China's northern province of Shanxi who specialize in northern, southern, and central Shanxi cooking. Their food, a bit on the salty side, is so delicious it appeals to Chinese palates educated in either the north or south of China. Of the more than 500 dishes and 40 wheat pastries in the repertoires of its chefs perhaps the best-known are "Succulent Duck," "White Fungi Peony Flowers," "Butterfly Sea Cucumbers," "Deep-Fried Meats," "Taiyuan-Style Braised Beef," and "Silkworm Cocoon Bean Curd." It also offers full imperial-style banquets with such rare delicacies as bear's paw and deer tendons.

Jin Yongchuan is the master chef of the Jinyang Restaurant. His apprenticeship began when he was 14. When he became interested in the Shanxi cuisine he went to the provincial capital, Taiyuan, and studied for two years before coming to Beijing to work with some 20 famous Shanxi cooks. Jin Yongchuan teaches in the Beijing Service School. He also gives lectures to nutrition specialists from the Chinese Medical Association. He is now cooperating with doctors in the study of the pharmacopoeia of his dishes.

The Beijing Vegetarian Restaurant 素菜餐厅

Don't be fooled by the menu, which lists gourmet dishes such as "Braised Shark's Fin in White Sauce," "Eight Treasure Whole Duck," "Croaker in Hot Sauce," and "Chicken Liver Rolls." Although they look (and even taste!) like meat, they are made exclusively from vegetables, soy beans, bean curd, nuts, roots, and edible fungi.

Chinese vegetarian cuisine originated in the monasteries, where Buddhist followers were not allowed to eat meat. By the 17th century, meatless dishes were also popular in the imperial as well as the commoner's kitchens. When the emperor offered sacrifices to heaven, he was supposed to abstain from eating meat. According to historical records, the Qing imperial kitchen could turn out more than 200 dishes made with gluten and dried bean curd. Subsequently, many vegetarian restaurants opened, serving delicious dishes from the monastery and imperial recipes.

Vegetarian food is light and not too oily, with high nutritional and medicinal value. Bean products contain a rich quantity of protein, while mushrooms and white fungi (tremella) are believed by some to have a nourishing and tonic effect in combatting hypertension, fortifying the heart and kidney, and preventing cirrhosis of the liver. As a result, more and more people—especially the middle-aged and elderly—have begun to enjoy vegetarian dishes.

Founded in 1964, the Beijing Vegetarian Restaurant is the only restaurant of its kind in Beijing.

Liu Yongshi is the manager of the Beijing Vegetarian Restaurant. After graduation he continued his study of culinary technique for eight years under Zhou Shuting, chief chef of the Beijing Vegetarian Restaurant. Zhou was the honor student of the famous Xiong Guangxing, Master of Vegetarian Cuisine. Liu Yongshi often cooks for visiting Buddhist guests and was recently invited to Shanghai vegetarian restaurants to exchange experiences.

Kangle Restaurant 康乐餐馆

The well-known Kangle Restaurant was founded in 1950 by four married couples. Foreign newspapers once referred to it as "Beijing's Three-Table Restaurant." However, it has now developed into a large enterprise in a new, unpretentious three-story building at Anding Gate.

This southern-style restaurant serves dishes from Jiangsu, Zhejiang, Jiangxi, Anhui, Yunnan, and Sichuan Provinces. The reason Kangle offers a greater variety of dishes than other

The Kangle staff of 100 serves the staggering total of 1,000 meals per day, many of them in-and-out, soup-and-beer lunches from its open street-level tables.

southern restaurants in Beijing is that its four founders came from four different places—Fujian, Sichuan, Yunnan, and Beijing. Three of the wives were expert cooks and were eager to learn recipes of other provinces. New dishes were constantly added to the menu.

The restaurant is famous for its "Sizzling Rice," "Fried Fish Slices," "Steam-Pot Chicken," "Stuffed Mushrooms," "Pickled Chicken Cubes," "Steamed Turtle," "Jade-Like Soup," and "Grape-Cluster Fish"—all of which were chosen to be included among the recipes in this collection.

Chang Jing, deputy manager of the Kangle Restaurant, is Beijing's most famous woman chef. Many beautiful and delicate dishes served in Kangle are to her credit—"Grape-Cluster Fish" and "Orchid Prawns," to name only two. She joined the restaurant when she was only 12, doing a variety of odd jobs. Later, when she grew up and became a waitress, she was greatly interested in the kitchen. She took every opportunity to learn by heart how the dishes were made—preparation of ingredients, sequence of cooking, and handling of the fire. One day a cook was absent for illness. She convinced her boss to let her try her hand in the kitchen. She was a great success. She has been a cook since then. She is now 65. Many of her apprentices have become famous, but she keeps working in the kitchen. She also teaches in a culinary school. Recently, she has been elected deputy to the People's Congress of the East District, Beijing.

Quyuan Restaurant 曲园酒楼

Though in front it is very plain, the inside design is original. Entering the restaurant, you will see a narrow passageway leading to a large dining room where one can get a quick meal. Connected to one end of the hall are several private rooms for banquets. Outside the back door is a small yard and a charming, little house. This is a quiet place at the innermost core of the restaurant where well-known personages and honored foreigners come to enjoy Hunan food at its best.

Quyuan Restaurant was originally built in Hunan's capital city of Changsha during the Qing Dynasty—more than one hundred years ago. Adequate for banquets of up to 160 tables at one time, this four-story restaurant was well-known in Hunan and Hubei provinces. The building was shaped like a gourd, hence its name *Qu Yuan* (or crooked circle). In 1938, the Japanese bombed Changsha and reduced this luxurious restaurant to rubble. Later, some of the chefs went to Nanjing and set up a restaurant with the same name there. Its business boomed and soon it became famous in the city. After the founding of the People's Republic in 1949, in order to let the capital's residents enjoy the Hunan-flavored food, the restaurant sent some of its chefs to Beijing to help set up a new restaurant.

The Quyuan serves the cuisine of Hunan Province, which borders on Sichuan, and has similarly flavored food. But there are distinct differences in seasoning and cooking style between the two. Most Sichuan dishes are spicy hot, while Hunan dishes are sourish hot. The former are fried or stir-fried, while the latter are braised in brown sauce or are cured before cooking. The

cured fish or meats are usually steamed before stir-frying and then seasoned with the well-known Liuyang *douchi* (fermented soy beans). The flavors are mellow and delicious, and leave an aromatic aftertaste. The quantities of oil and cornstarch for each dish should always be correct, so the dishes are never too greasy or too thick or thin. "Dongan Chick," "Braised Soft-Shelled Turtle," "Litchi Squid," and "Scallops with Two-Colored Eggs" are famous Hunan-style dishes. The scallops with eggs, in particular, is a specialty of the Quyuan Restaurant.

In recent years, the Quyuan Restaurant has employed some young cooks, waiters and waitresses from the province of Hunan, making Hunan Chinese feel even more at home.

Xue Baotian studied under the famous chef Lin Zhenjie of Hunan Province for 22 years. He's skilled at preparing imperial banquet delicacies such as shark's fins and bear's paw, but is also famous for his pastries. "Dongan Chick" and "Scallops with Two-Colored Eggs" are two of his original recipes that are unique in color and taste.

Ji, the Roast Meat Restaurant 烤肉季

Tucked away in a grove of willows on the northern banks of Shisha (Lake) is Ji, a Muslim restaurant that serves roast meat, mainly lamb, in the style of the Mongol sheepherders of the northern plains.

Roast Meat Ji has a history going back more than one hundred years. Sometime toward the middle of the 19th century people began to gather by the lake every year to see the lotus in bloom. These throngs naturally attracted merchants and peddlers. Soon an annual "lotus market" was formed there. A peddler named Ji Decai, from the outskirts of Beijing, was a frequent visitor. One day he set up a grill by the bridge. Before long the tantalizing aroma of the barbecued lamb attracted so many customers he began bringing his son along as an assistant and set up an open-air stand. As his fame spread, members of the imperial and aristocratic families who passed his way couldn't resist the aroma and would drop in for a plate or two. Eventually even the emperor got wind of it and the chef of Roast Meat Ji was summoned to the palace to demonstrate his skill, a performance that he was to repeat many times.

Ji's grandson's two-story restaurant now perches by the lake on the site of the old stand, serving an average of 12,000 customers per month (some even make reservations by phone from Tokyo). The atmosphere is electric—both hearty and beautiful. At night, lights flood the dining room and balcony. Diners are sometimes allowed to stir and toss the slivers of raw lamb on the hot charcoal grill and mix in the pungent fresh coriander themselves, while their friends sip wine and watch the moon and twinkling lights caught in the willow branches reflected on the rippling surface of the lake.

Kun Zhenchun, now 70, is the Master of Muslim cuisine at Ji, the Roast Meat Restaurant. He was apprenticed in a restaurant when he was 13, and over the past 50 years he has risen to master chef in famous restaurants in Tianjin, Shanghai, and Beijing. His beef and lamb dishes are famous, and he knows more than 40 different ways of cooking shrimp. His skill in tossing the frying pan is legendary. His push-and-toss can send 20 shrimp cakes flying two feet (0.5 m) in the air. They turn and land in the pan at the same time, without splashing the oil or breaking their original formation, and the dry condiments are evenly coated all over the cakes. Kun has a famous saying: "The dish is the chef's daughter." This, as his apprentices confirm, means only perfect dishes can be served.

Beijing Hotel 北京饭店

The Beijing Hotel, which enjoys a reputation among old China hands as the only hotel to stay at in Beijing, has become a paradigm of the ancient vs. the modern China.

This famous 600-room hotel juxtaposes the old and the new in contemporary China. The automatically controlled front doors open up to a luxurious lounge decorated with golden pillars, cream marble walls, and beautiful chandeliers. At the eastern end is a large restaurant, while at the western end there is a café, a post office, a bank, and a store—selling porcelain, rugs, textiles, Chinese and western medicine, calligraphy, painting, and handicraft articles.

The new gray wing (18 stories), added in 1974, is the tallest building along Changan Boulevard. The top floor commands a fine view of the Forbidden City, Tiananmen Square, and the rest of the city. This new wing (plus the two older sections of the hotel) can accommodate 1,800 guests.

There is a large dining room on the first floor and many smaller ones on the second floor of the new wing. The west wing boasts of a banquet hall large enough to hold 2,000 people and several small restaurants. The lords of the kitchens are masters of a remarkable variety of regional cuisines: Beijing, Guangdong, Sichuan, northern Jiangsu; but their specialty is the "Tan Family Cuisine," which originated from the house of Tan Zongjun, a high official of the Qing court. That Tan cuisine restaurant became part of the Beijing Hotel in the 1950s, and with it came honored recipes such as "Chicken with Straw Mushrooms," "Bound Sticks Duck," "Sunflower Pork," and "Braised Mushrooms." In addition to this noble Han cuisine, its chefs are famous for the Guangdong style of tropical South China, where Guangzhou (Canton) is the provincial capital. "Chicken in Oyster Sauce," "Stir-Fried Fish," and "Pork with Fermented Bean Curd" are among the Cantonese recipes selected for this collection.

Peng Changhai, now 62, is a technician special class in the Beijing Hotel, and representative of the Tan Family Cuisine. More than 100 years ago, there was a Tan Zongjun, a high official at the Qing court, who was a connoisseur in eating and drinking. He hired expert cooks to work in his kitchen. Gradually, the Tan Family Cuisine was formed, with chicken, duck, and sea food as the main ingredients. The dishes are thoroughly cooked, taste sweet and salty, and are served in the original sauce. Peng Changhai worked in Tan's kitchen when he was 17. After the establishment of the People's Republic in 1949, his "Chicken with Straw Mushrooms" appeared on state banquet menus. The late Premier Zhou Enlai invited him to prepare his best dishes for American presidents, British prime ministers, and Japanese premiers. Zhou Enlai received him several times.

Cuihualou 萃华楼饭庄

In Beijing's busiest shopping area, Wangfujing Street, you'll find a well-known restaurant with doors bearing three golden characters: *Cui hua lou. Cui hua* means outstanding and colorful, *lou* means great house.

Opened in 1940, Cuihualou has long been renowned for its Shangdong-style pastries and dishes from the cities of southern China. Its twelve chefs serve 1,000 customers on a normal day. They can choose from 200 cooked-to-order dishes, 50 cold meat dishes, and 30 varieties of pastries. Its stir-fried dishes are often flavored with scallions and garlic, which give the dishes a distinct southern aroma and taste. Coriander, the pungent Chinese parsley, and soybean paste are also used for flavor and texture. In common with masters of any trade, its chefs are conscientious about detail: exact measurements, the right order for adding ingredients, and the length of the stirring times are critical if the results are to be fresh, aromatic, tender, and crisp.

Since most of the Cuihualou chefs come from the coastal cities of Fushan and Yantai, their specialties include seafood such as "Fried Squid Rolls"—unique in color, flavor, and shape—and "Crispy Prawn"—distinguished by its bright red color and peppery taste.

The superb skills of these chefs are well known in Beijing and throughout the world. Recently, seven gave cooking demonstrations in the United States, the Soviet Union, Japan, the Philippines, and other countries.

Zang Weiduo, a chef at Cuihualou, is talented in several areas, but principally his technique is preparing Shangdong dishes. He is also famous for his pastries, cold dishes, and roast duck. Not confining his talents to cooking, Zang knows a lot about purchasing ingredients from their native places, doing cost accounting, and improving the management of the restaurant. Zang was born in Fushan, Shangdong Province. Many of his neighbors had been famous cooks in other parts of the country. He dreamed of becoming one, also. In 1950 he came to Cuihualou as a 16-year-old and finished a three-year apprenticeship course in two. Since 1979 Zang has traveled to New York and Washington, D.C., several times, demonstrating his skill to the American public.

The Quanjude Beijing Duck Restaurant 全聚德烤鸭店

In 1837 a young merchant from the county of Jixian in Hebei Province, named Yang Quanren, came to Beijing, bringing with him a famous roasting technique originated in the Ming (1368–1644) imperial kitchen.

The ducks at that time were from the Yangzi River (Changjiang) Valley. After the Ming Dynasty moved its capital from Nanjing to Beijing in the 15th century, the recipe for this dish gradually found its way into restaurants for the common people. The ducks raised in the city's outskirts were a small white breed; however, by the end of the 19th century, through careful selection and breeding, they have evolved into a new Beijing breed. Although the duck is still white, it is a much larger bird, with thin skin and tender flesh. Beijing's world-famous roast duck is golden brown and crisp on the outside and tender and succulent on the inside.

Large hotels from all over China send chefs to Quanjude to learn its unique roasting technique—a description of which is included under Poultry in the recipe section of this book.

Chef Chen Shoubin has invested thirty years inventing and perfecting recipes using roast duck. He has developed the traditional technique for roasting duck in the Beijing style and is capable of producing a "duck feast" complete with more than 50 dishes. Some new variations credited to him are "Singed Duck's Heart," and "Beijing Duck Rolls."

This seven-story restaurant has enough floor space for forty-one dining rooms that can serve Beijing Duck to 2,600 customers at one time.

At present, Senlong's Jiangsu-style menu offers more than 100 fried dishes and over twenty snacks and pastries. Travelers from Europe, America, and, as shown here, Japan, enjoy its reasonably priced natural foods.

Li Keqin is the number one chef of the Senlong Restaurant and is a master of the Jiangsu cuisine. He spent four years familiarizing himself with the ingredients of that province's cuisine, the cutting technique, the special features, and the relations between the main ingredients and the condiments. He took up the ladle only in the fifth year of his study.

Li Keqin considers patience the most important attribute for a cook and that a beginner can too easily get so nervous he even burns the ingredients in the wok. However, he must not lose confidence in himself. He has to watch the fire with his eyes, control the time with his hands, and tell the taste with his tongue. He is going to accumulate experience only through practice. That is the only way to learn.

Senlong Restaurant 森隆饭庄

Situated on a plain at the lower reaches of the Yangzi River (Changjiang), Jiangsu Province enjoys a temperate climate. Its network of rivers and lakes has an abundant supply of fish and provides excellent land for growing rice. Since ancient times, the residents of Jiangsu have been known for their superb culinary skills. In the 1920s, a talented native, Chang Senlong, opened the Senlong Restaurant in Beijing.

Senlong's food is known for its natural flavor. Jiangsu-style dishes taste rich but not greasy, soft but not pulpy, and the use of natural juices allows the food to retain its original flavors. Jiangsu chefs are especially good at making steamed foods and soups simply from fresh water and sea food. They also make an effort to seek out fresh vegetables that are found only in other parts of China such as bamboo, wild rice stem, green pea, and a type of preserved cabbage from the south. The dishes look shiny and taste a little sweet—quite different from northern foods, which are heavy, rich, and salty. The chief cooking methods used in this style are braising, stir-frying, and steaming. Senlong's menu offers 40 different ways of preparing sea food. For instance, when a shrimp is cut in half lengthwise, it may be cooked in two different ways: one half may be deep-fried until it turns golden brown; the other half may be stir-fried until it turns a beautiful red. "Braised shrimp," "Frog-Shaped Chicken," and "Coin-Shaped Shrimp Cakes" are a few of the restaurant's specialties.

Henan Restaurant 河南饭庄

The most famous Beijing restaurant specializing in Henan dishes was known to old timers as "Houdefu," when it was originally located on Dashalan outside the Front Gate (Qianmen). There it ranked with (and survived) "Nanweizhai" from Huaiyang, "Zuixionglin" from Guangdong, and "Xiaoyoutian" from Fujian—the three other most famous restaurants in Beijing at the time. It even opened branches in Xi'an, Harbin, Tianjin, Qingdao, Nanjing, Shanghai, and Kunming.

Most Henan cuisine originates from the cities of Kaifeng and Luyi. Kaigeng flourished as the country's political, economic, and cultural center when it was the capital of the Northern Song Dynasty (960–1127). According to historical records, the catering trade was highly developed in the ancient capital. Its streets were lined with restaurants that were open day and night. At one time, the Kaifeng style, not the Beijing style, was known as the "northern" cuisine. Unlike Beijing's court cuisine, though, its dishes are not elaborately sophisticated in form.

Because of the discriminating palate of the aristocrats and their strict demands on the imperial kitchen staff, Henan cuisine still stresses the selection of exact ingredients and their precise preparation.

Take, for example, the traditional "Sweet-and-Sour Fish Squares" dish in this book. Only the tender carp from the Yellow River (Huanghe) is used. It is regarded as a rare treat. It is said that the Empress Dowager Ci Xi lavishly praised this dish. "Daokou Fried Chicken" calls for a six-month to two-year-old chicken. Its preparation involves seven processes and requires eight different herbs. The stock (in which the chickens are cooked) is used over and over again; each time, more herbs are added, changing the taste of the chicken. The legendary Daokou recipe was first created in 1661 by a man named Zhang Ding (who was assisted by an imperial chef). Over the past 800 years, Zhang's descendants closely guarded the secret recipe. In fact, it was not until 1956 that his eighth generation descendants disclosed the recipe for the first time. When Daokou fried chicken first appeared on Hong Kong menus in 1962, the dish immediately became popular.

Other famous Henan dishes include "Pine Cone Carp," "Skillet-Baked Eggs," and "Two-in-One Shrimp." Some traditional dishes are still available only at the Henan Restaurant.

Its master chef, who once worked at the "Houdefu" in Xi'an, has 50 years of experience to guide his retinue of up-and-coming chefs.

Xue Yingfa has over fifty years' experience making Henan dishes. His fish and shrimp dishes, and his bear's paws, taste deliciously sweet and salty and are served in a heavy sauce. He has helped other famous restaurants develop their skills in the Henan style of cooking, and his many students now make up the backbone of the kitchen staff of the Henan Restaurant in the capital city of Beijing.

The Ingredients

原　料

Ingredients to a cook is like dresses and jewelry to a woman. A beautiful woman can do nothing with shabby dresses no matter how skilled she is in making herself up.

Yuan Xicai, Qing Dynasty

The Chinese eat every part of everything they buy or raise for food. Unless the meat weighs more than the chef, he or she would rather buy it live and slaughter it fresh so that no good parts are wasted. Many resulting delicacies that seem odd to westerners earn their place on the menu because they contribute to the balanced health of the body, in youth or later during old age.

Two categories of Chinese delicacies that seem unappetizing to western tastes are gristle and gelatinous foods. Many recipes in this book call for shark's fin, beef tendon, sea slug, duck's web, bird's nest (the nest is constructed from secretions ejected from the beaks of a swallow-like cliff-dwelling bird), jellyfish, and other materials similar in chemistry. Because they are believed to keep old bones from becoming brittle, Chinese in their early thirties start seeking out these delicacies.

Not all Chinese foods are purchased fresh. Fish, small meats, vegetables, and fruits are sold fresh in the markets (or sometimes frozen for transportation and restaurant use). Almost all delicacies are purchased dried, in bulk or prepackaged, however. Flavorings and oils are usually bottled and labeled if they are not homemade. Basic stock, cornstarch paste, and prickly ash are made up in batches by each chef for his or her own use. Recipes for these are given at the end of this section.

CHINESE NAMES   Even within China the same ingredient may be called by more than one name. This Ingredients Guide is based on the names used in Beijing and in the north. In Shanghai, for example, the Chinese names for flavorings or other ingredients might be different. The way flavorings are made also varies from region to region—even sometimes from city to city within the same province. Soy sauce, a common denominator of Asian cuisines, was homemade in the old days. The flavor and color varied from batch to batch, as well as from region to region or country to country. Now, even in China, soy sauce is commercially bottled in many varieties. (Light-colored soy sauce is the more refined and salty; the darker colored soy sauces go through a second fermentation process and are heavier in texture). In this section, the Chinese characters are given for each ingredient. When shopping for specific ingredients by mail or in an Asian specialty shop, it is helpful to show the Chinese name, even a photocopy, to the proprietor, because it may not be recognizable from the English name or from your attempt to pronounce the word in Chinese.

WESTERN NAMES   If Chinese characters are translated literally into another language, the words used sometimes give the impression that the original Chinese meaning is naïve, bizarre, or humorous —intentionally or otherwise. (Sometimes, too, the direct translation is refreshingly memorable; who can forget "cloud-ear" fungi?) For this reason, more than one English name may be given to the Chinese ingredient as cookbook writers, editors, menu-makers, food packagers, and store clerks try to find graceful or accurate translations of the literal Chinese. In this section the more commonly used name is given in the caption to the photographs. It is also given first in the listings of the Ingredients Guide, followed by other names for the ingredient.

Occasionally the translators must simply give up altogether and keep the sound of the Chinese words as the name without trying to come up with English words that mean the same thing. Some mushrooms, fungi, and a few other specialized ingredients can be identified by the Latin botanical names. In those cases, the Latin name is also given for precision.

PRONUNCIATION   In the Ingredients Guide the sound of the spoken Chinese word is given next to the Chinese characters. The spelling system used is one officially adopted by the Chinese government, called *Pinyin*. A guide to pronouncing *Pinyin* spellings for English-speaking people appears in the back of this section. Parallel spellings used under other pronunciation systems are given there as well. Unless one has experience in speaking Mandarin Chinese, much less the other dialects, it is unlikely that a Westerner will pronounce a word accurately in Chinese solely by following these Romanized spellings. (If you want to try, follow a dictum offered in *The Elements of Style,* a famous guide to writing in English: "If you don't know how to pronounce it, say it loud!") Therefore, when shopping, it would be wiser to rely on the written character to identify the ingredient for a Chinese vendor.

SUBSTITUTIONS   There is no way around it. Some foods native to China, or a region within China, are not native to this country. The Mandarin fish, for example, is *like* a fresh-water, small-mouthed bass or perch, but it isn't one. Chinese broccoli tastes *similar to* the small-clustered, mustardy greens sold by some fresh vegetable grocers as "Italian broccoli" or "collard greens," but there is a difference. Each cook who attempts to reproduce the famous, original dishes in this book must personally decide how much of a variation from the original to tolerate as a result of substituting ingredients. The Chinese define four elements that blend creatively in every successful dish: "color," "fragrance," "flavor," and "shape." A change in ingredients could affect the dish by changing the balance in one, some, or all of those four ways. As a practical matter, the need to substitute should not interfere with the exciting prospect of trying to prepare a new, interesting-looking dish, as long as the cook remains sensitive to the principles at work in the recipe.

Chinese cuisine also subdivides flavor into five tastes: "sweet," "sour," "bitter," "pungent," and "salty." For centuries China's chefs have understood the need to harmonize those flavors to prevent and cure disease and to prolong life. A substitution may throw out of balance a harmony of flavors that bears on health in the Chinese view. (The pharmacopoeia of Chinese cuisine is treated further in a separate section of this book.) For example, the body's lack, or excess of, "inner fire" must be kept in balance by the foods taken in. The Chinese eat crabs in the autumn, but always with ginger. Crabs alone are too "cooling;" ginger adds "fire" to balance them.

Some major ingredients are too costly or difficult to obtain or handle in most western home kitchens. Among them are dried shark's fin, bird's nest, fresh turtle, sea slug, fresh-water eels, and Beijing duck. Recipes that call for these ingredients are included because those dishes are highly honored in the repertoires of contemporary China's most accomplished chefs. Any reader seriously interested in the state of the art in Chinese cuisine will enjoy a description of the preparation of these dishes in China, whether or not the ingredients, skills, and equipment used travel conveniently to our culinary idiom.

SOURCES   More and more Chinese-style fresh vegetables are being grown for sale in this country. Packaged ingredients similar or identical to those used in China are imported from various Asian sources (and under various names) for sale through Asian food stores and to Chinese restaurants. Inquire at fruit and vegetable stands or grocery stores run by Asians, even if they are not Chinese. The manager of a local Chinese restaurant may be able to give you the names of suppliers or may even be willing to order your ingredients for you. As a last resort, send a photocopy of your list of dried or packaged ingredients to a friend in a large city who may have access to Chinese groceries. The friend's task will be much easier if you include the Chinese character for each ingredient as shown in the Ingredients Guide.

It is contrary to the will of God
to eat delicate food hastily.
Chang Ch'ao

Meat, Poultry, and Eggs

Hunters, a mural from a Tunhuang Grotto. Tang period.

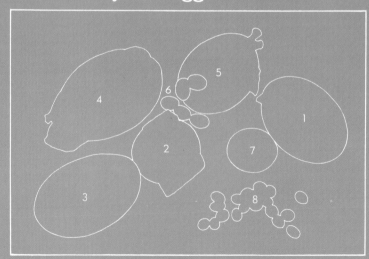

1. pork   **2.** mutton   **3.** beef   **4.** duck and eggs
5. chicken   **6.** chicken eggs   **7.** preserved eggs
8. quail eggs

Fish and Seafood

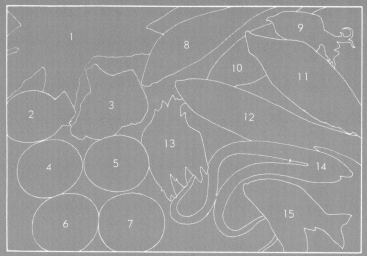

1. shark's fin, dried   2. jellyfish   3. fish maw
4. sea cucumber 5. scallop, dried 6. abalone, canned
7. shrimp, dried 8. carp 9. squid 10. yellow croaker
11. Mandarin fish 12. black carp 13. prawn 14. eel
15. crucian carp

A vegetable market during winter.

Vegetables

1. scallion 2. romaine lettuce 3. winter rape 4. rape
5. garlic   6. hair-fine sea moss   7. coriander
8. Chinese white cabbage 9. cabbage 10. white turnip
11. cucumber 12. carrot 13. potato 14. ginger root
15. hot red pepper, dried 16. onion   17. sweet green
pepper   18. broad bean (string bean)   19. mung bean
sprouts 20. pea sprouts 21. winter melon 22. tomato
23. hot pickled mustard tuber   24. cabbage, preserved,
dried   25. water chestnut, canned   26. peas, canned

Shoots, Mushrooms, and Fungi

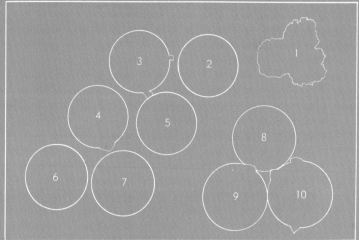

1. white fungus, *Tremella*, dried   2. tree or cloud ear fungus, *Auricularia auricula-judae*, dried   3. staghorn bamboo fungus, *Dictyophora phalloidea*   4. black winter mushroom, *Lentinus edodes*, dried   5. fresh white mushroom   6. black mushroom   7. St. George's mushroom, *Tricholoma gambosun*   8. asparagus
9. winter bamboo shoots   10. bamboo shoots, dried, soaked

净重250克

鲜味虾片

Xianweixiapian

浙江省金华市副食品加工厂

The workers pictured here are replanting rice stalks. This procedure—which takes place about the time the plants form "ears"—involves pulling up the original bunch of stalks, separating it into smaller bunches, and replanting these in even rows enough distance apart to allow for later weeding. The workers must take care to stand still and do as much of the replanting as possible from one position, so as not to stir up the bottom of paddy.

Proteins and Starches

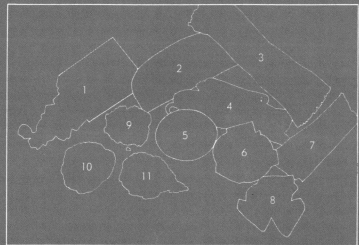

1. prawn crackers   2. bread   3. agar agar
4. dried bean curd stick   5. cooked flour gluten, fresh or canned   6. bean curd   7. dried soybean curd sheets
8. fried gluten   9. flour   10. rice   11. glutinous rice

A market in the South.

Fruits, Nuts, and Sweets

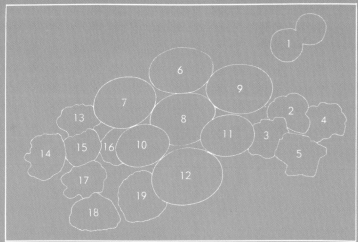

1. apple   2. tangerine, candied   3. date, candied
4. Chinese green plum, candied   5. winter melon,
preserved 6. tangerine sections, canned 7. longan fruit,
canned   8. pineapple, canned   9. litchi, canned
10. rose candy   11. osmanthus blossom candy
12. cherry, canned   13. lotus seed   14. peanut
15. date   16. almonds   17. walnut
18. black sesame seed   19. sesame seed

Seasonings

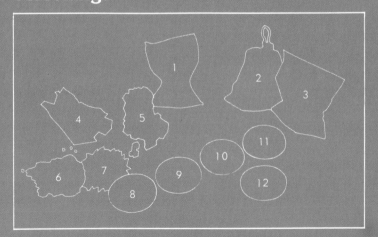

1. salt   2. cornstarch   3. MSG   4. cinnamon bark
5. rock candy   6. Sichuan peppercorn   7. star anise
8. cornstarch paste   9. malt sugar   10. powdered
dried hot pepper   11. prickly ash   12. sugar

Shaoxing rice wine jar.

Liquids, Pastes, and Oils

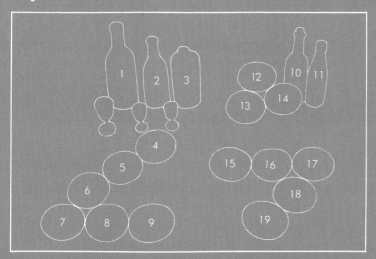

1. grape wine, red   2. liquor   3. Maotai liquor
4. soybean paste, salted and fermented   5. hot broad
bean sauce   6. sesame paste   7. fruit jam
8. fermented bean curd   9. red distiller's mash
10. shrimp sauce   11. oyster sauce   12. rice wine
13. soy sauce   14. vinegar   15. lard
16. chili pepper-flavored oil   17. peanut oil
18. chicken fat   19. peppercorn-flavored oil

Dry Spices

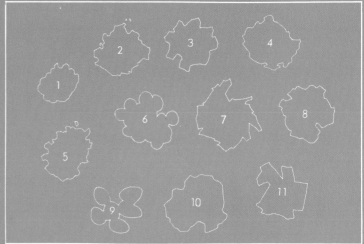

1. amomum seed clusters   2. amomum (caoguo) seeds
3. angelica root .   4. cloves   5. Chinese wolfberry
6. whole cardamom   7. cassia bark   8. galingale
9. nutmeg   10. orange peel, dried   11. Chinese cassia

*The grandfather is holding his grandson
  on his knees.
The grandfather says here are meat buns to
  dip in vinegar sauce.
When you have finished eating you will be
  saucy
And will come over to hit your grandfather
  three blows in the face.*

Anon

Ingredients Guide

The 192 native Chinese ingredients listed here are those used in the recipes included in this book. They are grouped in the same categories as those pictured at the beginning of this section. Each item is listed by Chinese character (to show the proprietor of your local Chinese market), in English transliteration (to help you pronounce the word or phrase correctly), and by common name (or names) in English, followed by the Latin botanical name as required for precise identification. Comments by the Western editors follow in italics, including suggested substitutions for ingredients that may not be easily obtainable in Western countries.

At the back of this listing you will find the instructions and recipes for ingredients that can be made up ahead of time by the cook and kept on hand for any cooking session. These are "cornstarch paste" (in three consistencies), "pepper-salt" and "stock" (three varieties). Substituting commercially canned broth will change the taste of the dish from its original.

Meat, Poultry, and Eggs

	MEAT		
猪肉	zhurou	**pork** *The meat preferred by Chinese chefs for uniform consistency and bland flavor*	
猪五花肉	zhuwuhuarou	**streaky pork (rashers)** *Thickly-cut, fresh, slab bacon*	
猪里脊肉	zhulijirou	**pork tenderloin**	
猪肘	zhuzhou	**pork shoulder**	
火腿	huotui	**cured ham** *The best come from Yunnan Province, sold sliced in cans outside China; subst. Smithfield, prosciutto, Westphalian ham*	
牛肉	niurou	**beef** *Rarely used in this form*	
牛里脊肉	niulijirou	**beef tenderloin**	
牛蹄筋	niutijin	**beef tendon** *Available fresh from a butcher or dried*	
羊肉	yangrou	**lamb (mutton)** *Not common except in the north; odor thought to be too strong; the same Chinese word is also used for goat*	
鹿肉	lurou	**venison** *Also refers sometimes to reindeer from the North*	
	POULTRY		
鸡	ji	**chicken** *Smaller in China; Western commercial birds need shorter cooking times per pound*	
鸡脯肉	jipurou	**breast of chicken** *Prized by chefs as a delicately-flavored meat of uniform consistency*	

笋鸡肉	sunjirou	**young tender chicken meat** *"Never eat a rooster after it has learned to crow," the chefs say*	
鸭	ya	**duck**	
填鸭	tianya	**Peking (Beijing) duck** *Ducks are raised especially for roasting in "Peking" style*	
鸭皮	yapi	**duck skin** *Crispy, when roasted correctly*	
鸭心	yaxin	**duck heart** *Subst. chicken heart*	
鸭肝	yagan	**duck liver** *Subst. chicken liver, which has a milder taste*	
鸭舌	yashe	**duck tongue**	
鸭胰	yayi	**duck pancreas**	
鸭胗	yazhen	**duck gizzard** *Subst. chicken gizzard*	
鸭掌	yazhang	**duck web** *The stretched skin that forms paddles of feet; a delicacy*	
鹌鹑	anchun	**quail** *An ancient Imperial delicacy thought to lengthen life; subst. Cornish game hen*	
	EGGS		
鸡蛋	jidan	**chicken egg, fresh** *Chinese eggs are small; use "medium" size in the U.S.*	
鸭蛋	yadan	**duck egg, fresh**	

| 松花蛋 | songhuadan | preserved egg
"1000-year-old eggs" are raw duck eggs covered with an alkaline mud for up to 100 days, then peeled, sliced lengthwise, and eaten with a ginger and vinegar dip | 鸽蛋 | gedan | pigeon egg
Subst. quail egg, or fresh pullet eggs |
| | | | 鹌鹑蛋 | anchundan | quail egg
Sold in cans already hardboiled |

Fish and Seafood

鲤鱼	liyu	carp *Subst. freshwater whitefish (same family as goldfish); myth relates them to dragons*	鱼翅	yuchi	shark's fin *Usually sold as dried shreds (requires blanching and soaking to soften to gelatinous texture) for eating in soup; an expensive delicacy*
青鱼	qingyu	black carp			
鲫鱼	jiyu	crucian carp (silver or European carp)	对虾(大虾)	duixia (daxia)	prawn
桂鱼	guiyu	Mandarin fish *Subst. perch, bass, or small freshwater fish*	青虾	qingxia	freshwater shrimp
			虾仁	xiaren	shrimp, shelled
			河蟹	hexie	river crab (freshwater crab)
黄鱼	huangyu	yellow croaker *Sea bass, or other meaty, light-fleshed fish*	蟹肉	xierou	crab meat
鳝鱼	shanyu	eel *Sold live in Chinese markets*	海参	haishen	sea cucumber *A flavorless kind of jellyfish; known in French cuisine as bêche-de-mer, or sea slug; sold dried or presoaked*
鱿鱼	youyu	squid *Fresh, frozen, or dried, which requires long soaking*	海米	haimi	shrimp, dried
			海蜇	haizhe	jellyfish, dried *Flavorless and chewy—even rubbery—in texture; used for contrasting texture*
鲍鱼	baoyu	abalone *A shellfish, usually canned in brine; if dried it must be boiled a long time; canned and fresh become tough if overcooked*	干贝	ganbei	scallop, dried (conpoy) *In China this cousin of Western scallops is called kanpei; always sold dried*
元鱼	yuanyu	soft-shelled turtle *Sold live in Chinese markets*			
鱼肚	yudu	fish maw *The fish bladder, sold dried; usually deep-fried, which is necessary before it is edible*			

Vegetables

油菜	youcai	rape (broccoli rabe) *Subst. celery cabbage, Italian broccoli, or collard greens*	生菜	shengcai	romaine lettuce
			苔菜	taicai	dried sea grass, *Enteromorpha*
油菜心	youcaixir	heart of rape *Subst. Napa celery cabbage*	香菜	xiangcai	coriander (Chinese parsley) *Used fresh in Northern dishes, especially with lamb; strongly pungent flavor*
白菜	baicai	bok choy (Chinese white cabbage) *Subst. Swiss chard, celery cabbage, white cabbage*			
			盖兰菜苔	gailan caitai	mustard greens *Subst. Italian broccoli or broccoli rabe*
菠菜	bocai	spinach			
青菜(油冬菜)	qingcai (youdongcai)	winter rape *Subst. spinach or green bok choy*	黄瓜	huanggua	cucumber

冬瓜	donggua	**winter melon** *Subst. firm winter squash*
扁豆	biandou	**broad bean (green or string bean)** *Subst. lentils; also called hyacinth bean*
青豆	qingdou	**green soybean** *Subst. green peas; fresh soybeans are always cooked before eating*
土豆	tudou	**potato**
豌豆	wandou	**pea** *Subst. lima bean; also called fava bean or green peas*
豆苗	doumiao	**pea sprouts** *The tops of very young soybean sprouts; subst. mung bean sprouts*
青蒜	qingsuan	**leeks (green tops of)** *Chinese leeks are closer to onions, hence stronger than Western leeks; used mostly in Northern cuisines; taste like green tops of garlic*
青柿椒	qingshijiao	**sweet green pepper**
红柿椒	hongshijiao	**sweet red pepper**
白萝卜	bailuobo	**white radish (Chinese turnip)** *Turnip*
胡萝卜	huluobo	**carrot**
红胡萝卜	honghu luobo	**orange-red carrot**
葱	cong	**scallion (spring, or green onion)** *A basic flavoring; whites more delicate but greens also used*
姜	jiang	**ginger root** *Always fresh; usually scraped or peeled before slicing or mincing; a "hot" yang ingredient; good for digestion*
蒜	suan	**garlic**
干辣椒	ganlajiao	**hot red pepper, dried**

黄豆芽	huangdouya	**soybean sprouts** *Sold fresh or canned; change water daily after opening can; always parboil or stir-fry fresh ones before eating to kill bitter flavor and odor*
绿豆芽	lüdouya	**mung bean sprouts** *Subst. alfalfa sprouts if eaten raw; tops are called silver sprouts*
西红柿	xihongshi	**tomato**
荸荠	biqi	**water chestnut** *Bullrush root; sold canned; refrigerate in constantly fresh water; also ground into flour for tender batters*
葱头	congtou	**onion**
冬菜	dongcai	**preserved dried cabbage** *Sold in cans*
榨菜	zhacai	**hot-pickled mustard tuber** *Turnip, green cabbage, or radish preserved by soaking in salt solution; sold in cans or jars*
云南大头菜	Yunnan datoucai	**pickled rutabaga from Yunnan Province**
腌雪里蕻	yanxuelihong	**pickled mustard greens** *Sold in brine in bulk or 16 oz. (500 g) jars and cans; subst. sauerkraut*
糖腌蒜头	tangyan suantou	**sweet pickled garlic bulb**
山药	shanyao	**Chinese yam** *Long, narrow sweet potato; a staple protein in common diet since the mid-18th century*
发菜	facai	**hair-fine, dark purple sea moss** *Sold dried; looks like black hair; used in new year's festival dishes*
	longxucai	**asparagus (see Shoots, Mushrooms, and Fungi)**

Shoots, Mushrooms, and Fungi

	SHOOTS	
龙须菜(芦笋)	longxucai (luxun)	**asparagus**
青笋	qingsun	**bamboo shoots** *Largest shoots are gathered in spring; summer shoots are tiny; a different type grows from the root and is packed in brine*
冬笋	dongsun	**winter bamboo shoots** *Smallest, most tender and most desirable; sold canned in plain water; look like white pine cones*

玉兰片	yulanpian	**dried bamboo slices, soaked** *Tips are salted and dried, sold in bulk and soaked before being used as flavoring in soups*
	MUSHROOMS	
香菇	xianggu	**black mushroom** *Sold dried; soak for half hour before cooking; used for flavor; subst. fresh white mushrooms for consistency, not flavor*
鲜蘑	xianmo	**fresh white mushroom**

口蘑	koumo	St. George's mushroom *Tricholoma gambosun* Whitish-colored, irregular in shape, from north of Beijing (40° longitude)

草菇	caogu	straw mushroom *Peaked cap; sold fresh, dried or canned; refrigerate opened can; change water frequently*

冬菇	donggu	black winter mushroom *Lentinus edodes* Sold dried; dark grey on top, light yellow beneath; always remove stems and soak for at least an hour

FUNGI

木耳	muer	cloud (mu-er) ears *Auricularia auricula-judae* Sold dried; also called tree ear or black fungus; soak in water brought to boiling, remove when cool; will swell into flower-shape; remove pithy stem

银耳	yiner	white fungus (silver fungus) *tremella* Sold dried; prepare like mu-er (above); used often in vegetarian Buddhist recipes; rare and expensive; believed to be a strong medicinal tonic

竹荪	zhusun	staghorn (or bamboo) fungus *Dictyophora phalloidea* Sold dried; extremely rare and expensive; looks like white lace; grows on bamboo only in Sichuan Province

羊肚菌	yangdujun	morels *Sold dried; reddish brown cap; looks like a sponge; soak to reconstitute shape and soften*

Proteins and Starches

PROTEINS

豆腐	doufu	bean curd (tofu) *The juice from a purée of soybeans is set into a custard with a coagulant; in firm form it is sold fresh in square cakes of 3 in. (7.5 cm), each 1 in. (2.5 cm) thick; refrigerate in water in a tightly covered jar, changing water daily; spoils in a week; instant bean curd powder is now becoming available*

付竹	fuzhu	dried soybean milk *Sold in yellowish, wrinkled sticks, dried; the surface skin that forms when soybeans are boiled is skimmed off and dried*

面筋	mianjin	gluten *A high-gluten flour-and-water dough is soaked and kneaded in water to wash out starch; remaining gluten is porous, like a sponge; it is cut into pieces and used like dumplings to carry flavor and give substance in liquid sauces*

油皮	youpi	dried soybean curd sheets *Yellowish translucent "skins" of dried soybean milk; wrappers for vegetarian dishes made to resemble meat; soluble in water*

燻麸	kaofu	wheat gluten (vegetable steak) *A vegetarian food, made from the protein extracted from flour; resembles beef steak; canned*

粉丝	fensi	cellophane noodles (bean thread) *Transparent noodles made from mung bean flour; soak before cooking*

龙虾片	longxiapian	prawn crackers (shrimp chips) *Thick, crispy, shrimp-flavored crackers; sold in cellophane bags; subst. potato chips*

洋粉 (冻粉、石花菜)	yangfen (dongfen) shihuacai)	agar agar *Dark green; product of seaweed, sold dried in paper-thin sheets, sometimes as powder or noodles; soak in cold water; subst. cellophane noodles for texture only*

STARCHES

面粉	mianfen	flour *Finely ground, white wheat flour used for making steamed breads and dumplings*

大米	dami	rice *Primary basic food accompanied by other foods*

江米	jiangmi	glutinous rice *A variety of white rice with short round grains that becomes sticky and almost clear when cooked*

大米饭	damifan	cooked rice		面包	mianbao	bread

大米饭 damifan **cooked rice**
Allow 2 oz. (60 g) per person, rinse until cold water is clear, add water in pot one-thumb-thickness above rice, cover tightly, boil suddenly; barely heat 15 to 20 minutes, stir only at end; grains will be individual but sticky enough to pick up

馒头 mantou **steamed bun**
To make at home: 1 Tbsp. sugar, ¾ cup (185 ml) of warm water, 1½ tsp. yeast, 2½ cups (300 g) white flour, 1 Tbsp. lard; mix sugar, water, and yeast; let rest until foamy; add flour and lard, knead, form buns; let rise 10 minutes; steam 10 minutes (makes one dozen)

面包 mianbao **bread**

咸面包 xianmianbao **salty bread**

酵面 xiaomian **fermented dough**
Dough leavened with yeast, kept like sourdough-starter

发面肥 famianfei **yeast**
Subst. baking powder

食碱 shijian **baking soda**

Fruits, Nuts, and Sweets

FRUITS

菠萝 boluo **pineapple**
Fresh or canned

荔枝 lizhi **litchi**
Fresh or canned; fragrance of fresh litchi changes within one day, then taste in two; texture resembles white grapes

樱桃 yingtao **cherry**
Usually maraschino, bottled; used mainly for decoration

桔子 juzi **tangerine**
Chinese generic word for fruit of the orange family; Mandarin orange has correct flavor

龙眼 longyan **longan (a fruit)**
Litchi family; smaller; sold fresh or canned

NUTS

花生米 huashengmi **peanut**

核桃仁 hetaoren **walnut**

芝麻 zhima **sesame seed**
White seeds used for sweet fillings, garnish, sesame paste

黑芝麻 heizhima **black sesame seed**
Used for soup or garnish

莲子 lianzi **lotus seed**
Lotus is a water lily; to prepare for cooking, blanch and steep for 5 minutes, remove brown wrapper and bitter germ, boil about 12 minutes; subst. almonds

SWEETS

瓜条 guatiao **winter melon, preserved**
Pickled in brine; bottled; subst. pickled cucumber, young marrow, or zucchini (courgettes)

桔饼 jubing **tangerine, candied**

枣 zao **date (jujube)**
Dried red date; subst. prune

蜜枣 mizao **date, candied**

青果 qingguo **Chinese green, fresh olive**

甜杏仁 tianxingren **sweet almond**

杏仁 xingren **almond**

糖桂花 tangguihua **osmanthus flower, candied**
Small white flowers, sweetly fragrant; preserved in alcohol and sugar solution; dry or bottled; subst. crystalized rose or violet petals

糖玫瑰 tangmeigui **rose candy**

青梅饯 qingmeijian **sour plum, candied**
Green plum, small; like an olive

山渣糕 shanzhagao **hawthorn jelly**
The hawthorn fruit is sour with a taste like cranberry, size and consistency of crabapple; Chinese children eat candied on a stick

蜂蜜 fengmi **honey**

Seasonings

花椒	huajiao	Sichuan peppercorn (wild pepper)	饴糖（麦芽糖）	yitang	malt sugar *Made from fermenting germinated grains of barley; golden, thick, strong-flavored; subst. corn syrup, molasses, honey*	
八角	bajiao	aniseed, star anise *Sold whole; tips may be broken off stars*				
白胡椒粉	baihu jiaofen	powdered white pepper	泡椒辣	paolajiao	pickled hot pepper	
花椒盐	huajiaoyan	prickly ash *A mixture of toasted peppercorns and salt ground fine; see recipe following Ingredients Guide*	辣椒面	lajiaomian	powdered dried hot pepper	
			腌韭菜花	yanjiucaihua	pickled chive flower *Small white flowers of sturdy-stalked variety of chive, pickled in brine*	
精盐	jingyan	salt	干淀粉 （玉米粉）	gandianfen	cornstarch (cornflour)	
味精	weijing	MSG (monosodium glutamate) *A flavor-enhancer that can cause physical discomfort in some people; for that reason all listings in the recipes are given in parentheses*	湿淀粉	shidianfen	cornstarch paste (cornflour paste) *A ubiquitous thickener made up fresh by the chef in consistencies to suit; see instructions following Ingredients Guide*	
冰糖	bingtang	crystal sugar *Rock candy*	水淀粉	shuidianfen	dissolved cornstarch (cornflour)	
白糖	baitang	sugar *Partly-refined, dark brown; pressed into cakes; subst. light brown sugar*	桂皮	guipi	Chinese cinnamon	

Liquids, Pastes, and Oils

	LIQUIDS		葡萄酒	putaojiu	grape wine, red *Not common; sweet*	
酱油	jiangyou	soy sauce *Sold in bottles; made by steaming soybeans until soft, kneading with flour, cutting into cubes, salting, and leaving them to ferment in a crock for 40 days; the first draining is light in color and flavor; darker sauce is sweeter and thicker*	桂元汁	guiyuanzhi	Longan fruit juice *Subst. litchi fruit juice*	
			牛奶	niunai	milk *Rarely used except in Mongol, Tibetan and Hunnan cuisines*	
			四川郫县豆瓣酱	Sichuan Pixian doubanjiang	broad-bean sauce *A thick, very spicy sauce made in Pixian in the province of Sichuan*	
辣酱油	lajiangyou	hot pungent sauce *Subst. Worcestershire sauce*				
米醋	micu	rice vinegar *Distilled from rice; dark brown, strong and sweet-flavored; subst. cider vinegar with a little sugar*	豆瓣辣酱	douban lajiang	hot broad-bean sauce	
			甜面酱	tianmianjiang	fermented flour sauce (sweet)	
			西红柿酱	xihongshijiang	tomato sauce	
料酒（黄酒）	liaojiu	rice wine *Yellowish; the finest quality is from Shaoxing; subst. dry sherry*	果子酱	guozijiang	fruit jam *A sweet, thick fruit preserve usually made of citrus fruits; subst. tangerine or orange marmalade*	
白酒	baijiu	liquor *A clear spirit distilled from sorghum or maize; subst. corn whiskey or vodka*	红糟	hongzao	red fermented mash *A colorful flavoring which adds substance to the taste of a dish; fermented rice is dried and packaged in small plastic bags*	
茅台酒	maotaijiu	Maotai liquor *Highly potent, clear spirit for toasting at banquets; distilled from millet; subst. vodka or tequila*				

蠔油	haoyou	**oyster sauce** *Dark brown flavoring and coloring made of fermented soy sauce and the liquor of oysters; keeps a long time*	芝麻油（香油）	zhimayou (xiangyou)	**sesame oil** *Nutty, strong aroma; used sparingly for flavor; used for cooking only in Northern cuisines; bottled; refrigerate*
卤虾油	luxiayou	**shrimp sauce** *Bottled; almost a paste; pungent and very salty; the fermented essence of pulverized shrimp*	辣椒香油	lajiao xiangyou	**sesame oil flavored with hot chili** *Bottled; made by frying red peppers in sesame oil until oil turns red*

PASTES

			花生油	huashengyou	**peanut oil** *The most commonly used vegetable oil; oil used once for stir-frying is preferred to fresh oil for its flavor*
黄酱	huang jiang	**soybean paste, salted and fermented** *Sometimes labeled "ground bean sauce"; sold in jars, cans, or in bulk; canned must be put in screw-top jar and refrigerated*			
芝麻酱	zhimajiang	**sesame paste** *Subst. peanut butter blended with sesame oil*	猪油	zhuyou	**lard** *Purified Pork fat used for frying; serve those dishes while they are very hot; solid shortening gives same consistency but different taste*
酱豆腐	jiangdoufu	**fermented bean curd** *Bean curd is soaked in saltwater and alcohol; while it ferments it softens into a paste; keep in a capped jar in refrigerator; quite salty*	鸡油	jiyou	**chicken fat** *melted; used for final flavoring*
			鸭油	yayou	**duck fat**
	OILS		花椒油	huajiaoyou	**peppercorn-flavored oil** *Peanut oil is heated with finely-ground Sichuan peppercorns; sold bottled*
油咖喱	yougali	**curry-flavored oil** *Sold in bottles; heat peanut oil mixed with curry powder; cool and bottle*			

Dry Spices

砂仁	sharen	**amomum seed clusters** *Cardamom family, native to Vietnam; bitter, aromatic, resinous flavor*	良姜	liangjiang	**galingale** *Subst. ginger*
豆蔻	doukou	**whole cardamom** *Native East Indies, grows in Guangdong Province; said to cure hangovers and dyspepsia*	白芷	baizhi	**angelica root** *Carrot family; subst. celery*
			枸杞	gouqi	**wolfberry** *Berries of matrimony vine, Lycium Chinense; honeysuckle family, a dry prairie shrub*
丁香	dingxiang	**clove**			
草果	caoguo	**amomum tsao-ko** *Elongated oval capsules from Yunnan Province with masses of angular seeds; said to cure stomach disorders*	山耐	shannai	**lily buds** *Dried buds from the Easter Lily; subst. any day lily*
			肉果	rouguo	**nutmeg**
肉桂	rougui	**Chinese cassia** *Rough bark like cinnamon; distinctive flavor; called sweet olive in southern U.S.; blossoms are preserved; subst. cinnamon*			

A note from the Western editors: We are not able to recommend a single source in this country from which non-Chinese-speaking people can reliably order an adequate range of dried, bottled, or canned Chinese ingredients directly by mail or telephone. Readers knowing of such sources are encouraged to write to the publisher or directly to: The Editors, Allen D. Bragdon Publishers, Inc., 153 West 82nd Street, New York 10024, USA.

陈皮	chenpi	**orange peel, dried** *Tangerine peel or Mandarin orange peel, is sun-dried naturally*

Clear Stock   Qing tang

You may substitute another chicken for the pork to make a pure chicken stock or substitute equivalent amounts of other meats in this stock to suit your needs.

- 1 chicken (2 lbs./1 kg)
- 2 lbs. (1 kg) fresh pork, with bone
- 3¼ oz. (100 g) scallions, white bulb only, chopped into 2-inch (5 cm) pieces
- 1¾ oz. (50 g) crushed peeled fresh ginger
- 3½ tablespoons rice wine
- ½ lb. (250 g) skinned, boned chicken breast, mashed for final, optional refining step

1. Place the meats in a dry wok and add cold water just to cover. Heat to boiling over an intense flame; skim off the broth.
2. Add the scallions, ginger, and rice wine. Lower the heat, cover, and simmer for 4 hours.
3. Remove and discard the solid ingredients, then strain the broth through gauze or fine-mesh cheesecloth.

To make a stock of the most delicate and refined quality, add the mashed chicken breasts to the strained stock after it has cooled. Place over an intense flame and heat, stirring steadily in one direction (clockwise or counterclockwise, but do not change direction), until boiling. Lower the heat and let boil gently for 15 minutes. Any remaining impurities in the stock will adhere to the chicken breast. Strain the stock again.

Stock to a cook is voice to a singer.

Milky Stock

Follow instructions for Clear Stock through step 1. Boil over a medium flame for 2 hours; keep at a low boil. During the second hour the soup will turn milky. Keep the flame low enough so the soup does not boil away. After 2 hours the soup will be thick.

An alternate recipe used by some restaurant chefs uses meat and bones only to make large batches. The alternate calls for a 3-pound (1.5 kg) cleaned and plucked chicken and 1 pound (500 g) each of pork meat, pork bones, and fresh pig's trotters (feet). They are boiled in water to cover, briefly, to clot any blood for easy removal. The meat and bones are transferred to a huge stock pot with 5½ quarts (5.5 L) of cold water. After it is brought to as fast a boil as possible, then boiled over a medium flame until two thirds of the liquid has boiled away, and it has turned white, (about 2½ hours), remove meat and bones.

Prickly Ash   Huajiaoyan

This is a dip for a variety of dishes. It is also called "Pepper–Salt" or "Toasted Salt and Sichuan Pepper." This recipe yields about ¼ cup.

- 4 tablespoons salt
- 1 tablespoon whole Sichuan peppercorns
- ½ teaspoon whole black peppercorns

Heat a heavy dry skillet or wok over moderate heat and pour in the peppercorns. Stir constantly until the heat releases the fragrance of the pepper, about 1 minute. Pour the peppercorns into a mortar and grind them to a fine powder. Reheat the skillet or wok and pour in the salt. Stir it constantly until it just begins to turn golden brown, less than 5 minutes. Pour it into a bowl to cool for 1 minute. If the peppercorns have not been ground uniformly fine, put them through a sieve and grind the larger pieces again. Mix ground peppercorns with the salt. Discard obvious husks. After the mixture has cooled, store it in a jar with a screw top so it will not pick up other aromas. It will keep indefinitely if kept dry.

White Soup   Bai tang

1. Heat a dry wok over a medium flame. When the wok is hot, add two handfuls of fresh soybean sprouts and fry briefly to eliminate the sharp smell.

2. Pour in water to fully cover the sprouts and let boil for 30 minutes. The soup should be quite thin, not reduced. Strain out the soybean sprouts and refrigerate the stock.

Vegetarian dishes commonly require a "stock" made from soybean sprouts. Standard stocks, made from meat and bones, are not allowed in the diet of Buddhist monks, who provide many of the most imaginative vegetarian recipes. This White Soup plays the same role that a meat stock plays in nonvegetarian cuisines.

Cornstarch Paste   Shuidiaufeu

Chinese chefs use a mixture of cornstarch and water as a final thickener and glaze in nearly every recipe that produces seasoned liquids. They also thicken liquids in preparation steps prior to the final stages. The standard proportions are 1 part cornstarch to 2 parts water. When different proportions are required, they are given in the recipe. A thin paste might call for 3½ parts water; a thick paste, equal parts of water and cornstarch. If the mixture sits for a while, the cornstarch may separate from the water, so stir again just before adding it to the recipe ingredients.

Pronunciation Guide

Chinese words in this volume are rendered in the *pinyin* system of romanization. The People's Republic of China has used this system in its foreign language publications since January 1, 1979, and most American publishers subsequently adopted it.

Many readers will be more familiar with renderings of the traditional systems—Postal Atlas for place names and Wade-Giles for personal names and other words. Below are guidelines on how to pronounce words rendered in *pinyin* (Wade-Giles equivalents are in parentheses).

a (a): as in far
b (p): as in baby
c (ts): as "ts" in its
ch (ch'): as "ch" in church, strongly aspirated
d (t): as in do
e (e): 1) as "er" in her, the "r" being silent
2) as in yes in the "ie" dipthong
3) as in way in the "ei" dipthong
f (f): as in foot
g (k): as in go
h (h): as in her, strongly aspirated
i (i): 1) as in eat
2) as in sir in syllables beginning with c, ch, r, s, sh, z, zh
j (ch): as in jeep
k (k'): as in kind, strongly aspirated
l (l): as in land
m (m): as in me

n (n): as in no
o (o): as "aw" in law
p (p'): as in par, strongly aspirated
q (ch'): as "ch" in cheek
r (j): as "r" but not rolled, or like "z" in azure
s (s,ss, sz): as in sister
sh (sh): as "sh" in shore
t (t'): as in top, strongly aspirated
u (u): 1) as in too
2) as in the French "u" in "tu" or the German umlauted "u" in "Muenchen"
w (w): as in want
x (hs): as "sh" in she
y (y): as in yet
z (ts, tz): as in zero
zh (ch): as "j" in jump

Pinyin	Wade-Giles
Zhang Aiping	Chang Ai-p'ing
Zhang Caiqian	Chang Ts'ai-ch'ien
Zhang Chunxiao	Chang Ch'un-hs'iao
Zhang Tingfa	Chang T'ing-fa

Pinyin	Wade-Giles
Zhang Zhixiu	Chang Chih-hsiu
Zhao Ziyang	Chao Tzu-yang
Zhou Enlai	Chou En-lai
Zhu De	Chu Te

Place Names

Pinyin	Postal Atlas
Baotou	Paotow
Beijing	Peking
Changsha	Changsha
Chengdu	Chengtu
Daqing	Ta-ch'ing
Dazhai	Ta-chai
Fengtian	Fengtien
Fujian	Fukien
Fuzhou	Fuchow
Gansu	Kansu
Guangdong	Kwangtung
Guangxi	Kwangsi
Guangzhou	Canton
Guiyang	Kuiyang
Guizhou	Kuichow
Ha'erbin	Harbin
Hangzhou	Hangchow
Hebei	Hopei
Hefei	Hofei
Heilongjiang	Heilungkiang
Henan	Honan
Hubei	Hupei
Huhehaote	Huhehot
Jiangsu	Kiangsu
Jiangxi	Kiangsi
Jilin	Kirin

Pinyin	Postal Atlas
Ji'nan	Tsinan
Lanzhou	Lanchow
Liaodong	Liaotung
Ningxia	Ninghsia
Qingdao	Tsingtao
Qinghai	Tsinghai
Shaanxi	Shensi
Shandong	Shantung
Shanxi	Shansi
Shijiazhuang	Shihchiachuang
Sichuan	Szechwan
Tianjin	Tientsin
Tiaoyudai	T'iao-yu-tai
Wuxi	Wu-hsi
Xi'an	Sian
Xiangtan	Hsiang-t'an
Xi'ning	Sining
Xinjiang	Sinkiang
Xizang	Tibet
Xuzhou	Hsuchow
Yan'an	Yenan
Yangzi	Yangtze
Yinchaun	Yinchwan
Zhejiang	Chekiang
Zhengzhou	Chengchow

TRIPLICATE ZENG-STEAMER

Belonging to the 12th century B.C., consists of four parts. The rectangular body, 42 inches (104 cm) long, 18 inches (45 cm) high, and 11 inches (27 cm) wide, is for holding water. The bottomless zengs are 10 inches (26 cm) high, and 13 inches (33 cm) wide. Ingredients are placed on a bamboo grate inside the zeng.

DING-CAULDRON

Ding-cauldron was popular two thousand years ago. This one, of the 12th century B.C., is of medium size—9 inches (22 cm) high, 10 inches (25 cm) in diameter, and weighs 25 pounds (10 kg).

The Tools and Techniques

用具及技術

You don't cut bamboo with a knife that has just cut scallions; you don't crush food with a pestle that has just been crushing pepper; nor do you use a dirty cloth or cutting board, the flavor of which can linger on the food. The good cook sharpens his knives, uses a clean towel, scrapes down the chopping-board, and washes his hands; he keeps tobacco ash, flies, ash from the fire, and his own sweat, all safely away from the food.

M. Yüan

üan Mei was an inspired scholar who lived during the later Ching period and wrote an often-quoted book of recipes called *Shih Tan*. In the passage quoted here he describes his personal chef, Wang Hsiao-yü, with the lively appreciation that makes him such an eloquent spokesman for the passionate Chinese attitude toward food. "... He insisted on doing all the marketing himself, saying, 'I must see things in their natural state before I can decide whether I can apply my art to them.' He never made more than six or seven dishes, and if more were asked for, he would not cook them. At the stove, he capered like a sparrow, but never took his eyes off it for a moment, and if when anything was coming to a boil someone called out to him, he took not the slightest notice, and did not even seem to hear... When he said, 'The soup is done,' the kitchen-boy would rush up the tureen and take it, and if by any chance the boy was slow, Wang would fly into a terrible rage and curse him roundly... I once said to him, 'If it were a question of your producing your results when provided with rare and costly ingredients, I could understand your achievements. What astonishes me is that, out of a couple of eggs, you can make a dish that no one else could have made.' 'The cook who can work only on a large scale must lack daintiness,' he replied, 'just as one who can handle common ingredients but fails with rare and costly ones can only be reckoned as a feeble practitioner. Good cooking, however, does not depend on whether the dish is large or small, expensive or economical. If one has the art, then a piece of celery or salted cabbage can be made into a marvellous delicacy; whereas if one has not the art, not all the greatest delicacies and rarities of land, sea or sky are of any avail'. "(Trans. Waley 1956 from K.C. Chang pp. 292-3).

The first cooking vessels were made of pottery and were developed in the New Stone Age. They were a *ge*-cauldron, which stood over an open fire, and a *zeng*-steamer, which had small holes in the bottom and fitted into the cauldron. The larger *ding*-cauldron was among the bronze utensils that supplanted the early pottery vessels. The bronze pots were more durable and quicker to heat. In turn, bronze utensils were supplanted by iron ones. Now kitchenware is made of metal, pottery, and bamboo.

The earliest cooking fires were made in holes dug in the ground. The *ge*-cauldron stood on three legs over the fire. By 200 B.C. brick stoves had been invented, and there appeared a new *fu*-cauldron that could sit directly on the stove. Today, most Chinese restaurants still burn coal in brick stoves, while a few use gas. Some Chinese dishes are cooked over charcoal or firewood—charcoal is used for the Mongolian hot pot; firewood, for roast duck. (The best firewood for cooking comes from fruit trees because it yields a fragrant smoke and an intense fire with minimum ash.)

This section is an illustrated, condensed chef's manual explaining the utensils, the techniques for preparing raw ingredients, the four levels of heat, and the nineteen cooking methods. The terms described here are also used in the recipes.

1. Five basic cooking utensils are used in China as well as cleavers and long cooking chopsticks. Three other cooking vessels are used in regional cuisines: the Hot Pot and grill for Mongol recipes, and the steam pot used in Yunnan Province.

2. There are ten basic motions used to cut raw ingredients. All of them are executed with cleavers or long cleaver-knives. Since Chinese master chefs must also be skilled at butchering meat, some motions may be only of academic interest to the Western home cook.

3. The *shape* of the pieces is one of the four classic components a Chinese chef must consider to create a skillfully balanced dish. The other three are *color*, *fragrance*, and *flavor*. This section illustrates the eleven sizes and shapes that raw ingredients are converted to in Chinese cuisine.

4. Most Chinese chefs work with coal, some with gas. The fire is kindled inside a brick stove with circular holes in the top. A wok sits down inside the hole so the heat of the flame comes in direct contact with the sides as well as the bottom of the iron vessel.

5. Each method is described in detail, and its English or Chinese names are given. The techniques are all known to Western chefs. Some of the cooking vessels are different, however, so the techniques vary.

1. Wok 2. Ladles 3. Strainer 4. Clay casserole 5. Steamer

The Utensils

Compared to Western kitchens with saucepans, frying pans, and mixing bowls in graduated sizes and a plethora of labor-saving gadgets, the Chinese home kitchen offers a sharp contrast. Most cooks prepare entire meals using only six utensils: wok, steamer, cleaver, ladle, strainer, and casserole.

The Wok

The wok is a very efficient cooking pan. Made of lightweight iron, it was designed with a rounded bottom to fit over a primitive brazier. It conducts and holds heat evenly. In Western markets woks are available in stainless steel, copper, aluminum, and porcelainized enamel over steel, but their sole advantage over the authentic iron wok is appearance. Iron rusts, but in a Chinese home the wok is used many times a day, so rusting is not a problem. At times of high humidity, or at the seashore, the wok can be stored in a heavy plastic bag.

The size of the wok is an important consideration for home cooking. Two sizes, 12 or 14 inches (30–35 cm) in diameter, 3½–4½ inches (8.5–11.5 cm) deep are the most practical. Larger sizes take too much space on a range and the heat input of domestic ranges is not adequate for cooking in large quantities. Woks are available with metal or wood handles on each side, or a single wood handle about 8 inches (20 cm) long. Many cooks like the long wood handles because they eliminate the need for potholders.

When shopping for a wok, it is a good idea to buy the lid and a ring (usually sold separately) at the same time. Lids are made of lightweight metal, usually aluminum, with a wooden knob on top. The domed shape allows for cooking a whole duck or chicken in the wok. A ring is essential in Western homes because ranges are flat on top. The ring fits over a gas burner and cradles the wok, preventing it from tipping during cooking. Rings come with round holes or notches to provide air for the gas flame. If your gas burner has a square grid, or the grid is large, it is a good idea to bring the grid when you shop so you can have the ring cut to fit over it.

For homes equipped with electric ranges, a flat-bottom wok, designed to be used on electric burners, is now available. It is slightly shallower than the regular wok and it does not require a ring because the bottom of the pan must touch the electric unit for it to work. An electrified wok is also on the market, but the temperature range is limited; this model is best for small recipes, such as those for two portions. Since electric heat lingers after a control is turned off, food must be removed from the pan immediately to prevent overcooking. Electric rice cookers, automatically controlled, are excellent for cooking large quantities of rice.

How to Clean and Season a Chinese Wok

A new wok is coated with grease to keep it from rusting. That coating must be thoroughly removed before starting to cook. To remove the heavy film, wipe the wok with crushed paper towels.

Place the wok on the ring and fill it with boiling water. Let it soak for 30 minutes. Wash in warm, soapy water and use a stiff brush to remove adhering coating. When the surface is smooth and clean, rinse well, wipe with a paper towel and place over low heat to dry. Using more paper towels, rub vegetable oil (peanut or corn oil) on the surface of the wok. Keep the heat low so you can continue the rubbing action. Do not let oil sit in the wok. Heat about 10 minutes, then wipe the pan clean. Repeat the oil treatment, heating ten more minutes. Use a fresh paper towel and wipe out the wok, removing excess oil. It is now ready for use.

After cooking in a wok, soak it in hot water and clean as you would an omelet pan. Never use detergents or abrasives as they will remove the seasoning and cause foods to stick to the surface. If food sticks, use a stiff brush or steel wool without soap. Always dry the wok thoroughly over very low heat.

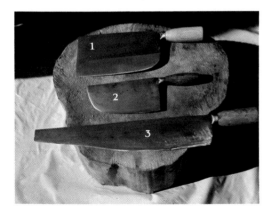

1. Chopper **2.** Slicer **3.** Dual Purpose

Cleaver

In the Chinese kitchen cleavers are used for peeling, pounding, crushing, slicing, and even transporting food from chopping board to wok. They are available in a variety of materials and weights. An all-purpose cleaver is of medium weight with a blade somewhat over 8 inches (20 cm) long and 3 to 4 inches (8 to 10 cm) wide. A heavier cleaver, weighing almost two pounds (1 kg) is convenient for chopping bones such as drumsticks and ribs. A smaller, lighter cleaver is useful because a thinner, sharper blade is good for slicing vegetables and meats. The medium-weight cleaver is preferred by most Chinese cooks; blades made of tempered carbon steel are preferred, as they hold a sharp edge. The wood handle on these cleavers gives them a crude appearance that belies their efficiency. Stainless steel cleavers with metal handles, while nicer in appearance, require more frequent sharpening and the handle gets slippery.

A cleaver should always be razor sharp and polished. To prevent rusting, wipe it with a dry cloth after use. Sharpen it frequently on a fine-grained whetstone. Hone the cleaver evenly on both sides to keep the blade straight and sharp. After cleaning the blade and wiping it dry, hang the cleaver by the handle to keep the blade from becoming dulled on other metal in a drawer. A cutting board is an important accessory and in most Chinese homes a cross-section of a tree trunk, several inches thick, is used.

Steamer

Bamboo and metal steamers are designed to stack in layers on top of a wok. Water is placed in the wok and live steam circulates through the layers so an entire meal can be cooked over a single burner. Steamers are easy to improvise, however, in Western kitchens. Use a large kettle, or a roaster with a trivet to lift food above the boiling water. Collapsible stainless steel and aluminum steamers can be used in this manner.

Ladle

Also made of iron, the ladle has a long metal handle with a wood tip. It is used for adding ingredients, stirring during cooking, and transferring food from wok to serving bowl. It is now available in aluminum, which weighs less and does not rust. A spatula or shovel is often sold with the ladle and it is handy for cooks unaccustomed to chopsticks. It fits the bottom of a wok and is used for lifting and tossing foods during stir-frying.

Strainer

Made of copper or steel wire with bamboo handles, or of perforated metal, strainers are used to scoop foods blanching in hot oil or water. The disc-like shape allows for transferring large quantities of food quickly to avoid overcooking.

Casserole

Made of earthenware or stoneware, this utensil comes in a variety of sizes and shapes. It is often unglazed on the outside and glazed on the inside, with a snug fitting lid. Foods such as rice and sausages or chicken are placed in the casserole, then cooked in a water bath—not unlike cooking in a double boiler. Food simmers slowly in this utensil, resulting in concentrated flavor.

Regional Cooking Utensils

Minority peoples have contributed distinctive utensils and methods of cooking to the Chinese cuisine. The following are three utensils often encountered at Chinese markets that originated among non-Han minorities.

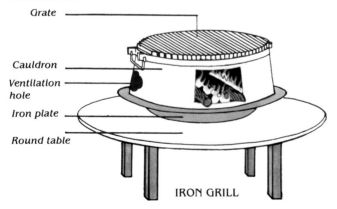

Grate
Cauldron
Ventilation hole
Iron plate
Round table

IRON GRILL

An iron cauldron sits in the center of an iron-covered round table. The grate, made of iron rods rests on an iron ring.

Iron Grill

Broiling (cooking foods by dry, intense heat) is not often done in China. Occasionally, you may be served very thin slices of meat, marinated in soy sauce, chili peppers, garlic, scallions, and the like. Such dishes are cooked quickly on sturdy iron, charcoal-burning grills. The little stove resembles a hibachi, the grate made of welded iron rods resting on an iron cauldron.

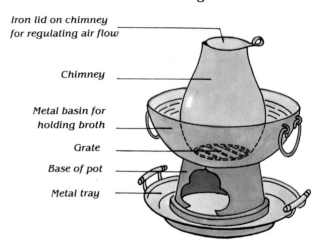

Iron lid on chimney for regulating air flow
Chimney
Metal basin for holding broth
Grate
Base of pot
Metal tray

THE MONGOLIAN HOT POT

The Mongolian Hot Pot, a brass vessel, is used for cooking lamb in the style of the Northern herdsmen.

Mongolian Hot Pot

This pot was designed by nomadic northern tribes for cooking meat and vegetables in broth. The flared base with a chimney is the stove. Since it uses charcoal for fuel, and the bottom gets very hot, it must be used on a heatproof surface. The cooking pan is shaped like a doughnut, with a large hole in the middle to let it slip over the chimney. Broth is placed in the cooking pan and heated. Each diner is furnished with a small wire strainer or a pair of chopsticks to pick up thinly sliced meat or vegetables to cook in the boiling broth. (Thinly sliced lamb is usually offered in northern China.) Ingredients such as sesame seed oil, soy sauce, wine, fermented bean curd, ginger, and garlic are assembled nearby for each diner to mix a dipping sauce for seasoning the cooked ingredients.

When all the sliced meat is consumed, cellophane noodles and leafy greens are added to the broth, then eaten as a finishing touch, as a flavorful soup.

The base of the pot has a sliding door that serves as a draft for controlling air for the fire. A grate on top of the base forms the bottom of the chimney. A metal basin, shaped like a doughnut holds the broth.

Steam Pot

This pot-bellied kettle originated in Yunnan Province, close to Vietnam. It is made of earthenware and features a funnel rising in the center, resembling the tube pans used for sponge cakes in Western kitchens.

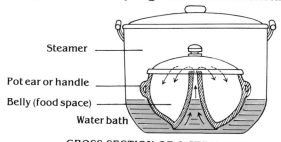

CROSS-SECTION OF A STEAM POT

This pot-bellied earthen steamer has a funnel that rises in the center.

The Four Levels of Flame

Chinese cooks use all five senses—sight, sound, taste, touch, and smell—while preparing food. The sound of a big sizzle when food is added to a preheated wok is important. If there is no sizzle, the wok and oil are not hot enough. When preparing to fry in deep fat, cooks watch for movement of little waves on the surface of oil to determine that the proper temperature has been reached. They may test the temperature by adding a slice of ginger root to the heating oil. If the oil bubbles actively around the ginger slice, the temperature is right.

Inexperienced cooks are dependent upon precise directions and recipes when cooking. They learn to cook using automatic controls, thermometers, and other measuring devices. Deep-fat frying, for instance, is often done in an automatically controlled fryer; or a frying thermometer may be clipped to the side of the frying pan. When the temperature reaches 375 F (190 C) degrees, the oil has reached proper frying temperature. But cooks who rely on such devices seldom observe changes in the appearance of foods during cooking. Neither can they recognize signals that indicate what is happening during the cooking process. They can be quite helpless when mechanical cooking aids fail.

Serious cooks worldwide realize that observation brings dimension and judgment to food preparation. They know that an intense blue flame is desired when cooking with natural gas; a red or orange flame indicates the burner needs adjusting. When they use charcoal as fuel for outdoor cooking, they preheat it until the flames disappear, because heat from flames

is uneven. When flames subside, the hot coals provide intense, even heat, perfect for cooking. Every fuel has its special characteristics that seasoned cooks identify without the help of gadgets.

The amount of heat necessary for cooking depends on the method of cooking, the size of the pieces, and the nature and amount of ingredients. Foods such as snow peas, mushrooms, bean sprouts, and scallions cook quickly. Denser foods such as green beans, carrots, lotus root, and bamboo shoots take longer for heat to penetrate; they must be cut thinner and given more cooking time. Since oil reaches higher temperatures than water, foods cooked in oil require more intense heat; cooking time will be shorter. Conversely, foods cooked in water or steam require less intense heat.

For most Chinese recipes the following range of temperatures is adequate:

375 F (190 C) degrees for deep-fat frying
325 F (163 C) degrees for stir-frying
300 F (149 C) degrees for oil blanching
212 F (100 C) degrees for boiling and steaming
194 F (90 C) degrees for simmering

The following color illustrations show the four intensities of flame—weak, low, medium, and intense—used in the recipes selected for this book. Traditionally, the Chinese cook over charcoal. In restaurant kitchens brick stoves are built to waist height. When stoked the flames reach the woks through large holes in the stove top in which the wok sits solidly. Gas flames of comparable intensity are also shown.

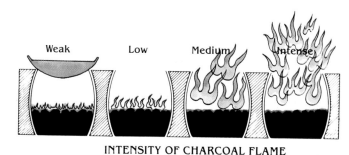

INTENSITY OF CHARCOAL FLAME

INTENSITY OF GAS-FLAME

The Basic Methods of Cooking

Chinese dishes are prepared in a variety of ways, to suit the many ingredients used. Techniques for preparing food with heat vary according to region, taste, and the desired color. Some of the principle methods used in Chinese cooking are listed here.

Chao, or stir-frying, can be compared to sautéeing, except it is done in a wok instead of a flat-bottom frying pan. The food is tossed continuously during frying, while during sautéeing it is turned once. Because of its flared sides, the wok exposes a larger surface to direct heat. Yet it requires less oil than a flat-bottom pan as the oil moves to the bottom of the pan and ingredients are continuously tossed with it. Cooking by this method is quick, seldom more than 2 or 3 minutes. Success depends on proper cutting and preparation of ingredients, preheating wok and oil (heat the wok a little before adding the oil), the sequence of adding each ingredient, and sensitivity of the ingredients to the amount of heat. Stir-frying over a low flame is called *Pa*.

Jian is slow frying. The food is cooked on one side, then turned to the other, as in Western sautéeing. The flame is much lower than in stir-frying.

Ao is stir-frying meat. The meat is cut up, seared, then simmered in a thick broth, like a stew without vegetables.

Bao is precooking. Ingredients are dipped into boiling water or oil before stir-frying. Green vegetables, for instance, are blanched to intensify color and release acids. They are drained and quickly cooled, then thoroughly cooked by brief stir-frying.

Ja is deep frying in hot oil, often done as a two-step process: The first frying precooks the food at a lower temperature, 300 F (150 C) degrees; a second frying, in hotter oil of 375 F (190 C) degrees, produces an appetizing color and texture.

Peng is a method of cooking shellfish. It starts with deep frying, then stir-frying in a sauce. This combination of cooking methods lends a velvety texture to the food.

Jing is steaming. Food is cooked by live steam under and around a bowl, a platter, or a rack of food resting above boiling water or broth inside a covered wok or pot. Fish and minced meats are sometimes marinated first. They are usually served in the dish in which they were cooked.

Cuan is boiling or parboiling meat quickly in broth or water, as in Mongolian hot-pots prepared at the table by diners.

The preparation of rice illustrates how Chinese cooks determine cooking stages. Rice starts cooking in cold water over an intense flame in an uncovered pot. When the boiling point is reached, the flame is reduced to simmer and the lid goes on the pot. After 15 to 20 minutes, large holes called "fish eyes" appear on the surface of the rice. These indicate the rice has finished cooking—all the water has been absorbed. But this rice isn't served immediately: it must stand at least 15 minutes while each grain of rice fully plumps itself. If stirred immediately after cooking, rice grains break up and become sticky. After the resting period, the rice is fluffed using a chopstick or pair of chopsticks. Only then is it ready to be served.

Suan boiling. This method is used only for meat and simple primitive boiling (as with a whole sheep).

Dun and *Wei* is stewing food in its own juice in a clay casserole, either vigorously or simmered over a very low flame for a long time.

Men is stewing. Food is simmered in a tightly sealed casserole over low flame. Usually meats are browned first, then cooked in a small amount of liquid. "Red-cooked" foods are prepared in this manner.

Hui is similar to *Men*, but meats are blanched instead of browned and cooked in broth over low heat. The cooking is done in a saucepan, Dutch oven, or casserole, and vegetables are usually included. Meat, vegetables, and soup are eaten at the same meal.

Ju is quick boiling—like blanching, only the time is extended 3 to 5 minutes, then the heat is reduced for simmering. This method is used for preparing meat. The fast boil removes blood and pieces of bone, insuring a clear, flavorful broth.

Kao is roasting. This may be grilling on a rack or over charcoal, wood, or gas. Strips of meat may be toasted or tossed on a grill, or they may be broiled from below on a skewer.

After several hours of marinating, meats are seared at high heat to crisp the skin and seal in juices. Heat is then turned down to low to finish cooking. Unlike Western methods of roasting, in which meat is placed on a trivet in a roasting pan, the Chinese hang the meat so each piece is surrounded by dry heat. A pan containing water is placed under roasting meat to catch the drippings. Meat may be basted with the marinade during final stages of roasting.

Guo Qian is a finishing touch used with many methods of cooking. A cornstarch paste is added to cooking juices. This thickens juices so they adhere to the other ingredients. It yields additional distribution of the sauce as well as a tempting shiny appearance.

Combined Cooking Methods

To achieve subtle nuances of texture and flavor, the Chinese combine numerous cooking methods. The silky, melting texture of Velvet Chicken, for instance, is achieved by poaching or blanching the chicken and egg white in warm oil. This coagulates the egg white without toughening it. The blanching oil is drained off and the blanched meat is subjected to a second frying at a higher temperature. The result is a true delight. Following are some additional samples illustrating how cooking methods are combined to produce special effects:

Xiu—ingredients are first fried or steamed, then brought to a boil in water. The pot is then covered and the heat reduced to simmering. After ingredients are cooked, the lid is removed, heat is increased, and juices are condensed to thicken the sauce.

Liu—ingredients are coated with cornstarch or flour, then fried or steamed, and finally added to a sauce and simmered to finish the cooking process.

The Cutting Techniques

In Chinese cooking all ingredients are cut into small pieces. One reason for this is that fuel was so scarce, the people invented ways to cook it quickly before the precious sticks of firewood were consumed. Bite-sized pieces are also easier to eat with chopsticks. Since knives have never been used on Chinese tables, foods have to be manageable with chopsticks and the meat separated from bone or shell in the mouth with nimble manipulation of tongue and teeth.

Preparation of raw ingredients is a major part of the technical challenge in Chinese cuisine. The size of the pieces into which an ingredient is cut must be uniform—not only to create aesthetic harmony but because each piece must be cooked evenly; larger ones will be undercooked and smaller ones burned. The judgment of cooking is also a consideration. Thin slices cook faster than chunks. Tender ingredients may be cut larger than tough ones that require more cooking time. Thick pieces such as kidney or squid may be scored to permit more heat and sauce penetration. And less tender cuts of meat can be tenderized by cutting across the long fibers that run lengthwise.

For these reasons a Chinese chef must be able to cut a given ingredient into pieces of uniform size, command a repertoire of a wide variety of shapes, and work very quickly. A spectrum of techniques has been developed to suit the physical characteristics of differing ingredients. A chef must master all the basic ones described here.

Straight Cutting

When cutting straight slices, the cutting motion is up and down. The cleaver is held at a right angle to the chopping board. Using both hands, the stronger hand manipulates the cleaver, the other hand guides the ingredient into the cutting path. Press the knuckle on the middle finger of the hand holding the ingredient against the flat side of the blade. This facilitates feeding the ingredient into the knife at an even rate, resulting in equal-sized pieces.

Push Cut For compact or tough foods, such as meat, push the cleaver down and forward while cutting straight down.

Pull Cut For tender ingredients like bean curd, pull the cleaver back toward the body while cutting straight down.

Saw Cutting For cutting fibrous ingredients such as ham, beef or bread, use a sawing motion. Like straight cutting, the cleaver is held at right angles to the ingredient and is moved forward and backward instead of cutting straight down. Cut slowly and steadily, keeping the blade straight up and down.

Rock Cutting This cutting method is used for mincing ingredients such as water chestnuts, onion, or breast of chicken. Grasp the handle of the cleaver with the stronger hand. Line up the blade at a right angle to the ingredient. Rest the heel of the other hand on the blunt back of the blade, near the tip. (Chefs often use a cleaver with a rounded blade and this facilitates a pivoting action.) The cleaver never leaves the chopping board as the cutting edge pivots from one side to the other while cutting up and down. This results in a rocking motion; thus the name, rock cut.

Diagonal Roll Cutting

This cut achieves a distinctive appearance for round or oval shaped ingredients such as asparagus and carrots. One hand rotates the vegetable as the blade moves up and down diagonally, slicing off oblique-shaped pieces.

Heavy Chopping

A heavy cleaver is used for butchering meats or severing fish heads. Hold the handle of the cleaver with the stronger hand and chop straight down, cutting completely through with the first blow.

Slap Chopping

For lighter bones such as young poultry and fish, hold the blade on the cutting line and slap the back of the cleaver with a mallet, a block of wood, or your hand.

Lock Chopping

Thick, solid bones, such as pig's feet, may need two or three blows. A heavy cleaver is used and the first blow should lock the cleaver blade into the bone. A properly locked cleaver will pick up the entire ingredient and both material and cleaver swing down together on subsequent blows.

Two Blade Mincing

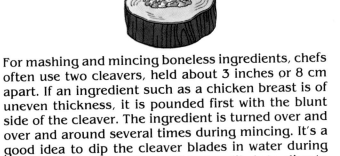

For mashing and mincing boneless ingredients, chefs often use two cleavers, held about 3 inches or 8 cm apart. If an ingredient such as a chicken breast is of uneven thickness, it is pounded first with the blunt side of the cleaver. The ingredient is turned over and over and around several times during mincing. It's a good idea to dip the cleaver blades in water during mincing so the ingredient will be less likely to cling to the blades.

Horizontal Slicing

For boneless foods, such as pork kidney and chicken breast, and soft foods such as bean curd, the cleaver moves parallel to the chopping board to make thin, even slices. Hold the cleaver horizontally and push it straight forward from the bottom up or the top down, cutting the full length of the ingredient. Hold the ingredient securely with the other hand to prevent it from slipping.

Pull Slice For slicing meat, such as ham or beef, slash it, then pull the cleaver toward the body as indicated by the arrow.

Push Slice For fleshy vegetables like bamboo shoots, first make a cut in the ingredient, then push the cleaver forward and inward as indicated by the arrow.
Diagonal Roll Slice Used for thick slabs such as fish fillet, the cleaver forms an acute angle to the chopping board. Basic movements are similar to those used in horizontal slicing.

Forehand Diagonal Slice The back of the cleaver faces outward. The cutting movement is toward your body.

Backhand Diagonal Slice This is for slippery items like squid, and for tender leaves like cabbage. If you are right-handed, incline the cleaver to the left with the back facing inward, toward you, and slice away from your body. Rest the fingertips of your left hand on the

block so your hand is at the same angle as you want the slice to be. Let the flat side of the blade ride on the knuckles of the guide-hand so the angle stays the same for each slice. Move the fingertips back on the board the same distance for each slice so as to get uniform thickness.

Combination Cuts —Scoring

This technique slashes diagonal lines or cuts across ingredients with long fibers such as chewy seafood, kidneys, squid, and some meats. Cutting across fiber tenderizes it. The cuts also let sauces and heat penetrate more evenly. The cutting movements are variations on those used in horizontal slicing, combining forehand and backhand diagonal slicing. Keep the slashes as uniform as possible and a diamond pattern results on the ingredient, resembling an ear of corn or a bunch of grapes.

The Eleven Shapes

The shape of each ingredient in each dish served at a Chinese meal is an important consideration. To achieve variety among the dishes served at a banquet, one dish may consist of diced ingredients, while another might feature roll-cut chunks of uniform size. A whole fish would offer something completely different, so the fourth dish might be slivered, sliced, or minced. The shape of each ingredient is determined by its nature, the method of cooking, and the specific aesthetic requirements of a recipe.

Western cooks use slicers, graters, shredders, grinders, and food processors for shaping ingredients. But Chinese cooks rely on the cleaver, achieving amazing results in uniformity and appearance. A sharp cleaver cuts through fibers without bruising or crushing. Too often the cutting edges of household utensils are not sharp enough to achieve the crisp shapes that a cleaver does.

Slices, Strips, Cubes, Slivers, Diced pieces Thick, thin, and diagonal slices are basic for a variety of other shapes. By stacking and turning slices the Chinese cook will cut strips and cubes, starting with thick slices. Thin slices can be maneuvered into slivers and

The people of Fukien are called san Pa Tao which means that they are skilled in three crafts that depend on the use of sharp blades: barbering, tailoring, and cooking.

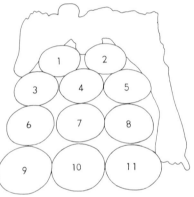

THE ELEVEN SHAPES

1. Strips 2. Scallion sections 3. Diagonal pieces 4. Diced pieces 5. Cubes 6. Gear-shaped pieces 7. Bits 8. Consecutive pieces 9. Slivers 10. Mash (chicken) 11. Vegetable sections.

diced pieces—and even bits in the same manner. Diced ingredients should be about the size of a grain of rice. When cut even more, they become bits—the size of a millet kernel.

In stir-fry cooking the dominant ingredient determines the cutting shape. For instance, in Pepper Steak, beef is cut into strips, so green pepper is cut in a similar way. For Shrimp and Peas, shrimp is diced to harmonize with peas. Cubes of pork are the dominant ingredient when combined with bean curd. So the bean curd is cubed like the pork. Ham and scallions are often cut into slivers or diced to be used as garnishes.

Consecutive Slicing, Gear-shaped Slices Sometimes vegetables like cucumbers and radishes will be sliced diagonally, but the cut doesn't go entirely through the vegetable; slices are still attached consecutively. The slices are then fanned out, or twisted, to create an unusual looking garnish. Sliced vegetables may be cut into shapes like willow leaves, oblongs, and other geometric forms. A gear-shaped slice is achieved by slashing grooves the length of a cylindrical shaped vegetable, such as a cucumber, before slicing. This results in indentations around the circumference of each slice.

Diagonal Slice, Roll Cut Rolling while cutting an ingredient creates an irregular, oblique-shaped chunk that exposes considerable surface to heat and sauce. This is a variation of diagonal slicing and is used for vegetables like carrots, asparagus, and green and yellow beans. The first cut is at a 30-degree angle, then the vegetable is rolled ¼ turn and the next diagonal cut is made. The cutting and rolling are continued until all the vegetables are sliced.

Mash Fish and chicken are often minced (or mashed) extremely fine and ingredients such as egg, starch, fat, or chicken broth are added to adjust the consistency. This type of mixture is used for various "meatballs" and for stuffing vegetables. Seasoning ingredients such as pickled vegetables, mushrooms, scallions, and ginger are often added to mashed mixtures for flavor and texture.

Crushing Ingredients such as garlic and ginger root are often crushed, using the broad side of the cleaver. Crushing releases the flavor; at the same time the ingredient does not fall apart, so it can be removed intact before serving. Radishes are also crushed in this manner, then marinated and served as a cold dish. The handle of the cleaver is used as a pestle for crushing seeds such as Sichuan pepper and coriander seeds.

Sections, Pieces Leafy vegetables, like Chinese cabbage, mustard greens, and spinach are cut in sections or pieces as determined by the recipe. Scallions are cut in pieces or slivered vertically in 3-inch (8-cm) long pieces. These are often slivered on both ends to be used as a garnish or as a brush for spreading hoisin sauce on doilies (pancakes or crêpes) served with Beijing Duck.

Scoring Large pieces of meat and fish are slashed on the surface in opposite directions to allow seasoning and heat to penetrate evenly. Scoring the surface produces attractive diamond patterns. Bowed shapes, like roof tiles, are created by scoring and undercutting the surface of the ingredient. Scoring also helps to tenderize meats made up of long fibers, as the cuts sever the fibers.

Cuts of meat

The principal sources of animal protein in the Chinese cuisine are pigs, sheep, cattle, chicken, ducks, and fish. The Chinese refer to the flesh of beef, poultry and fish alike as "meat." Freshness is perhaps the most important consideration of Chinese cooks in selecting meat for a meal. This accounts for the number of food markets that offer live poultry, fish, rabbits, and turtles throughout the country. It also means that home cooks, as well as chefs, must know how to slaughter and butcher meat.

For home use, meat is purchased in relatively small amounts, enough for one or two family meals. Because of lack of refrigeration, salted and dried meats are used as well as fresh cuts. Two or more different meats often appear in a single menu. However, meat is the main ingredient in only one or two dishes, such as red-cooked pork or a white-cooked chicken. In stir-fry (or *chao*), vegetables are often the dominant ingredient, i.e., Chicken with Mung Bean Sprouts and Beef with Cellophane Noodles (often called "Ants on a Tree"). In such dishes meat furnishes flavor and textural contrast, but it may be less than one third of the ingredients.

The method for cooking meat depends on the quality of the meat, the part of the carcass it comes from, and the skill of the cook. Because many homes have no facilities for roasting or baking, roasted pork, duck, ribs, and chicken are usually purchased ready-to-eat. In many Chinese cities, such meats are available from itinerant peddlers, as well as at restaurants and meat stores.

The less tender cuts of meat are usually scored or cut against the grain, or fiber, severing the long, tough strands; then they are often marinated before cooking in a savory sauce. Long-fibered cuts, such as flank steak, are sliced into strips against the grain and marinated before stir-frying. Cuts that have tendon strips throughout, such as beef shins, are treated with long, slow cooking. The tendons absorb flavors such as curry, anise, and ginger and provide an interesting texture for the Chinese palate. Tender meats, such as a whole fish, are often steamed or deep fried.

The most highly prized meats are pork, chicken, and carp. Their light color, even texture, and mild flavor are the qualities that have endeared them to Chinese cooks.

BURN-THE-TAIL FEAST During the Tang Dynasty (618-907), a "Burn-the-Tail Feast" was always held after the inauguration of ministers newly appointed by the emperor. The custom was for each new official to bring rare, elaborately prepared delicacies to the feast in order to show that his wealth and power would contribute to a glorious future for the emperor who appointed him. The name given to this feast came from an ancient legend called, "Carp Jump Over the Dragon Gate."

The Dragon Gate (also called Longmen) is a narrow, turbulent stretch of the Huanghe (Yellow River) between Hancheng of Shaanxi Province, and Hejin of Shanxi Province. Two imposing peaks, swathed in clouds, rise steeply on either side forming a

natural gate through which the Huanghe furiously roars and tumbles. An old legend describes how, in the spring, carp came swimming upstream against the current to spawn. But at the Dragon Gate the current, alas, was too strong for them. No matter how fiercely they swam, they were always swept back short of their goal. Then one day a carp learned to leap and taught the others. Joyously, they flew in shimmering arcs through the Dragon Gate amid boiling spray that rose to meet great sheets of rain bursting from thunder claps. As they leapt through the clouds the deity burned their tails in recognition of their feat, transforming the carp into scaly dragons with long sinuous tails so powerful they could fly forever. A "burned tail," therefore, came to signify a promising future.

The Customs
風 俗

THREE LEGENDS

BOILING THE TWO MINISTERS During the Tang Dynasty (618-907) there were two powerful bureaucrats in the court of the Empress Wu Zetian. One, named Zhou Xing, was heavy-jowled, potbellied, and as greedy as a pig. The other, Lai Junchen, was notoriously corrupt and quacked incessantly in high-pitched, contemptuous tones when he presided over meetings in the court.

One day the two powerful and infamous ministers dined together at the Zhangjialou Restaurant on Changan Street. An apprentice of the good Master Chef Liu served a dish to them incorrectly. The ministers immediately had the apprentice taken away by the police guards and beaten to death. Chef Liu, helpless before the great power of the ministers, said nothing and went back into his kitchen. There he cut the intestine from a pig and the gizzard from a duck. He dipped them into boiling water and served them to everyone else in his restaurant, calling his new dish "Two Ministers, Boiled."

When the customers spread the word about the meaning of the name for Liu's new dish others came to the restaurant and ordered it. As the fame of the dish spread the people took courage and began to lodge complaints against Zhou Xing and Lai Junchen. Empress Wu, hearing of these mounting complaints, sentenced the corrupt minister Lai to death and sent the greedy minister Zhou into exile.

IMPERIAL CONCUBINE YANG AND THE LITCHI Palates of great discernment notice that the exquisite fragrance of the fruit of the litchi tree changes within one day after the fruit is picked; the taste changes after two.

A favorite dish of the Imperial Concubine, Yang, who served the emperor during the latter days of the Tang Dynasty, was "Litchi with Wild Duck." Her power was such that she could command the imperial couriers, who had the fastest horses in all China and which were used only to deliver the emperor's most urgent dispatches to and from the imperial palace at Beijing in the north of China. Each year when the litchis began to ripen to perfection in the subtropical south of China, relays of imperial couriers were seen riding furiously the length of China and back again.

Through history it is frequently the poets who foresee the true trend of things and are able to say so safely by veiling their insights in verse. A Tang poet named Du Mu—who observed the extravagant imperial excesses during the period in which Concubine Yang was indulging her taste for litchi and wild duck—published a short verse memorable mainly for these lines, "The Concubine smiles at the dust-covered horse, but no one knows it is litchi it carries."

Should you ever have the good fortune to savor "Litchi with Wild Duck," be reminded of those lines and the decline of empires.

Folk Nutrition

There is an old Chinese saying: "All illnesses originate
from what is taken into the mouth; all disaster
emanates from the mouth."

The Chinese view of cosmic harmony—the delicate,
marvelous balance of things that allows the universe
to function—applies as well to the balanced harmony
of the human body. Its normal state, like all nature's,
is optimally functioning health. When the harmony is
disturbed by introducing foods into the body that un-
balance it, ill health shows itself. The "cool" *Yin* and
the "hot" *Yang* forces in the body's nutrition must be
maintained in a dynamic balance.

Throughout their 3000-year history, the Chinese
have shown a powerful, sensually joyous preoccupa-
tion with food—a result, perhaps, of both famine and
philosophy. China occupies an area about the same
size as the United States, for example, yet only 12% of
its land is arable (vs. 80% in the U.S.), and China's
population is five times larger. The struggle to wrest
sufficient food from the land has been unremitting. As
a result, the Chinese people have learned to maximize
the nutritional yield from whatever the land can be
made to produce. Much care was given to planting
and harvesting every product of the land and every
part of every comestible was utilized to its utmost.
Food should naturally be pleasing to the taste, but
can also be beneficial to the health, if properly man-
aged. Very early in Chinese recorded history, the five
flavors of food—sweet, sour, bitter, pungent, and
salty—were associated with the five basic elements of
all matter—earth, wood, fire, metal, and water. In
some texts as late as the Ming dynasty, these were
linked back into the human body by identifying them
respectively with the five "viscera"—stomach, liver,
heart, lungs, and kidneys. By this route, what the
palate discerns, the bodily systems use to govern and
sustain life.

Although ancient texts taught the effects various
foods have on health, these rules were never, charac-
teristically, incorporated into religious dietary laws.
As early as 510 A.D. the book *Food Cure* taught the
principles of good health, based on Doctor Sun
Simizo's maxim: "Treat the patient with curative food.

Use medicine only when the patient fails to respond."
The noted pharmacologist of the Ming Dynasty
(1368-1644), Li Shizhen, recorded in great detail the
medicinal value of plants and animals in his *Compen-
dium of Materia Medica*, explaining the importance of
nutritious food in preventing and curing diseases.
One of the most thorough of all early works that de-
scribe the medicinal value of foods was called *Essential Knowledge for Eating and Drinking*, compiled by
Chia Ming.

The wealthy scholar, Chia Ming, was in his hundredth
year in 1368 when the Ming dynasty was founded, and
the Ming Founder summoned him to the court to
honor him for his longevity. In the polite conversation
that ensued, the emperor of course asked him the
secret of his long life, to which Chia replied: "The
essential is to be most cautious about what one
drinks and eats." When the emperor asked further
about that, Chia replied that he had written a book on
the subject, which he would be happy to submit to the
throne. He did so; it is the book named above, which
has been widely printed in the centuries that followed.
Chia returned to his home after this encounter and
died there at the age of 106, not (of course!) of any ap-
parent ill health, but in response to an auspicious
dream.

Drink and food are relied upon to nourish life, yet if
one does not know that the natures of substances
may be opposed to each other and even incompatible
with each other, and (one) consumes them all
together indiscriminately, at the least, the five viscera
will be thrown out of harmony, and at the most,
disastrous consequences will immediately arise. Thus
it is that persons (successfully) nourishing their lives
have always avoided doing such damage to life.

Soybeans: their flavor is sweet; raw, their character is
warm, and when fried (or cooked) it becomes hot. They
are slightly poisonous. Eaten in excess they block the
lungs, produce phlegm and arouse coughing, induce
ulcerated sores, and cause a person to become yellow
of face and heavy of body. They must not be eaten
together with pork. Small greenish black beans, also
red and white beans, are similar to soybeans in flavor
and character. None should be eaten with fish or mutton.

Fragrant leeks (chiu ts'ai; Allium odorum): their
flavor is pungent and slightly acid; their character is
warm. Eaten in the spring season, they are fragrant
and quite beneficial. Eaten in the summer, they are
malodorous. Eaten in the winter, they cause a person
to arise during the night to get a drink. Eaten during

the Fifth Moon, they cause a person to become dizzy and weak. In the winter, before the shoots have emerged from the soil, they are called blanched leeks (*chiu huang*); those forced in cellars are called yellow-sprout leeks (*huang ya chiu*). Eating these impedes the *pneuma*, apparently because they retain in them some of the suppressed force of latent growth. Eating fragrant leeks after the frost has fallen on them causes vomiting; eaten to excess, they dull the senses and dim the eyes. One must especially avoid them after drinking wine. If one suffers from a chronic chill of the chest and abdomen and eats them, it will worsen that condition. If eaten ten days following a fever, they may induce drowsiness. They must never be eaten along with honey or beef, for that will cause intestinal blockage. Eating fragrant leeks causes bad breath; that can be dispelled by sucking candy. (Ibid.)

Spinach: its flavor is sweet, and its character is cold and slippery. Eaten to excess it may cause a weakening of the feet and will bring about pains in the waist and arouse chills. If a person who has previously been afflicted by stomach chills should eat spinach, it certainly will rupture his stomach. It must not be eaten together with eels, for that can induce cholera. If northerners, after eating meat and noodles cooked over a coal fire, should eat spinach, that will neutralize the (bad) effects. If southerners eat moist fish with rice and then eat spinach, that will gain a cooling effect. Spinach makes the small and large intestines cold and slippery. (Ibid.)

Distilled spirits (*shao chiu*): its flavor is sweet and pungent; its character is very hot. It is poisonous. Drunk to excess it damages the stomach and injures the spleen, disintegrates the marrow and weakens the muscles. It injures the spirit and shortens life. Persons who have *huo cheng* (tendency to have local fevers) should avoid it. If one consumes it together with ginger, garlic, or dog meat, it will induce hemorrhoids and will activate any chronic illnesses. If a pregnant woman drinks it, it can cause the child to have convulsions. Should one drink it to excess and develop a fever, he can be restored to clarity by being placed in cold water newly drawn from a well, or by having his hair soaked in that. Persons who have been poisoned by it can be somewhat restored by drinking cold salt water with green-pea flour. Or take a pint of large black beans and boil them to make one to two pints of soup. This, drunk in large quantities to induce vomiting, will dispel the poison." (Excerpted from Fredrick W. Mote's chapter and translation in *Food in Chinese Culture*, edited by K.C. Chang (Yale University Press, 1977.))

Many of these folk beliefs about the effect of foods as cures or causes were the product of practical empirical observations that worked: Some beliefs do not seem to mesh at all with modern nutritional science. The ancient texts advised: *Do not eat scallions with beef or honey. Do not eat plums with honey or the flesh of small songbirds.* —Meng Shen. *Do not eat animals that faced north as they died or meat refused by a dog.* —Ch'en Ts'ang-ch'i

Yet in ancient times, night blindness and anemia were treated with vitamin-rich lamb's liver; goiter was treated with high-iodine seaweed. In modern times, high-vitamin celery, eggplant, and dates are believed effective in the treatment of high blood pressure and arteriosclerosis. The following is a discussion of a few of the many beliefs about the medicinal value of the most frequently used Chinese cooking ingredients.

The Balance of Yin and Yang

The Chinese emphasis on the balance of *Yin* and *Yang*—the "moist" and the "dry" of the body system—influences their choice of food. Yin-Yang represent the interaction of opposites in nature which, when at one with itself, achieves harmony and tranquility—consequently, good health. *Yin* means cool, shaded, hidden, or covered. It also means the weaker force. *Yin* represents female, moon, dark quiescence, absorption, valleys.

Yang comprises heaven, sun, light, vigor, male, penetration, mountains, and all that is strong and hot. For example, people lacking *Yang* look weak, lack energy, appear undernourished, and have indigestion. They need to add high-protein sources, such as beef, into their diet. People lacking *Yin* look strong, but tire easily and get sick often. Ginseng, lamb, and herbs will be helpful to them. When the weather is humid, people feel tired; it is thought that this is caused by a dominance of *Yin*. It is believed that the body retains too much of this moisture. Sometimes, the tongue gets coated and small blisters appear on the skin. *Yang* foods like ginger, pepper, and spicy hot food will stimulate the perspiration to void the body's excess moisture. Conversely, if the body system is too dry, the *Yang* is overstrong; the nose bleeds and the lips crack. *Yin* foods like jellyfish and white tree fungus will help soothe and moisturize the system. Centuries ago, the Chinese stated that an excess of deep-fried food and chocolate would cause the dry symptoms of *Yang* dominance; whereas too much *Yin* food, such as asparagus, persimmons, and watermelon, lets the body become too damp and too cool.

Ginseng

Ginseng plays an important role in balancing the *Yin* and *Yang*, the dry and moist. There is both wild ginseng and cultivated ginseng. The wild variety is thought to be more potent. It grows in cool, mountainous regions. Ginseng roots are more valued the more they have the shape of the human body—with a head, a torso, and two legs. Such symbolism is important, for it is believed that ginseng has holistic curative powers for the entire human body.

This ancient wonder-herb is taken to help circulation, to energize and, it is said, to maintain the capacities of youth. It is taken in small amounts, and once taken, the effects are believed to last a long time. One way to prepare it is to simmer small pieces in water to make a broth—sometimes with pieces of chicken meat or bones added—thereby to transfer and reduce all of the essence of the root into this broth. Another way to take ginseng is to soak pieces of it in liquor—such as brandy or clear Chinese spirits distilled from sorghum—for a year or more. Drinking a small amount before bedtime is thought to confer the same benefits as the broth.

There are white and red Chinese ginseng and American ginseng. White ginseng is thought to be best for lowering blood pressure. Red ginseng helps build up circulation, stimulate the appetite, and strengthen people who are weak. The American ginseng is for cooling and soothing the body system; it is thought to be good for ridding the body of impurities. The wild ginseng are historically hard to find. Accordingly, one wild ginseng root is worth thousands of dollars. Its value, too, is increased by its correspondence to the human form.

> *Taking the five cereals as nutriment, the five fruits as assistants, the five meats as chief benefactors, and the five vegetables as supplements, and combining together the ch'i and the wei (tastes) in the diet; this blending is what benefits the mind and body.*
> Su Wen

Soybeans

They are the pivot-point of Chinese flavor and nutrition, yet soybeans are never consumed raw because they are indigestible at best and (perhaps because of their evolved resistance to pests and blight) may be poisonous. In the traditions of Chinese health and cuisine, soybeans rank highest—the one plentiful and inexpensive food with a venerable reputation for powerful nutritious value. Generations of chefs have devised ingenious and pleasing ways to include them in their cooking. Because of the high protein content of soybeans, vegetarian Buddhist monks—who may not eat flesh—have depended on soybean protein in many forms to keep them nourished, and to trick their palates by flavoring bean curd to resemble fish or meat. Recent studies of protein chemistry indicate that soybeans consumed with rice have a higher cumulative protein value than by soybeans alone.

Recipe: To make soybean milk, soak soybeans overnight, then grind them with water to make a thick mash. Dilute with enough water so the mash can be strained through a cheesecloth. The liquid becomes soybean milk. It contains the same nutrients as cow's milk, for which it is a substitute for allergic babies.

Recipe: To make the curdled bean curd, bring soybean milk to a boil; then use calcium sulphate to set it. Silky-textured bean curds will form into a soft solid. Cut the curds into square pieces and wrap them with cheesecloth. Put some weight on them to press out and drain excess water. The square curds will become firmer and the consistency will change with heavier or longer pressure. If you then deep-fry the bean curds, you get bean curd puffs. If you press out almost all of the liquid, pressed bean curds are formed. These can be preserved by cooking in soy sauce and spices.

If bean curd milk is boiled for a long time, a scum appears on top of the boiling liquid. This scum can be sun-dried to become bean curd sheets. The concentrated liquid, after further boiling, will be thick enough to pour onto fine bamboo mesh to dry. The result is dried bean curd pieces. Mock chicken, duck, meat, and fish dishes are cleverly concocted with these bean curd products. An ingenious chef can present a banquet of ten different "meat," "fish," and "game" courses—solely from bean curd products.

Garlic

Garlic is a wonder, in taste and conferred benefits. Garlic improves circulation, stimulates the appetite, and kills bacteria. How much can one eat aside from using it in seasoning? One cunning suggestion: if garlic cloves are soaked for several days in vinegar with a little sugar and salt, they are delicious and will not cause bad breath. Chinese doctors use cloves of garlic as an antibacterial in the treatment of tuberculosis and skin diseases.

> *Apart from foods which are poisonous in themselves, there are many which should not be eaten together as they do not harmonize and are apt to cause great discomfort and inconvience.*
> *Yin Shan Cheng Yao*

Ginger

Ginger taken internally produces warmth and helps to purify. It is widely used with seafood to counter the fishy odor. The most common culinary use of ginger is cooked with dark wine vinegar and pig's knuckles. It is thought to work wonders for mothers of newborn children, when taken for the month following childbirth. The vinegar releases the calcium from the pig's knuckles to replenish the mother's calcium. The pig's knuckle sinew repairs the mother's tissue; the ginger purifies the blood.

It is a Chinese custom that after feasting on crabs one must drink a ginger broth simmered with dark brown sugar. This combination not only offsets the cool, moist *Yin* of the crab and stimulates the digestion, but performs an antibacterial function as well, since crabs roam the lake bottoms and the seashore, where they might easily carry some sort of bacteria. The ginger and sugar are believed to help counteract the effects of these bacteria.

Mushrooms and Fungi

Chinese black mushrooms are used to treat high blood pressure and high cholesterol. They can be included in almost any dish. Black mushrooms and chicken feet, simmered in broth for hours, are a delicacy. In addition, chicken feet are a fat-free protein source.

Tremella (a white fungus), tree ear, tree fungus, or cloud ears (a black fungus) all have the same qualities as the black mushrooms. They are also used to build up vitality and promise the hope of longevity. They are a vegetable protein, easily digested and absorbed. Hot and Sour Soup and Mo Shu Pork have made the black tree fungus famous in Chinese cuisine. The white tree fungus is more rare than the black. Soup of white fungus and jujubes, taken daily, is believed to enhance youth and promote longevity.

Shen Nong tasted one hundred herbs to tell their properties—hunger allying, health keeping, and disease curing. The principle of Chinese medicine is "harmonization"—a proper mixture of ingredients. The essence of Chinese cuisine is synthesis—the artistic view of the Chinese nation and its philosophy.

Jujubes

Jujubes are little dates with red skin. Sweet, aromatic fumes fill the house when jujubes are cooked. They are called the food of harmony. They calm the nerves, induce sleep, and build up red blood cells. They are widely used as a filling in Chinese desserts, soups and stews.

Recipe: For a restorative beverage, bring ten jujubes, a few scallion bulb whites, and two cups of water to a boil. Continue to boil until the liquid is reduced to one cup. Taken two hours before bedtime, this brew can be used as a remedy for insomnia and anemia.

Barley

A nutritious barley soup is often served to children. It is believed to increase the metabolism rate and cleanse the digestive system. It has been reported that barley soup, consumed daily, can prevent overweight and lower blood pressure. In addition, its high vitamin content is respected by many health practitioners. Strong in calcium, protein, thiamine, and amino acid, it is widely considered a "wonder" grain.

Ch'en Ts'ang-ch'i included among tabooed meats the flesh of a black ox or goat with a white head, a single-horned goat, domestic animals that had died facing north, deer spotted like leopards, horse liver, and meat that a dog had refused to eat.

Poultry and Meat

Chicken meat is valued in China as a good source of protein, partly because it is also believed to nourish the five internal organs: the heart, liver, spleen, lungs, and kidneys. All parts of the chicken are used to build up health by stimulating the functions of the spleen and stomach, strengthening the bones and muscles, quickening blood circulation and, in women, regulating the menstrual cycle. Chicken broth is regular fare in Chinese kitchens. When chicken is simmered for a long time, the nutritious properties transfer into the broth. When the liquid cools, a gelatin forms—providing that it contains protein. Ancient lore, shared by many peoples, that home-made chicken soup is a cure-all remedy is not merely a saying in China.

Duck is also highly prized by many Chinese. A stew of duck meat, ham, and cucumber not only tastes delectable, it is used to improve urinary regularity, cure consumptive diseases, and relieve coughs. A porridge of glutinous rice and duck stock is prepared to nourish the stomach, enrich the blood, and help produce saliva.

Quail used to be wild game. No newcomer, it appeared on the Chinese menu three thousand years ago. Later, it was served exclusively at the royal table. The delicious, short-fibered quail meat is thought to increase energy, benefit the five organs, strengthen muscles and bones, and help reduce fever. New cooking techniques have increased the use of quail and quail eggs in Chinese cooking.

Quail meat, when cooked with red beans and ginger root, has long been considered a cure for dysentery. Recent data indicate that quail meat contains 20 to 30 percent more protein than chicken meat and 15 to 25 percent less cholesterol.

Lamb is considered an ideal "tonic"—higher in calcium and iron content than pork or beef. It is believed to stop pain, stimulate the appetite, and build up vigor. It is used in the treatment of asthma and tuberculosis.

Gelatin Protein Sources

Why do the Chinese people consider slimy, gelatinous foods delicacies?

Shark's fins, sea cucumber, bird's nests, duck's web, bear paws, and tree fungus are only a few of the many popular foods of this type. Thousands of years of experience have seemed to demonstrate that the bones and sinews of those who ate them did not become brittle as they aged. As a result these foods have become delicacies that health-conscious Chinese in their early and mid-thirties begin to make a regular part of their diet as a source of high-protein gelatin.

Shark's fins, for example, are needle-shaped gelatin pieces, held together to form the fin. Sea cucumber is a flavorless sea urchin called *bêche de mer* in the West that looks like a cucumber and has a consistency like jellyfish. Bear paws, the center pads of the bear palm, are thick pieces of gelatin.

Bird's nests are the skeleton of cliff-swallows' nests, made of secretions from their mouths, and lined with a delicate sea moss gathered from the surface of the waves and the feathers of the bird. These nests were obtained with great effort and difficulty by men who were carefully suspended by ropes from the summit of cliffs of Java, Sumatra, and the coast of Malacca where the nests were perched. Soup made from bird's nests is easily digested and nourishing. It is considered the best remedy for recovery after long illness. Also, bird's nest is believed to help reduce coughing. Because of the difficulty in acquiring them, the price for a good swallow's nest is quite high.

Shark's fins, sea cucumbers, bear paws, and bird's nests are all animal protein. Tree fungus, on the other hand, is a gelatinous secretion from trees, and as such is vegetable protein. None of these proteinous foods have any fat content. They are used for the repair of body tissue and the production of energy. After they have been sun-dried, they can be preserved for years without refrigeration, but require careful cleaning and soaking to return them to their gelatinous condition and make them edible.

From the Sea

Fish are noted for their nutritional value, especially carp, crucian carp, black carp, and eel.

Carp is good to eat by itself—praised for its beneficial effects on the liver, gall bladder, and spleen, and its benefits for the pregnant woman and foetus alike. But, the Chinese believe, if carp is cooked with winter melon peels it will also do wonders for inflammation of the kidneys. A quantity of carp stewed with half that quantity of red beans, taken once daily, is used to treat ascites, a condition caused by cirrhosis of the liver.

Eel, another delicacy, also has its medicinal value. *Recipe:* Place a generous portion of cut-up eel meat in a bowl; mix it with about four times that much dried pork; and steam the mixture briefly over an intense flame. Drink the broth, and eat the eel and pork. This delicious, single-portion combination is thought to cure kidney weakness. In addition to helping the kidneys and lungs, it has recently been concluded that eels are effective in treating diabetes.

These are but a few examples of the many ways the Chinese believe the food they eat can help maintain their health and restore nutritional balance. These beliefs are fundamental to Chinese culture. For that reason, an understanding of the properties of certain ingredients, used alone or in specific combinations, an appreciation of what foods the Chinese consider delicacies, and insight into the preparation of their food, all help us to see food as the Chinese see it—as a form of preventative and curative medicine.

"Don't eat carp with dog meat"
Chinese Proverb

The fire glows and the smoke puffs and curls;
From the incense-burner rises a delicate fragrance.
The clear wine has made our cheeks red;
Round the table joy and peace prevail.
May those who shared in this day's delight
Through countless autumns enjoy like felicity.

"The Golden Palace," anon., c. 1st century A.D.

Banqueting Protocol and Traditions

Tableware and Manners

From the archaeological findings and such books as the *Yi Jing* (the *Classic of Changes*), we learn not only how much the Chinese people enjoyed food and the rituals of eating, but also how important a role dining traditions and tableware played in their culture. Bronze vessels made to hold grain, water, and wine were embellished with beautiful and symbolic designs. Platters for meat, vegetables, soups, and sauces were adorned with decorations that show the great attention paid to eating and the importance of tableware for reflecting social status and formality.

In primitive society humans ate with their hands, and to this day the Chinese still refer to the index finger as the "eating finger." As cooking techniques developed and the varieties of food increased, utensils of bone, shell, horn, and pottery were used.

Table   77

Records from the 11th century B.C. show that King Zhou prized a pair of ivory chopsticks. Later, lacquer and porcelain wares were developed. About the time of the Ming and Qing (Ch'ing) dynasties, gold, silver and ivory were found in elaborate table settings. It is not all that surprising to learn, then, that the Empress Dowager Ci Xi of the Qing dynasty had an enormous collection of 1,500 pieces of gold tableware weighing 290 kilograms (about 640 pounds) and silver tableware weighing 529 kilograms (1160 pounds). Emperors and empresses customarily ate six times a day and presumably used a great many serving pieces.

Yet for many reasons, it was not precious metals but porcelain ware which proved to be the most practical and functional, as well as aesthetically pleasing, for serving at table. Ornate color pictures of people

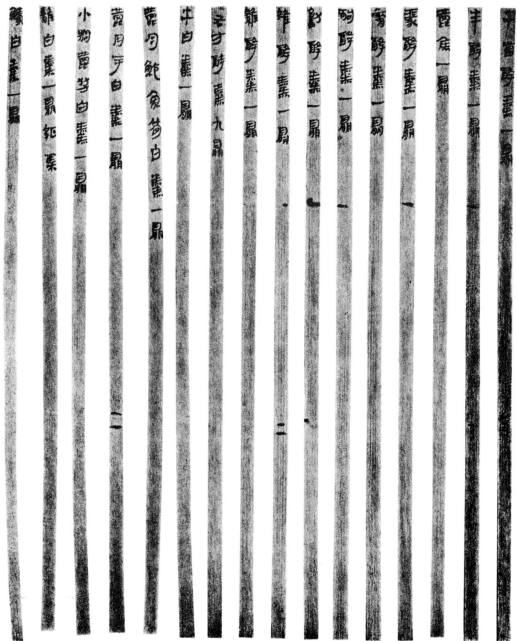

Bamboo slips from the Han tomb at Ma-wang-tui, listing names of food dishes furnished in the tomb

3000 YEARS OLD

Ivory cup, 12 inches (30 cm) high, belonging to the Yin and Shang Dynasties (12th century B.C.)

and scenery could be permanently baked on this delicate medium. Unlike gold and silver, porcelain reacts to neither acid nor alkali. Furthermore, it does not conduct heat as quickly as gold or silver—an important consideration since the Chinese people like to consume steaming hot soups, foods, and teas. To continue to use exquisite dinnerware made with gold and silver, the Chinese later developed a technique of lining dinnerware sets with porcelain.

Unlike the tableware of the ruling class, the common tableware used by most Chinese families is quite simple. Most important is the bowl to hold rice. The term "lose your rice bowl" is a euphemism for losing one's job. To hold a rice bowl in the palm of your hand is considered bad manners; instead, one should hold it with the thumb on the rim and the rest of the fingers supporting it at the bottom.

The second most important item are the chopsticks, used instead of forks and knives. Elaborate chopsticks are made of ivory or silver; now that ivory is largely unavailable, whale bone has become a

substitute. The most commonly used chopsticks, however, are made of wood or bamboo. Originally, the length of the chopstick was determined by notches in the natural bamboo. One may feel expert if one is able to pick up and hold a cherry with them. Because Chinese food is prepared in bite-size pieces, cutting is not necessary. Chopsticks allow one to reach for and pick up food, as well as to help push food like rice into the mouth. When taking food with chopsticks you should reach only for the part nearest to you, and never cross chopsticks with another diner when reaching toward a platter of food.

A variety of plates, spoons, and serving platters complete the setting. Small individual plates are used for condiments, or for bones left after eating. Each diner needs a porcelain spoon for soups and sauces. Unlike Western-style spoons, the handle on a Chinese spoon is an extension of the bowl of the spoon itself. An oval platter is designed to serve a whole fish. Round, shallow platters are used for dishes without a sauce; dishes with a sauce are usually served in a deeper dish similar to a large soup plate. A tureen is used for soup, which is customarily served at the end of the meal.

To set the table, the small plate is placed in front of each setting. The chopsticks are placed either to the right or below the plate. For convenience, the chopsticks are placed vertically next to the small plate with the lower half, or the eating end of the chopstick, at the top. The Chinese discourage the use

DRAGON LADLE

Lacquer ladle, 25 inches (62 cm) in length, embossed with a dragon design. It belonged to an aristocratic family living sometime between the 2nd century B.C. and 1st century A.D.

Table 79

of the left hand for chopsticks (not unlike Western discouragement of left-handedness). The soup bowl is placed to the upper right of the plate, with the soup spoon in it. The bowl of rice is placed on the plate. When banquets are served, the rice bowl is not set in place before the guests are seated. Instead, a full rice bowl is served to accompany each appropriate course. The meat and vegetable dishes all go to the middle of the table with the soup tureen in the center. Family members then help themselves as well as others. This practice is also followed in Chinese restaurants.

When a banquet is served, additional courses necessitate a more involved place setting. Still, only one pair of chopsticks is given to each person. A chopstick rest is helpful to prevent the chopsticks from soiling the tablecloth. During the course of a banquet, the small plates are changed with each new dish to keep the flavors from interfering with one another. Each person has a soup spoon (which should be held by the thumb, index, and middle fingers), a small plate on which to rest the spoon, and a very small sauce dish. All are set at the top of the small plate. The wine cup or glass goes on the right. Each service also has a smaller bowl, for shark's fin or dessert soup, and tea cups, with or without covers.

The serving pieces include a long, oval platter for fish or for cut-up whole fowl. A very large, deep, round platter is for delicacies, such as shark's fin and sea cucumbers, that have a lot of sauce. The 8-inch (20-cm) round plates are for cold dishes that come before the hot ones. The 10-inch (25-cm) round plates are for the stir-fry dishes. There is always a soup tureen with a cover and a ladle. (After serving oneself from the soup bowl, leave the spoon in it with the handle pointed toward the others at the table.)

There are also serving pieces for condiments: soy sauce and vinegar dispensers and dishes for mustard, hoisin sauce, and spiced salt. A tea pot and wine pot complete the setting. Traditionally, a complete set of china comes in a service for ten since, it is said, only ten people can convivially be seated around a table.

HAN XIZAI'S NIGHT FEASTING

Han Xizai was a bureaucrat during the Southern Tang period (923–936 A.D.). During a political crisis the Emperor needed a new prime minister so he appointed the prudent Han Xizai. That wily court politician knew that in troubled times one does not want to be in high office: one is more vulnerable to being put to death by the faction opposing the emperor should that group succeed. Yet a court bureaucrat could not refuse the current emperor on whose favors he depends for power and wealth. If Han Xizai said no to the appointment he would certainly lose more than just his career. A stratagem was needed that would cause the emperor to change his mind and withdraw the appointment voluntarily, without ever suspecting that Han Xizai was less than eager to serve his emperor. So, to that end, the prime minister-designate began indulging himself in riotous and carefree living — feasting, singing, and dancing the nights through. The emperor heard of this behavior and, because it was not true to Han Xizai's character, he sent Gu Hongzhong, a painter from the Royal Academy of Art, to spy out what Han was up to and document what he saw. When Gu returned from his mission he put down his observations in this painting. When the emperor saw it, he changed his mind. (This painting has never before been reproduced.)

Altogether this dinnerware service may consist of more than one hundred pieces.

In a Western household, one can usually find dishes to substitute for the traditional Chinese place settings. For instance, the salad plate can be used as the small plate; dinner plates can be used for serving the cold dishes and the stir-fry dishes. The meat platter can be used for fish and whole cut-up chicken or duck. With a little imagination, one will have no trouble serving a Chinese banquet with graceful settings.

> *In the triennial great sacrificial feast, one places the water goblet in the highest place, lays out raw fish on the offering table, and offers unflavored soup; thus showing honor to the unadorned basis of food and drink.*
>
> Hsün Tzu

Banqueting

According to legend, Chinese feasts took place as early as the 21st century B.C. At periodic intervals during the Shang (or Yin) dynasty (16th century to 11th century B.C.) the king, and each of his ministers, would offer sacrifices to ancient ancestors one by one. After the ceremonies they would partake of the offerings as part of the feast. By the Zhou dynasty (11th century B.C. to 771 B.C.), feasts honoring living dignitaries

INSTRUCTIONS TO THOSE SERVING AT A FORMAL BANQUET

Prepare a round table for ten—each guest will occupy a space of 24 inches (60 cm). Four articles are placed at each plate—a dish, a spoon, a pair of chopsticks, and a wine glass. The dish is placed in the center ¾-inch (2-cm) inside the edge of the table. The spoon is in the dish or on the table to the right of the dish. The chopsticks are to the right of the spoon; the wine glass is in front of the chopsticks. There may be more than one glass if wine and spirits are served depending on the occasion. In addition, there will be two sets of dishes, spoons, and chopsticks for the guests to serve themselves from platters.

The lefthand side is more important than the righthand side. The guest of honor sits to the left of the host. If he is with his wife, she will sit on the left and he on the right.

If the guests have come from distant places, the host invites them to take a rest before dinner. When the guests are seated, they will be served with scented towels to wipe off the dust from their faces and hands. When all the guests have arrived, the host will invite them to sit by the table. The first round of wine is poured, from the guest of honor and around to the right. Then the host will help his guests with the cold dishes using the serving chopsticks. After that, he will propose a toast. Another round of scented towels is served at the end of the dinner. After the eating, according to tradition the host is not permitted to leave the table before his guests.

Table 81

and heroes became popular. Banquets celebrating the coming of spring and the hunt were also observed. Gradually, festival feasts for weddings and birthdays became traditional. By today's standards, however, a banquet was a very solemn affair.

According to ancient books, many rules were established. During the Shang and Zhou dynasties, the arrangements were as follows. The people sat or knelt on mats placed in front of low oblong tables. Small dishes of food and cups of wine and water were placed and removed by attendants. The cooked meat with bones was placed on the left and sliced meat on the right. The cups with which the guests toasted were placed on the left and when emptied were placed on the right. Each guest would be served four large bowls of food made with grain. The number of dishes to go with the grain varied. The high-ranking officers would have more than the lower-ranking officers. A ninety-year-old gentleman would have more than an eighty-year-old, in accord with traditions of veneration for age, status, and so forth.

RULES OF ARRANGEMENT AND MANNERS AT THE DINING MAT FOR GENTLEMEN OF THE LATE CHOU PERIOD IN NORTHERN CHINA

1. "If a guest be of lower rank (than his entertainer), he should take up the (grain), rise and decline (the honor he is receiving). The host then rises and refuses to allow the guest to retire. After this the guest will resume his seat."
2. "When the host leads on the guests to present an offering (to the father of cookery), they will begin with the dishes which were first brought in. Starting from the meat cooked on the bone they will offer all (the other dishes)."
3. "After they have eaten three times, the host will lead guests to take of the sliced meat, from which they will go on to all the other dishes."
4. "A guest should not rinse his mouth with spirits until the host has gone over all the dishes."
5. "When (a youth) is in attendance on an elder at a meal, if the host should give anything to him with his own hand, the youth should bow to him and eat it. If he does not so give him anything, he should eat without bowing."
6. "When feasting with a man of superior rank and character, the guest first tasted the dishes and then stopped. He should not bolt the food, nor swill down the liquor. He should take small and frequent mouthfuls. While chewing quickly, he did not make faces with his mouth."
7. "When eating with others from the same dishes, one should not try to eat (hastily) to satiety. When eating with them from the same dish of (grain), one should not have to wash one's hands."
8. "Do not roll the (grain) into a ball; do not bolt down the various dishes; do not swill down (the soup)."
9. "Do not make a noise in eating; do not crunch the bones with the teeth; do not put back fish you have been eating; do not throw the bones to the dogs; do not snatch (at what you want)."

10. "Do not spread out the (grain) (to cool); do not use chopsticks in eating millet."

11. "Do not (try to) gulp down soup with vegetables in it, nor add condiments to it; do not keep picking the teeth, nor swill down the sauces. If a guest add condiments, the host will apologize for not having had the soup prepared better. If the guest should swill down the sauces the host will apologize for his poverty."

12. "Meat that is wet (and soft) may be divided with the teeth, but dried flesh cannot be so dealt with. Do not bolt roast meat in large pieces."

13. "When they have done eating, the guests will kneel in front (of the mat), and (begin to) remove the (dishes) of (grain) and sauces to give them to the attendants. The host will then rise and decline this service from the guests, who will resume their seats."

Li Chi, trans. Legge 1885 from K.C. Chang

These are only a few of many such admonitions.

It was not until the Northern Song dynasty (960–1126) that tables and chairs became popular. The commonly used table at this time came to be referred to as the "Eight Saints Table," since its square shape could seat two on each side. These tables are still in use in some old Chinese restaurants.

Traditions were passed down from the generations, yet many new rules were added. By the Qing dynasty (1644–1911), new rules of etiquette and new recipes were adopted from China's minority peoples—the Mongolians, Manchus, Hui, and Tibetans. It was said that the early officials of the Zhou courts would have over 30 dishes (18 cold dishes, 8 entrees, and 4 delicacy dishes); but by the Qing dynasty, the dinners and feasts became even more elaborate. The Qian Long emperor (1736–1795) was said to be served with 108 separate courses at dinner. During the twentieth century—after the imperial period in China had come to an end—feasts and banquets were simplified and reduced in extravagance, limited usually to only 20 courses.

At present, a feast or banquet contains 10 to 20 courses. A standard restaurant banquet menu will present the dishes in the following sequence: a group of about four cold dishes to go with the wine and first toastings; the first and main course containing the rarest delicacy; a group of hot dishes representing a variety of tastes, methods of cooking, and ingredients (poultry, meat, vegetarian, fish) served with wine; sweet dishes; dishes that go with rice; and, finally, soup.

THE MENU OF A MEAL SERVED TO EMPEROR CH'IEN-LUNG IN 1754

Main Course Dishes

A dish of fat chicken, pot-boiled duck and bean curd, cooked by Cheng Er

A dish of swallows' nests and julienned smoked duck, cooked by Cheng Er

A bowl of clear soup, cooked by Jung Kui

A dish of julienned pot-boiled chicken, cooked by Jung Kui

A dish of smoked fat chicken and Chinese cabbage, cooked by Cheng Er

A dish of salted duck and pork, cooked by Jung Kui

A dish of court-style fried chicken

Pastries

A dish of bamboo-stuffed steam dumplings

A dish of rice cakes

A dish of rice cakes with honey

Pickles (served in a ceramic container patterned with hollyhock flowers)

Chinese cabbage pickled in brine

Cucumbers preserved in soy

Pickled eggplant

Rice

Boiled rice

CONTEMPORARY IMPERIAL-STYLE BANQUET MENU FOR 14 GUESTS

Four Cold Dishes
Stewed Shark's Fins
Abalone with Mushrooms
Dong An Chicks
Crisp and Fragrant Duck
Stewed Soft-Shelled Turtle
Fried Eel Threads
Chicken Cubes with Hot Pepper
Braised Prawns
Dried Scallops and Eggs
Squirrel-shaped Mandarin Fish
White Fungus and Egg White Soup
Fish Maw and Pigeon Eggs Soup

Here is a sample of how a full banquet unfolds. First, four to eight cold dishes are placed on the table before the guests are seated. Similar to Western hors d'oeuvres, these are light vegetable and meat dishes to tease and induce the appetite. This course gives the chef more time to prepare the hot dishes that come later; it also allows more time for conversation and toasting. The cold cooked and raw foods are sliced and arranged on platters in brightly vivid and delicate patterns frequently copying nature. They are symbols of welcome. (The "Peacock Spreads Its Tail" and the "Dragon and Phoenix" are two examples shown in this book.) According to a Chinese saying, it is good for the appetite and digestion first to take cold and then hot dishes. When there are four cold dishes, put them on the corners of an imaginary square; when there are five, arrange them in the shape of a plum blossom.

THE PLUM-BLOSSOM TRAY MADE BY SHEN FU'S WIFE, YUEN

I am very fond of a little wine with my meals but I do not like elaborate food, nor too many dishes at a time. Yuen made a plum flower tray, for which she used six deep white porcelain dishes, about two inches in diameter, arranging five of them about the centre dish in the manner of a five-pointed star. When the box had been painted a light grey, the whole thing looked like a plum blossom, the tray and its cover both having indented edges, and the cover having a handle like the stem of a flower. When it was placed on the table, the tray looked like a fallen plum blossom, and the lifted cover showed the vegetables served in the petals. One of these trays, with its six different dishes, contains enough for a pleasant meal for two or three close friends. If the dishes are emptied, they can always be refilled for second helpings.

We also made another tray, a round one with a low border, which we found handy for holding our cups, chopsticks, wine pots and such things. These trays could be carried to any place one wished and were easy to remove again afterwards. This is an example of economy in the matter of food.

Yüan Mei (F. Shen, 1960 ed.)

Hot dishes are served when two thirds of the cold dishes are consumed. The first hot course is the main course, consisting of the most precious ingredient. (It is the most carefully cooked in order to give the guests a good impression of the host's effort to honor them.) At a bird's nest banquet, for example, the first course must be the bird's nest, and it is to be followed by the tremella (silver fungus or silver ear mushroom) because no matter how carefully the chef has cleaned the nests before cooking them, some tiny bits of down may be left in the nests. This kind of fungus will "collect" stray feathers and carry them through the digestive system.

After the rare delicacy to honor the guests has been served, the platters of cold dishes may be removed. The "fired" meats are then brought to the table, first the poultry, then the fish. If they are cut into pieces to cook, they are rearranged on the serving platter to resemble their original forms before being brought to the table.

When a whole duck or chicken is presented, the servant is careful not to place the platter so its head points directly at either the host or guest. It should correctly point to the right of the host. If it is a whole fish, it is turned to present with its belly, not its back, showing to host and guest, as a sign of respect. In ancient times, the Chinese would never offer their guests "the head of a chicken, the back of a fish, and the pad of a duck." One reason for turning the belly toward the diner is that the soft, tender, relatively boneless belly is considered the choicest part of the fish. There is another reason, however, a tradition that sprang from the legend of the king of Wu and the assassin-chef named Zhu.

THE DEATH OF KING WU

In 515 B.C., He Lu, the crown prince of Wu, planned to kill the king of Wu, King Liao, and seize the throne. He hired the clever assassin, Zhuan Zhu, to carry out the mission. Since the king liked fish, Zhuan Zhu trained himself hard in the technique of cooking. One day, He Lu invited the king of Wu to dinner. Zhuan Zhu prepared a delicious fish, and hid a dagger inside the abdomen. When he entered the room, he presented the fish with its back to the king, so as to hide the dagger. As he came near, he suddenly took the dagger and stabbed the king of Wu to death.

Felicitous-sounding Chinese words are also part of food lore. The pronunciation of "fish" in Chinese is identical to the word meaning "more than enough." Thus, this final main offering to guests symbolizes endless blessings and increasing prosperity. Altogether, there can be eight to ten main dishes.

A sweet course is usually served before the rice dishes. It is placed in small bowls, one for each diner.

HOW TO EAT CANDIED FRUIT

A favorite sweet course is hot, candied fruit—pears, apples, pineapple, and so on (see recipe for Hot Candied Apples). The trick to eating this dish is deftly demonstrated by the host, quickly, since the deep-fried sections of fruit have been deep-fried then coated with melted sugar, so they will stick together if not eaten immediately. Each diner has been given a small bowl of iced water. The host demonstrates by picking up a piece of fruit from the platter with chopsticks, dipping it for two to five seconds into the water, and popping it into his mouth. The sugar caramelizes into a crispy coating and the fruit inside is still *very* hot.

The sweet dish is followed by bowls of rice and, finally, soup. The rice is served first to the guest of honor. If the banquet occasion is a birthday, noodles (signifying longevity) will be served after the soup. Steamed buns and pastries are served in two plates. By this time, all the toasting with wine is done, finishing with the traditional "Bottoms up." When the host lifts his glass to a guest and says, "*kan pei*" (or, in Cantonese dialect, "*yum sing*") the guest is compelled by tradition to empty the glass set before him, and so must the host empty his. This exchange may take place many times during the meal. If the glasses being kept full by the host or waiter contain the lovely rice wine

from Shaohsing, that is one thing. If they contain the clear white, distilled spirit called *Maotai*, beware; it is at least the equal of brandy.

Banquets last a minimum of three hours. In ancient times, members of the party challenged each other to recite poetry. Years later, finger guessing games became popular.

DRINKING GAME

The rules of the Chinese finger-throwing contest for two contestants are simple. Each contestant raises and lowers his clenched hand while counting "one," "two," and on "three," each opens his hand showing one to five fingers and simultaneously shouts a number from two to ten. If one shouts the number equivalent to the exact total of both sets of fingers showing—the other loses and, usually, is compelled to "*kan pei*" his glass of beer, wine or spirits. Things tend to become noisily cheerful after a while.

Whatever the contest, the loser always "suffered" the penalty of more "*kan pei*." The after-dinner activities were a lively contrast to the formality of the banquet presentation. For special occasions such as weddings and birthday celebrations, entertainers were called in to perform between courses. These activities often extended the banquet through the entire night.

In recent years, banquets were shortened both to save time and avoid consumption of the prodigious amounts of food that were often eaten, or wasted, at imperial banquets.

Food Sculpture

Dough sculpture *The chefs of the imperial kitchens are skilled at moulding figures from dough, then baking and painting them. These dough sculptures are placed in the center of the main dish as a decoration. They often illustrate, in some way, the name of the dish, its mythical origin, or its main ingredients. Top left: "Mu Guiying Takes Command" (from the Beijing Opera) Top right: "Pulling Radishes" Bottom right: "The Katydid and the Ear of Corn"*

Food carving *Chef Chen Aiwu carves the prize-winning Lotus Blossoms and Cranes centerpiece from raw vegetables.*

The Recipes

製 方

Harmony may be illustrated by soup. You have the water and fire, vinegar, pickle, salt, and plums, with which to cook fish and meat. It is made to boil by the firewood, and then the cook mixes the ingredients, harmoniously equalizing the several flavours, so as to supply whatever is deficient and carry off whatever is in excess. Then the master eats it, and his mind is made equable. Yen Tzu (521 B.C.)

Notes for Western Cooks

he recipes on the following pages have been developed by the most honored professional chefs in the capital city of China. They represent the state of the art in contemporary restaurant cuisine. They have been organized here into the categories and presented in the sequence traditionally characteristic of a "banquet" menu—which simply means an occasion to which guests have been invited.

The ingredients and proportions in these recipes have not been changed for Western consumption. The preparation instructions have been expanded in detail after testing the recipes in Western home kitchens. The photographs that show preparation steps were all made in China inside the restaurant kitchen over which the chef who contributed that recipe presides. For that reason the pots, utensils, quantities, and staff sometimes appear larger and more numerous than those available to an amateur home cook.

An introduction to each recipe has been added by the Western editors in an effort to help Western cooks acquaint themselves with specific Chinese preparation procedures, crucial steps, optional substitutions for unusual ingredients, and real or mythical lore about the origin of the dish. The quantities have been set to serve five diners (the Chinese tend to use odd, rather than even, generic numbers) on the assumption that four or five different dishes will be served, as is the custom. The flavor-enhancers—MSG and "Gourmet Powder," which contains MSG—have been set in parentheses to alert those readers who cannot tolerate them.

The terms used for ingredients and preparation instructions are defined and illustrated in detail in, respectively, "The Ingredients" beginning on page 34, and "The Tools and Techniques" beginning on page 58. Native Chinese ingredients, grouped by type, are pictured in color photographs. An Ingredients Guide in chart form, on pages 49 through 55, defines all the ingredients used in the recipes selected for this book. Each entry gives the Chinese character, the romanized pronunciation, the English term(s), the Latin botanical name if appropriate, suggested substitutions, and other facts of potential use to Western cooks. A Chinese/English pronunciation guide appears on page 57 as an aid to non-Chinese-speaking people. Instructions for preparing the basic stocks and cooking soups called for in the recipes are given on page 56. Since cornstarch (cornflour) paste and "prickly ash" (a salt-and-pepper flavoring) are also compound ingredients which are made up by each chef for his or her own use, instructions for making those are also provided on page 56.

Vegetable oil (usually peanut or rape-seed) is the basic cooking fat, though lard is often specified in quick-frying for its flavor and crisping properties. Relatively large quantities of oil are called for in recipes that require deep-frying, but very little of it is absorbed by the food because of, among other factors, the short cooking times. Used oil may be reserved for another time by ladling it, after it cools down, onto three layers of loosely-stretched cheesecloth and straining it through twice. (It is extremely dangerous to try to pour hot oil directly from the pot or wok.) Oil that has been used for cooking fish or shellfish should be kept in a separate container. Although some Chinese chefs even prefer the flavor imparted to food by "cooked" oil—oil that has been heated at least once before using—oil that has taken on a flavor should not be used to prepare another dish in which that flavor would be incompatible.

Throughout China's 3000 years of civilization the simple act of sharing food has always been an excuse for a joyful occasion. Some insights into the ways food has been appreciated, presented, and enjoyed in China are described in "The Customs" section of this book beginning on page 70. May the gift of these favored recipes from the chefs of China bring you happiness.

Dragon and Phoenix Cold Dishes
Longfeng chengxiang 龙凤呈祥

This masterful presentation of food-as-sculpture was served at royal banquets as the first group of as many as 100 dishes. The dragon and phoenix, which symbolize the emperor and the empress respectively, are presented on a large platter surrounded by ten plates containing forms composed of meats and vegetables. Four of these plates (two meat and two vegetable) hold food arranged in the shape of Chinese characters meaning "dragon," "phoenix,"

"offer," and "good luck," a propitious proverb translating into *excellent good luck*. The food on the other six side plates (three meat and three vegetable) is arranged to look like flowers, birds, fish, and crabs.

To make the egg wrappers for this dish, follow the instructions in the recipe for Fried Five-Shred Rolls, but use 5 eggs and 3 tablespoons cornstarch, to make 6 instead of 5 egg wrappers.

1.

2.

Ingredients for the Dragon and the Phoenix platter

1 lb. (500 g) white-fleshed fish fillets

6 egg whites

(1 teaspoon MSG)

1 teaspoon salt

1 tablespoon minced scallion

1 teaspoon minced peeled fresh ginger

1 large sheet dried dark seaweed

6 fried egg wrappers (see Editor's Note)

3¼ oz. (100 g) carrots, shredded

Bread dough to sculpt the dragon's head and the head and tail of the phoenix

7 oz. (200 g) soaked dried bamboo shoots

¾ oz. (25 g) jam

1¾ oz. (50 g) cherries

2 lb. (1 kg) cooked duck meat, sliced

12 pigeon eggs, steamed

Ingredients for the ten plates

3¼ oz. (100 g) cooked crab meat

1¾ oz. (50 g) soaked dried scallops

8 oz. (250 g) cooked sliced white-fleshed fish fillet

7 cooked prawns

5 oz. (150 g) longan

7 oz. (200 g) jellyfish

5 oz. (150 g) fresh black mushrooms

5 oz. (150 g) sweet red pepper

5 oz. (150 g) cucumber

3 preserved eggs

3.

4.

5.

6.

Preparation of the main platter

Mash the fish fillet and combine in a bowl with the egg whites, (MSG), salt, scallion, and ginger. Cut the sheet of dried seawood into five strips. Spread half the fish batter on three seaweed strips, cover with fried egg wrappers, and roll up. Add the shredded carrots to the remaining batter, spread on the remaining egg wrappers, and roll up. Steam the rolls.

Arrangement

Sculpt the dragon's head and the head and tail of the phoenix out of bread dough. Place them at opposite sides of a platter. Form the dragon's body with bamboo shoots. Cover each side of the body with a line of overlapping scales sliced from two fish rolls of dark seaweed sheets. Slice scales from two of the carrot-rolls, and overlap them down the center of the back. Save a few carrot-roll slices to make the four short legs. Form the claws with a base of jam and slivers of red cherries.

For the phoenix, slice the duck meat to form the body and wings. To form the tail, cut toothed edges around the remaining carrot and fish rolls. Slice the pigeon eggs; form the center of the tail with overlapping slices down the center. Decorate each side of the egg slices with the tooth-cut seaweed slices. Finish with tail with cucumber peelings and the remaining cherries.

7.

8.

9.

10.

11.

12.

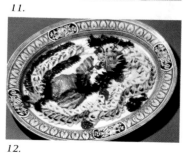

Peacock Spreads Tail
Kongque kaiping 孔雀开屏

An impressive and beautiful cold dish, this peacock is actually not, with time and patience, very hard to create. Various foods, including eggs, abalone, shrimp, and canned fruits are cut and arranged to look like a peacock roaming through the grassland. The head and neck are carved from a white radish and colored to look like the real bird. Cucumber peel and slices conceal any rough edges.

1¾ oz. (50 g) 1-inch-by-
   1-inch-by 5-inches
   (2.5 x 2.5 x 12.5 cm)
   agar-agar, rinsed
¾ oz. (50 g) chicken
8 eggs
1 lb. (500 g) prawns
7 oz. (200 g) cucumber
5 teaspoons rice wine
¼ teaspoon salt
¼ teaspoon prickly ash
   (see recipe following
   Ingredients Guide)
1 white radish
Food colorings

11 canned cherries, halved
3 canned black mushrooms
5 oz. (150 g) canned abalone
2 canned mandarin orange
   segments

1. Rinse the agar-agar in cold water; squeeze dry and chop. Cook the chicken in lightly salted boiling water just until tender; drain and discard the water. Cut the chicken meat into shreds. Hard-boil the eggs; cool in cold water and remove shells. Cut three of the eggs in half lengthwise. Separate the yolks from the whites. Cut the whites lengthwise into 24 to 30 thin "feathers" and set aside. Cut off the prawn heads; shell, devein, and cut the prawns in half lengthwise. Peel the cucumber, reserving the peel. Cut in half crosswise, then slice it lengthwise into flat thin feathers like the eggwhites. Pickle a few of the peelings in a brine of salt and sugar.

2. To 2 cups (500 ml) water in a wok or pot, add the rice wine, salt, and a pinch of prickly ash. Heat to boiling; add the prawns and simmer for 10 minutes; remove the prawns and drain.

3. Mound a layer of the agar-agar and chicken on the platter as a base for the head, neck and body. (It will be covered with other things.) Carve the head, neck, beak, and crown from white radishes. Dye them with food coloring and assemble them as shown in the photograph. Use prickly ash for the eyes. Place the head and neck on the mound of agar-agar. Cover the neck with alternating rows of cucumber slices and blade-like slices of the white part of the egg. Ruffle and fan them to resemble feathers.

4. Following the arrangement in the photo, place the pickled cucumber peelings in the center of the platter in line with the head. Place the mushrooms on top of the cucumbers. Top the mushrooms with slices of egg yolk. Slice one of the eggs, notch edges around the whites, place these around the mushrooms, and top each with a cherry half.

5. Slice the abalone into oblong pieces and notch the edges; tint with food coloring. Decorate them with the sliced-off rounded ends of the egg whites. Place the prawns, cut side downward, and top each with a melon seed-shaped piece of pickled cucumber. Cut the remaining eggs crosswise into 14 thin slices. Arrange them around the edge of the platter. Place a cherry half on the yolks and arrange the slices of abalone, prawn, eggs, and cucumber around the body, fanning out like feathers.

6. Nestle the orange segments and carved cucumber flowers near the wings, suggesting a peacock with tail fanned out, roaming in the grassland.

Assorted Cold Dishes
Hunsu pinpan 荤素拼盘

At the beginning of a banquet restaurant meal or special dinner, an assortment of goodies is served cold, often accompanied by wine, beer, or toasts with Maotai, a strong, clear spirit. Lamb, shrimp, chicken, duck, vegetables, and refreshing fruits comprise this festive platter.

Spiced lamb is leg meat, parboiled, then steamed over a mixture of sauce, wine, and hoisin sauce, flavored with scallions, garlic, ginger, sugar, coriander, and anise. *Egg yolk lamb* is spiced lamb dipped into egg yolk and then deep-fried. Substitute cold roast pork, if necessary.

3 tablespoons rice wine
Pinch of salt
(Pinch of MSG)
1¾ oz. (50 g) spiced lamb, cooked and chilled
1¾ oz. (50 g) egg yolk lamb, cooked and chilled
1¾ oz. (50 g) chicken meat, cooked in water and chilled
1¾ oz. (50 g) duck meat, cooked in water and chilled
1¾ oz. (50 g) soaked dried black mushrooms
3¼ oz. (100 g) cucumber
1 sweet red pepper

1¾ oz. (50 g) canned or fresh pineapple
1¾ oz. (50 g) canned or fresh mandarin orange sections
1 pickled duck egg, shelled
5 teaspoons soy sauce
2 teaspoons vinegar
2 teaspoons sesame oil

1. Cut each shrimp into 5 or 6 thin slices. Combine ½ cup (125 ml) water, the rice wine, salt, (and MSG). Heat to boiling in a small pot. Add the shrimp and cook until done, about 30 seconds. Remove the shrimp and set aside; reserve the broth.
2. Slice the spiced lamb and egg yolk lamb. Cut the cooked chicken and duck into strips of equal length.
3. Wash the black mushrooms and remove the stems. Cook the mushrooms in the reserved shrimp broth until tender, 15 to 20 minutes. Remove from broth and cut into slices.
4. Cut the cucumber and pepper into thin slices. Arrange the shrimp in a pile

in the center of a serving platter and top with the cucumber and touches of red pepper. Arrange the lamb, chicken, duck, mushrooms, pineapple, and mandarin orange sections symmetrically around the shrimp. Cut the duck egg into eight sections and place at the four corners of the arrangement. Garnish with additional red pepper accents.
5. Combine the soy sauce, vinegar, and sesame oil. Pour into a small bowl as a dip for the chicken and duck.

"Goldfish and Lotus"
Jinyu xilian　金鱼戏莲

This elaborately presented example of imperial court cuisine is served as a cold first course for a banquet. It is a master chef's tour de force because of the intricate carving of the shapes that are symbolic of objects in nature. The "goldfish" is fashioned from pieces of cooked crabmeat and assorted vegetables, using steamed egg white and egg yolk mixtures for the scales. The features of the "goldfish" are made from cherries, tangerines, and egg slices. The "lotus" is sculpted from a whole tomato.

6 eggs, separated

5 teaspoons water chestnut powder

1 teaspoon salt
   (Pinch of MSG)

10 oz. (300 g) cooked and drained crab meat

4 tangerine sections

2 canned cherries

1 hard-boiled egg

1 lime-preserved duck egg

1 cucumber (1 lb./500 g)

1 carrot (7 oz./200 g) peeled

1 green pepper (7 oz./200 g)

7 oz. (200 g) winter bamboo shoots, sliced

1 tomato

2 teaspoons sesame oil

1. Lightly beat the egg yolks. Gradually add 2½ teaspoons water chestnut powder, ½ teaspoon salt, (pinch of MSG), mixing until well blended. In a separate bowl lightly beat the egg whites with the remaining water chestnut powder, salt, (and pinch of MSG) until well blended. Pour the egg mixtures into separate 8-inch (20-cm) plates with raised lips.

2. Cover the plates and steam until the mixtures are firm, about 20 minutes. (Check that the water does not completely evaporate.) Remove the plates and let the egg cakes cool. Cut each cake into thin rounded slices to resemble fish scales.

3. Shape the crabmeat into the shape of two fish bodies on a serving platter. Cover one fish with the white and one with the yellow egg-cake scales. Each fishes' mouth is formed with two tangerine sections. Slice the small ends plus two more slices off the hard-boiled egg and the preserved egg; use these egg slices, and the cherries, to form eyes for each fish.

4. Blanch the cucumber, carrots, pepper, and winter bamboo shoots for 4 minutes in boiling salted water. Drain under cold water. Cut half the cucumber and the remaining vegetables into slices to form the long fish tails. A few slices of cucumber make the fins.

5. To make the lotus flower, stem and leaves, slice the tomato into 5 wedges and remove the pulp. As shown in the photograph, arrange the wedges to form a lotus flower. To make the stem, cut some of the remaining cucumber into long, rounded strips, then chop it into hairfine segments, but not severed, so it can be laid down in curves, like a snake. To form the lotus leaves feather the chunk ends of cucumber with lots of very thin slices and fan them out. Brush the sesame oil carefully onto the "goldfish" and "lotus" and serve.

Red Shark's Fin

Haihong yu chi 海红鱼翅

Shark's fin, which is a great delicacy, is prized for its contribution to good health and its ability to absorb the flavors of the foods with which it is cooked. In this dish it is first steamed for several hours in a sauce with chicken and pork, then stir-fried with delicate crabmeat and served with sweet sauce made by sauteeing grated carrots which also serves to give the shark's fin mixture a reddish color. It is important to thoroughly clean and rinse the shark's fin to remove the fishy taste.

If for the sake of economy you wish to halve the quantity of shark's fin and make a smaller amount of this dish, halve the amounts of the chicken, pork, and crab as well, but not the amounts of the remaining ingredients.

Almost all shark's fin is sold dried, in needle-like shreds. Fresh fins are rarely available, even in China.

2 lb. (1 kg) dried shark's fin "needles"

2 lb. (1 kg) skinned and boned chicken meat, cut in two pieces

1½ lb. (750 g) pork

1 tablespoon rice wine

10 scallions

1¾ oz. (50 g) sliced peeled fresh ginger

2 cups (500 ml) clear stock

1 carrot, grated (7 oz./200 g)

3¼ oz. (100 ml) melted lard

3 to 4 fresh river crabs (3 lb./1.5 kg)

2 tablespoons peanut oil

(¼ teaspoon MSG)

1 teaspoon salt

1 tablespoon cornstarch paste

Two fins from freshly caught red sharks; a rare delicacy.

1. Soak the dried shark's fin needles in 3 quarts (3 L) cold water for 24 hours to soften, changing the water three or four times. Remove from water, then boil the shark's fin in fresh water to cover for 3 minutes; drain and rinse in cold water. Repeat, drain, and place on a deep, heatproof plate.

2. Add 1 lb. chicken, the pork, 2 teaspoons rice wine, 5 scallions, half the ginger, and ⅔ cup (175 ml) clear stock to the shark's fin in the deep plate. Steam until the shark's fin is tender, for 7 to 8 hours. (Check to see that the water does not completely evaporate.) Drain the shark's fin in the plate and discard the cooking liquid.

3. Add the remaining chicken and scallions, half the remaining ginger, and ⅔ cup (175 ml) clear stock to the shark's fin. Steam for 30 minutes more.

4. Heat the lard in a wok over a low flame. Add the carrots and sauté until they become saucelike; set aside.

5. Plunge the crabs into a large pot of boiling water with a steaming rack above the water, and cover. Steam until just cooked, (they will turn red) in 10 to 20 minutes. Remove the crabs, drain, and pick out crabmeat and roe; cut into bite-size pieces.

6. Heat the oil over a medium flame until hot. Stir-fry the crab pieces for

2 minutes. Add the remaining clear stock, rice wine, and ginger, (the MSG), the salt, and the shark's fin. Reduce heat to a low flame and simmer until the liquid thickens. Stir in the cornstarch paste. Transfer the shark's fin mixture to a platter, spoon on the sautéed carrots and serve.

Shark's Fin in the Shape of a Citron
Foshou wei yuchi　佛手围鱼翅

This elaborate dish is based on shark's fin—an exquisite and exotic ingredient—surrounded by citron-shaped rolls. According to Chinese legend, a fruit that resembles a large, well-endowed lemon, the citron, has magical properties. Even today in south China, people like to keep a drying citron in their homes for its pleasant fragrance.

Four slashes are made in the shaped rolls before they are cooked. The five "fingers" puff up when stir-fried, as can be seen in the photograph. Because the Chinese variety of citron looks somewhat like a hand, its name in Chinese also means "Buddha's Hand."

Since shark's fin is such an expensive delicacy, you may want to modify this recipe by cutting the quantity of shark's fin. Even when you halve the shark's fin, you need not reduce the other ingredients. The results will be just as tasty, only less costly.

Editor's note: To make the egg wrappers for this dish, follow the instructions in the recipe for Fried Five-Shred Rolls, but use 8 eggs and 5 tablespoons cornstarch paste, to yield 10 wrappers.

2½ lb. (1.25 kg) shark's fin
1 tablespoon minced scallion
1 tablespoon minced peeled fresh ginger
3 tablespoons rice wine
2 lb. (1 kg) chicken meat, cubed
1 lb. (500 g) duck breast meat, cubed
¾ oz. (25 g) dried scallops
⅓ oz. (10 g) ham, chopped
6 tablespoons peanut oil
3¼ oz. (100 g) hearts of rape
1¾ oz. (50 g) bamboo shoots, sliced
1¾ oz. (50 g) chicken breast meat, minced
(5 teaspoons MSG)
2 teaspoons salt
½ lb. (250 g) pork, minced
2 medium eggs
3 tablespoons cornstarch paste
1 teaspoon soy sauce
½ teaspoon sesame oil
4 tablespoons flour

20 egg wrappers (see *Editor's note)*
5 teaspoons melted chicken fat

1. Soak the shark's fin in 3 quarts (3 L) cold water for 24 hours to soften and thoroughly eliminate the fishy taste, changing the water three or four times. Rinse the fin in cold water. Add the scallions, ginger, and 1 tablespoon rice wine to 2½ quarts (2.5 L) boiling water; immerse the fin in the boiling liquid then remove when the fin is more pliable.
2. Combine the chicken meat, duck breast meat, scallops, and ham in a pot and add water just to cover; heat to boiling. Meanwhile, wrap the shark's fin in fine cheesecloth; add to the pot. Reduce heat to a weak flame, cover, and simmer until the fin has softened, 6 to 7 hours. Remove the fin from the pot, unwrap, and place with the chicken, duck, scallops, and ham on a serving platter.
3. Heat 3 tablespoons peanut oil in a wok over an intense flame. Add the hearts of rape, bamboo shoots, chicken breast meat, (2 teaspoons MSG), and 1 teaspoon salt and stir-fry. Spoon over the shark's fin mixture.
4. Combine the pork, eggs, 1 tablespoon cornstarch paste, the soy sauce, (remaining MSG), 1 tablespoon rice wine, and the sesame oil.
5. Mix the flour with enough water to make a thin paste. Cut each egg-wrapper in half and spread the flour paste around the rounded edge. Spread a small amount of the pork mixture in the middle.

Starting with the straight edge, roll up each pancake half into a cylinder about 1½ inches (3.5 cm) in diameter. Make four slits crosswise in each cylinder (being careful not to cut all the way through), creating five sections that will resemble five stubby fingers when they are stir-fried.
6. Clean the wok, then heat 2 tablespoons peanut oil over a medium flame until hot. Fry the stuffed egg wrappers until evenly golden, 5 to 10 minutes. Remove the stuffed wrappers from oil, drain, and arrange on the platter around the shark's fin mixture.
7. Clean the wok again, then heat the remaining peanut oil over a medium flame until hot. Add the remaining rice wine, salt, and cornstarch paste and stir until a thin sauce is formed. Sprinkle with the chicken fat, pour the sauce over the shark's fin mixture, and serve.

Shark's Fin Casserole
Shaguo yuchi 砂锅鱼翅

Shark's fin is an expensive delicacy and consequently is served only at banquets. Most recipes calling for large quantities of the fin and complex preparation come from the cuisine developed in the imperial court for the emperor. Shark's fin is sold dried in long needle-like strips of cartilage that give the real fin its structure. Whole fins are also sold dried, and are more desirable for their nutrients and texture, much more expensive, and more difficult to rid of their strong fishy smell in the soaking process.

It is important to thoroughly clean and rinse the fin to remove the fishy taste and allow it to absorb the flavors of the other ingredients in the sauce. The recipe for the clear duck and chicken stock is included, with some other basic recipes, following the Ingredients Guide in this book. The cooked shark's fin "needles" become soft and tender with a pleasantly slippery texture. This dish offers a decorative counterplay of colors with its red, green, yellow, and white ingredients.

1 lb. (500 g) dried shark's fin "needles," or whole fin

6 scallions

8 tablespoons minced peeled fresh ginger

6 tablespoons peanut oil

6 cups (1.5 L) chicken and duck stock

2 tablespoons rice wine

1 cup (250 ml) Milky Stock (see recipe following Ingredients Guide)

¾ oz. (25 g) ham, sliced

⅔ oz. (20 g) soaked black mushrooms, steamed

5 teaspoons melted chicken fat

½ teaspoon salt

(½ teaspoon MSG)

⅔ oz. (20 g) bamboo shoots, sliced

¾ oz. (25 g) hearts of broccoli rape, cut into 2-inch (5-cm) sections.

and remaining teaspoon ginger juice. Heat to a boil, then lower the flame, cover, and simmer for 1 hour. Discard the cooking liquid. Rinse the shark's fin again, in boiling water.

4. Heat the remaining oil in a wok over an intense flame. Add the two minced scallions, the remaining ginger, rice wine, chicken and duck stock, and the salt, (MSG), bamboo

1. Soak the shark's fin in 3 quarts (3 L) cold water for 24 hours to soften, changing the water 3 or 4 times, then add it to a wok filled with cold water. (If you are using a whole fin, scrub it with a brush to help eliminate its strong fishy smell.) Slowly heat to boiling, then remove the fin and place in cold water again. When it has cooled, rinse and place in a bowl. Cut four of the scallions into fine shreds; mince the remaining scallions. Wrap 2 tablespoons minced ginger in fine-mesh cheesecloth or put them into a hand-held garlic press, and squeeze to

extract the juice. Pour 4 tablespoons water over the squeezed pulp and squeeze again. Set the 2-teaspoon yield of ginger juice aside.

2. Heat 2 tablespoons oil in a wok over an intense flame. Add 2 shredded scallions, 2 tablespoons ginger, 2 cups (500 ml) chicken and duck stock , 2 teaspoons rice wine, and 1 teaspoon ginger juice and heat to boiling. Pour over the shark's fin in the bowl, then steam shark's fin for 3 hours. Remove the fin and rinse in hot, boiled water three times to remove the fishy smell. Discard the cooking liquid.

3. Heat 2 tablespoons oil in a wok over an intense flame. Add the shark's fin, the remaining shredded scallions, 2 tablespoons ginger, 2 cups (500 ml) chicken and duck stock, 2 teaspoons rice wine,

slices, and chicken fat; heat to a boil and add the shark's fin. Pour the mixture into a clay pot and stew over a weak flame for 20 minutes. Add the hearts of rape and heat through. Serve in a clay pot.

Deep-Fried Meats
Shao zahui 烧杂烩

3¼ oz. (100 g) soaked sea cucumbers, cleaned (see instructions)

3¼ oz. (100 g) fish maw

4 cups (1 L) peanut oil

3¼ oz. (100 g) boiled chicken breast

3¼ oz. (100 g) boiled pork

1¾ oz. (50 g) bamboo shoots

1¾ oz. (50 g) soaked shark's fin

1¾ oz. (50 g) pork, minced

1 teaspoon cornstarch paste

½ teaspoon salt

1 teaspoon shredded peeled fresh ginger

2 teaspoons soy sauce

½ teaspoon rice wine

(¼ teaspoon Gourmet Powder)

1 teaspoon shredded scallion

1 teaspoon melted chicken fat

Chicken, pork, fish maw (the air bladder, sold deep-fried and dried), and sea cucumbers are prepared in various ways, then deep-fried with little pork balls, bamboo shoots, and shark's fin. They are served with a sauce flavored with ginger and scallions.

1. After soaking the sea cucumbers in water for at least 24 hours, cut them open at the abdomen and clean. After soaking the shark's fin in cold water for 24 hours, changing the water three or four times, rinse the fin in cold water.

2. Deep-fry the fish maw in 2 cups (500 ml) peanut oil over a weak flame for 1 hour, stirring occasionally. Turn up the heat and continue to deep-fry, stirring and press-ing, for 10 minutes. Remove from the oil and drain. Soak in cold water until soft, about 10 minutes. Soak in warm salted water 5 minutes to remove the excess oil; rinse thoroughly with cold water.

3. Cut the sea cucumbers, fish maw, boiled chicken breast, and boiled pork into slices at 45 degrees. Cut the bamboo shoots crosswise into slices. Tear the shark's fin into small pieces and rinse with boiling water to clean; drain.

4. In a small bowl mix the minced pork, cornstarch paste, salt, and ½ teaspoon shredded ginger and form in-to balls the size of cherries. Heat the remaining peanut oil over a medium flame in a clean wok and deep-fry the balls until browned, about 1 minute. Raise the heat and add the sea cucumbers, fish maw, chicken, pork, bamboo shoots, and shark's fin; deep-fry for 30 seconds. Remove all the ingredients from the oil, drain, and place on a platter.

5. Mix the soy sauce, rice wine, (Gourmet Powder), scal-lion, and remaining ginger with 1 tablespoon water; pour into a clean wok and heat. When the mixture is hot, pour the sauce over the balls and other deep-fried ingredients, sprinkle with chicken fat, and serve.

Dragon with Pearls
Wulong tuzhu　乌龙吐珠

Sea cucumbers, known in the Western countries as *beche de mer* or *sea slugs*, are parboiled and cooked in a sweet sauce flavored with scallions and ginger: they have a gelatinous texture and no flavor or taste of their own. They are served with rape hearts, and pigeon eggs are placed around the platter to resemble pearls.

1½ lb. (750 g) dried, soaked sea cucumbers

15 pigeon eggs

2 teaspoons salt

15 two-inch (5-cm) pieces of rape heart, each cut in half lengthwise

1 teaspoon soy sauce

5 teaspoons rice wine

¾ cup (200 ml) clear chicken stock

3 tablespoons sugar

(1 tablespoon MSG)

2½ teaspoons chopped scallions

1 teaspoon minced peeled fresh ginger

2 teaspoons cornstarch dissolved in 2 teaspoons water

1 teaspoon melted chicken fat

⅓ cup (85 ml) peanut oil

1. Soak the sea cucumbers in water for at least 24 hours; cut them open at the abdomen and clean. Place the pigeon eggs in a pot and cover with cold water. Heat over a gentle flame until the water boils; then cook for 5 to 6 minutes. Cool in cold water, then remove the shells.

2. Sprinkle the sea cucumbers with 1 teaspoon salt. Heat water to boiling; add the sea cucumbers and cook for 2 minutes. Rinse the sea cucumbers, drain, and place in a wok. Then dip the rape in the boiling water for 10 seconds, remove and drain.

3. In a bowl, mix the soy sauce, remaining salt, rice wine, chicken stock, sugar, (and MSG); add to the sea cucumbers in the wok along with the scallion and ginger. Heat to boiling, and cook for 2 minutes, stirring to cook evenly. Add the rape heart pieces and stir in the dissolved cornstarch until thickened. Remove the sea cucumbers and rape hearts to a serving platter and sprinkle with the chicken fat.

4. Heat the peanut oil in a wok over a medium flame and add the pigeon eggs. Stir until they turn light golden. Remove, drain, place around the sea cucumbers, and serve.

Fish Hot Pot
Sisheng yuguo 四生鱼锅

Chicken, fish, pork, sea cucumber, black mushroom, bamboo shoots, and other ingredients are cooked at table to make this delicious soup. The broth is made with chicken and duck stock, cellophane noodles, rape leaves, and parsley.

5 oz. (150 g) sea cucumber

1 black mushroom, soaked and halved

2 teaspoons (⅓ oz. / 10 g) bamboo shoots, sliced

2 cups (3¼ oz. / 100 g) loosely packed rape leaves

10 cups (2.5 L) duck and chicken stock

½ teaspoon salt

5 teaspoons soy sauce

5 teaspoons ginger juice

2 teaspoons rice wine

1¾ oz. (50 g) cellophane noodles

(½ teaspoon MSG)

3¼ oz. (100 g) skinned boned chicken, sliced

3¼ oz. (100 g) white-fleshed fish fillets, sliced

3¼ oz. (100 g) pork tenderloin, sliced

⅓ cup (¾ oz. / 25 g) minced parsley

½ teaspoon pepper

1. Soak the sea cucumber for 24 hours; drain and slice crosswise. Dip the mushroom and bamboo shoots into boiling water; squeeze dry. Wash the rape leaves; squeeze dry and cut into 1-inch (2.5-cm) pieces.
2. Heat the stock in a wok over an intense flame until it is hot, then add the salt, soy sauce, ginger juice, rice wine, mushrooms, and bamboo shoots. When it boils skim off the froth, then add the noodles, rape leaves, (and MSG). Pour into a hot-pot.
3. Pour the fuel into the pot chamber and light it. Add the chicken, fish, pork, and sea cucumber slices to the broth. When it boils, sprinkle with the parsley and pepper. Serve.

Three Delicacies Hot Pot
Sanxian huoguo 三鲜火锅

This hot pot meal is simple to prepare. The stock is filled with ''three delicacies''—sea cucumbers, chicken, and prawns—and bamboo shoots, mushrooms, and cellophane noodles. This dish is a favorite winter treat in Shanxi Province.

1 lb. (500 g) dried sea cucumber, soaked

3 prawns

8 oz. (250 g) boiled chicken breast meat

5 oz. (150 g) bamboo shoots

1 lb. (500 g) cellophane noodles

3¼ oz. (100 g) fresh mushroom caps

2 cups (500 ml) clear chicken and duck stock

1 teaspoon rice wine

½ teaspoon salt

(¼ teaspoon Gourmet Powder)

1 teaspoon sesame oil

1. Soak the dried sea cucumbers for 24 hours. Drain. In a pot, heat to a boil enough water to cover sea cucumbers; drop in sea cucumbers and cook for 1 minute. Remove and clean. Cut them into strips about 1¾ inches (4 cm) long.

2. Shell and devein the prawns. Split down the center of the back and cook in boiling water for 1 minute; drain. Cut the chicken and bamboo shoots into slices.

3. Cook the cellophane noodles in boiling water for

2 minutes; rinse under cold running water. Place the noodles in the basin of a hot pot and arrange the sea cucumbers, prawns, chicken, bamboo shoots, and mushrooms on top. Pour the chicken and duck stock over all.

4. Light the charcoal under the hot pot. When the liquid begins to boil, add the rice wine, salt, (Gourmet Powder), and sesame oil. Stir to mix, and serve.

Arrange sea cucumbers, prawns, chicken, bamboo shoots, and mushrooms on top of noodles in hot pot.

Butterfly Sea Cucumbers
Hudie haishen　蝴蝶海参

Sea cucumbers come dried, and though they must be soaked for 24 hours before they are used, they retain a distinctive texture and flavor. In this dish they are formed with a chicken batter into butterflies and decorated with ham and rape leaves. Dried shrimp form the eyes, and dried, needle-like strands of shark's fin form the antennae. The butterflies then decorate a soup made with additional sea cucumbers. Strands of shark's fin are sold cleaned and dried ready for use.

1½ lb. (750 g) soaked sea cucumbers

5 oz. (150 g) chicken breasts, mashed

4 medium egg whites

6 tablespoons peanut oil

(2 teaspoons Gourmet Powder)

½ teaspoon salt

½ cup (50 g) flour

20 dried shark's fin strands

20 dried shrimp

1¾ oz. (50 g) ham, finely chopped

1 tablespoon finely chopped rape leaves

1 cup (250 ml) chicken and duck stock

6 tablespoons rice wine

½ teaspoon soy sauce

½ teaspoon sugar

2 teaspoons melted chicken fat

1. After soaking the sea cucumbers for 24 hours, rinse, then boil for 2 minutes. Rinse them again under cold running water, drain, and pat dry. Pound the chicken into a purée and place in a bowl. Add the egg whites, peanut oil, (1 teaspoon Gourmet Powder), and ¼ teaspoon salt, and mix well.

2. Cut 5 oz. (150 g) sea cucumbers, at a 45-degree angle, into 40 slices. Dip them first into the flour and then into the puréed chicken mixture. Form 10 butterflies on a platter with 4 sea cucumber slices as the wings, and the remaining chicken mixture as the bodies. Make antennae from the shark's fin strands and the eyes from the dried shrimp. Dot the ham and rape leaves on the "wings" as markings. Steam the butterflies for 5 minutes over an intense flame.

3. Score the remaining sea cucumbers crosswise. Place them in a wok, then add ⅞ cup (200 ml) chicken and duck stock, the rice wine, and soy sauce; stir over a medium flame until it comes to a boil. Transfer the mixture to a shallow serving bowl and arrange eight butterflies around the edge and two in the middle. Heat the remaining chicken and duck stock over a medium flame; add the remaining salt, (Gourmet Powder), and the sugar. Heat, stirring, until the soup comes to a boil. Pour the soup over the sea cucumbers, sprinkle with the chicken fat, and serve.

Swallow's Nest Soup

Qingtang yanwo yunpian 清汤燕窝云片

This colorful soup is made with swallow's nest and pigeon eggs. The eggs are decorated with ham and parsley and steamed, then added, with the swallow's nest, to the soup. To make the ginger juice that flavors the soup, peel and mince about 2 tablespoons of fresh ginger; squeeze it in a twist of fine-mesh cheesecloth, or a garlic press, into a bowl. Pour two teaspoons of water into the squeezed pulp and squeeze it again. Use twelve heatproof shot or wine glasses for steaming the pigeon eggs.

4 oz. (125 g) soaked swallow's nest (see "Bird's Nest Rolls" for information)
1½ teaspoons baking soda
1 teaspoon sesame oil
12 pigeon eggs
1½ teaspoons minced ham
12 coriander leaves
5 cups (1.25 L) clear stock
2 teaspoons ginger juice
1 teaspoon rice wine
(½ teaspoon MSG)
¼ teaspoon salt

1. After soaking the swallow's nest in warm water to cover for 1 hour, clean the nest and remove any feathers. Dissolve the baking soda in a bowl filled with hot water. Add the soaked bird's nest, cover tightly, and let stand for 5 minutes. Pour off the liquid; rinse the nest under cold running water to eliminate the alkaline taste, then squeeze out the water and set aside.

2. Brush each of 12 tiny wine cups with the sesame oil and break 1 egg into each cup, being careful not to break the yolk. Sprinkle the eggs with the ham and place a coriander leaf on each. Steam for 5 minutes over a low flame. Slip the eggs into cold water to set.

3. Heat the stock in a wok over a medium flame. When hot, add the ginger juice, rice wine, (MSG), and salt. Heat the soup to boiling and skim off the froth. Pour into a serving bowl, add the nest and eggs, and serve.

Add eggs and swallow's nest to soup just before serving.

Bird's Nest Rolls
Sansi yancaijuan 三丝燕菜卷

¾ oz. (25 g) soaked bird's nest

¾ oz. (25 g) dried shelled
   shrimp

3¼ oz. (100 g) ham

3¼ oz. (100 g) soaked black
   mushrooms (12 mushrooms,
   each 1 inch / 2.5 cm in
   diameter)

3¼ oz. (100 g) bamboo shoots

2 teaspoons baking soda

3¼ oz. (100 g) chicken
   breast meat

3 egg whites

3 tablespoons melted lard

2 tablespoons rice wine

(½ teaspoon MSG)

1½ teaspoons salt

1⅔ cups (400 ml) clear stock

5 teaspoons cornstarch,
   dissolved in 3 tablespoons
   water

1 teaspoon sesame oil

"Bird's Nest," the structural skeleton of a swallow's nest, is made of a white gelatinous substance secreted from the bird's mouth. When soaked in water, it becomes soft and is very nutritious. It is an expensive delicacy, used only for special dishes. In this recipe portions of the bird's nest are covered with a chicken batter, and rolled into individual portions by hand. These are covered with minced ham, mushrooms, and dried shrimp, steamed, then served with a simple sauce made from clear stock.

1. After soaking the bird's nest in warm water to cover for 1 hour, clean the nest and remove any feathers. Mince the dried shrimp. Mince one quarter of the ham, black mushrooms, and bamboo shoots; slice the rest into 2-inch (5-cm) strips. Mince the chicken breast, then pound with the back of a cleaver until mashed.

2. Dissolve the baking soda in a bowl filled with hot water. Add the soaked bird's nest, cover tightly, and let stand until the nest swells, about 5 minutes. Pour off the liquid; rinse the nest under cold running water to eliminate the alkaline taste, then squeeze out the water.

3. In a separate bowl, mix the chicken breast, egg whites, lard, 2 teaspoons rice wine, (a pinch of MSG), and ½ teaspoon salt to make a batter. Divide the nest into 24 portions. Cover one portion at a time with the chicken batter and hand-roll into a ball. Place the balls on a heatproof plate and sprinkle with the minced ham, black mushrooms, and dried shrimp. Steam over an intense flame for 5 minutes; then keep them warm.

4. Arrange the strips of ham, black mushrooms, and bamboo shoots in a heatproof bowl. Add 1 cup (250 ml) clear stock, 2 teaspoons rice wine, (a pinch of MSG), and ½ teaspoon salt, and steam for 15 minutes. Remove from the steamer and arrange on a serving platter; arrange the bird's nest rolls on top.

5. Heat a wok over a medium flame. Add the remaining clear stock, rice wine, (MSG), and salt and heat to boiling. Stir in the dissolved cornstarch until the sauce thickens, then sprinkle with the sesame oil. Pour the sauce over the bird's nest rolls and serve.

Venison with Black Mushrooms and Ham
Sanxian lurou 三鲜鹿肉

Though this is a dish that is more likely to be served on an imperial hunting trip than in an ordinary home, the seasonings and sauce are simple. The strongest flavor comes from the game itself, so the quality and freshness of the venison meat are very important. This dark, hunter's dish is garnished around the edge with the contrasting colors and textures of mushrooms and bamboo shoots. The pieces of bamboo shoot are notched so that when they are sliced into rounds, they have sunburst edges.

1½ lb. (750 g) venison
3¼ oz. (100 g) soaked black mushrooms, stems removed
3¼ oz. (100 g) bamboo shoots, sliced
5 oz. (150 g) ham
1 tablespoon rice wine
2 teaspoons soy sauce
2 teaspoons salt
2 teaspoons melted chicken fat

2 scallions, cut into 2-inch (5-cm) sections
2⅛ -inch (0.3-cm) slices peeled fresh ginger
1⅔ cups (400 ml) clear stock
4½ tablespoons cornstarch paste
(¼ teaspoon MSG)

1. Place the venison in a pot with enough cold water to cover. Heat to boiling, then skim off the froth. Cover, reduce the heat to a low flame, and simmer for 40 minutes. Remove the venison and cut into 3-by-2-inch (8 x 5-cm) strips. Discard the cooking liquid.

2. Cut the ham and about three quarters of the black mushrooms and bamboo shoot slices into strips the same size as the venison. Cut the remaining mushrooms and bamboo slices into small rounds. Blanch the mushroom and bamboo shoot strips in boiling water for 2 to 3 minutes; drain off the water and squeeze dry.

3. Arrange the strips of venison, black mushrooms, bamboo shoots, and all but 4 strips of the ham in a heat-proof bowl. Add 2 teaspoons rice wine, 1½ teaspoons soy sauce, 1 teaspoon salt, 1 teaspoon chicken fat, scallions, ginger, and ⅔ cup (150 ml) clear stock. Steam for 30 minutes. Drain off the liquid; discard the scallion and ginger pieces. Carefully turn the mixture onto a serving platter.

4. Blanch the mushroom and bamboo shoot rounds with the remaining ham for 3 minutes. Drain and arrange around the venison on the platter.

5. Pour the remaining clear stock into a pot and heat to boiling. Add the remaining rice wine, soy sauce, (the MSG), and the remaining salt. Stir in the cornstarch paste until the sauce thickens. Sprinkle the sauce with the remaining chicken fat, pour the sauce over the venison, and serve.

Fried Quail
Zha anchun 炸 鹌 鹑

Master chefs who labored many generations ago in the kitchens of the imperial palace prepared this dish as only one of over 100 sumptuous offerings in banquets laid out for the emperor's pleasure. Twelve tiny quail are dipped in a cornstarch batter and deep-fried. As with many Chinese deep-fried dishes, lowering the heat for several seconds and then raising it again ensures that the quail are thoroughly cooked inside while remaining crispy on the outside. The quail are served with Chinese onion salt. For the authentic taste of this dish, the called-for quail should be used; if quail are not available, subsitutute six Cornish hens each about one pound, cut in half before cooking.

A small covey of live quail investigate an arrangement of carved-vegetable flowers.

3 tablespoons cornstarch
  paste
12 quail, heads and feet
  removed, cleaned
4 cups (1 L) peanut oil
2 teaspoons Chinese
  onion salt

1. Place cornstarch paste in a large bowl. Add the quail and mix to coat well.
2. Heat the oil in a wok over an intense flame. When hot, place each quail in a strainer and lower, one by one, into the oil. When they begin to turn golden, about 10 minutes, lower the heat for 20 seconds, then turn the flame back up. When the quail turn a deeper golden color, remove and drain. Arrange on a serving platter, season with the onion salt, and serve.

Longevity Quail

Shouxing anchun 寿星鹌鹑

The Chinese began eating quail 2,000 years ago. From ancient times through the Qing Dynasty (1644–1911) it was a delicacy prepared exclusively for the royal house.

Here the quail are steamed in a richly aromatic marinade and then deep-fried. The platter can be decorated with a dough sculpture of the God of Longevity in the center (as in the photograph)—hence the name "Longevity Quail." If you wish to make such a sculpture, follow the instructions in the recipe for "Maid Marrying Herself Off."

If all of the quail and the marinade do not fit in one bowl, use two; steam in a two-tier steamer or in two batches. It is very important to thoroughly drain and dry the quail after steaming—excess moisture in the quail will produce a tremendous splattering when they are placed in the oil for deep frying. If necessary, add more oil while frying the quail.

Chinese quail are smaller than those available in this country, so if you find that the given marinade ingredient quantities do not make enough to cover the quail, simply double them. Substitute six cornish hens if quail are not available.

12 quail (½ lb. / 250 g each)
3 tablespoons sesame oil
2 tablespoons soy sauce
2 tablespoons chopped peeled fresh ginger
2 tablespoons cardamom
5 whole cloves
10 strands (2.5 g) lily buds
½ teaspoon ground nutmeg
½ teaspoon salt
(¼ teaspoon MSG)
2 scallions, cut into 2-inch (5-cm) sections
2 cups (500 ml) peanut oil

1. Clean the quail. Rinse with cold water and drain thoroughly.
2. In a bowl combine the sesame oil, soy sauce, ginger, cardamom, cloves, lily bud strands, nutmeg, and salt. Gently toss the quail in this marinade to coat thoroughly, then top with the scallions.
3. Steam the quail in the marinade over a weak flame for 30 minutes. (Check to make sure the water does not completely evaporate as the quail steam.) Thoroughly drain the quail; reserve the marinade. Pat dry—gently, but thoroughly.
4. Heat the oil in a wok over a medium flame until it is hot. Gently place two of the quails in the oil and fry until the skins are golden and crisp. Remove from the oil and drain. Fry the remaining quail two at a time. Meanwhile reheat the marinade. Arrange the quail on the platter, pour the marinade over the quail, (sprinkle with MSG), and serve.

Tian Dan Recovering the Qi Territory
Tian Dan fu Qi　　　　田单复齐

In the war against the Yen State during the Warring States Period (475–221 B.C.), the Qi State lost scores of cities. Tian Dan, a Qi general, won back all of the lost territory. The ingenious general burned the tails of a large herd of oxen, forcing the animals to stampede and put to rout the Yen army. When the King of Qi gave a banquet to celebrate, the cooks concocted a dish of "flaming red" beef commemorating the stampede.

Strips of beef are stuffed with chicken, ham, bamboo shoots, and water chestnuts, then coated with a breadcrumb batter, deep fried and served on a bed of deep-fried rape leaves. Partially freeze the tenderloin to facilitate cutting it into very thin slices.

5 oz. (155 g) beef tenderloin

2 oz. (60 g) cooked ham

2 oz. (60 g) chicken breast meat

2 -inch section (2 oz./60 g) bamboo shoot

½ lb. (250 g) rape leaves, washed

6 (2 oz./60 g) water chestnuts

4 slices (¼ lb./125 g) bread

1 egg, separated

5 teaspoons rice wine

Pinch of salt

(¼ teaspoon MSG)

2½ tablespoons sesame oil

⅕ cup (35 g) flour

4 cups (1 L) peanut oil

1. Slice the beef into 3-by-2-by-¹⁄₁₆-inch (7-by-5-by-0.2-cm) pieces. Cut the ham into thin strips. Mince the chicken and mash it with the flat side of a cleaver. Cut the bamboo shoots and rape leaves into thin strips and slice the water chestnuts. Dry the bread slices in a 250 F (120 C)

degree oven for 30 minutes and roll into coarse crumbs.

2. In a medium-size bowl, combine the chicken, egg white, rice wine, salt, (and MSG). Add the ham, bamboo shoot, water chestnuts, and sesame oil and mix well. Spread a little of this mixture on each slice of beef and roll into 2-inch rolls about ¾-inches in diameter.

3. In a small bowl, combine the flour and egg yolk, adding enough water to make a thin batter. Dip each beef roll first into the batter and then into the breadcrumbs; set aside. (Letting the breaded rolls stand before frying helps set the coating so that it does not fall off during frying.)

4. Heat the peanut oil in a wok over a medium flame until hot. Gently lower the rolls into the oil and deep fry until golden brown, about 3 minutes. Scoop out and drain; keep warm.

5. Deep fry the rape leaf strips until they turn bright green, about 5 seconds; remove from oil and drain.

6. Arrange the rape leaf strips on a serving platter, place the beef rolls on top, and serve.

Taiyuan-Style Braised Beef
Taiyuan men niurou 太原焖牛肉

Beef is fried with scallions, then seasoned with an intriguing blend of Sichuan peppercorn infusion and star anise. (The infusion is made by pouring boiling water over Sichuan peppercorns and steeping for a few minutes.) The meat is then braised in a chicken and duck stock.

1 teaspoon Sichuan pepper-corns

¼ cup (60 ml) soy sauce

2 tablespoons cornstarch paste

¾ lb. (375 g) lean beef, thinly sliced

8 scallions, cut into 1½-inch (4-cm) pieces

½ cup (125 ml) sesame oil

1 anise star

½ cup (125 ml) clear chicken and duck stock

2 teaspoons rice wine

(¼ teaspoon Gourmet Powder)

Pinch of shredded peeled fresh ginger

1. Pour 1 tablespoon boiling water over the Sichuan peppercorns; let steep 5 minutes.
2. Combine the soy sauce with the cornstarch paste; stir in the beef and scallions.

3. Heat the sesame oil in a wok over an intense flame until hot. Add the anise star, then the beef mixture and stir-fry for 15 seconds. Add the chicken and duck stock, rice wine, (Gourmet Powder), and ¼ teaspoon Sichuan peppercorn infusion. Cover the wok and cook for 1 minute. Sprinkle the shredded ginger on top and serve.

Beef Steak
Niuroupa 牛肉扒

Patties of minced beef are dipped in egg, deep fried, and served with onions. The preparation of these tender, slightly peppery delights is simple and quick. They go well with wine.

7 oz. (200 g) beef tenderloin

1 teaspoon rice wine

3 teaspoons soy sauce

1 teaspoon white pepper powder

(½ teaspoon MSG)

½ teaspoon minced peeled fresh ginger

2 egg yolks

2 medium-size onions

½ cup (125 ml) vegetable oil

1½ teaspoons peanut oil

1. Cut the tenderloin in strips; pound them with a wooden mallet and mince. Sprinkle a few drops of water over the minced beef to hold the meat together. Mix the meat with the rice wine, soy sauce, white pepper, (MSG), and ginger. Form the mixture into ⅛-inch-thick (0.3-cm) rectangular patties each 2 inches (5 cm) long and 1½ (4 cm) wide. Beat the egg yolks and dip the meat patties into them, letting the excess yolk drip back into the bowl.

2. Peel and chop the onions, stir-fry them in a few tablespoons of oil, with the wok over an intense flame, until golden. Transfer to a serving platter and keep warm.

3. Clean the wok and heat the remaining vegetable oil over a low flame. Add the meat patties and fry slowly, until both sides are light brown. Brown for 1 minute more and drain off the vegetable oil.

4. Sprinkle the patties with the peanut oil, toss the wok, transfer patties to the serving platter with the onions and serve.

108 Beef

Home-Style Beef Tendon

Jiachang shaozi niujin 家常绍子牛筋

Dry beef tendon may be hard to find outside China. Fresh beef gristle from the beef shin can be used, instead. While it may take as long as four hours of gentle simmering to make the tendon properly tender, the finished product is absolutely delicious, with a very slight peppery tingle, and well worth the effort. Ancient Chinese folk-medicine recommends that the middle-aged start eating gristle and cartilage (such as shark's fin) to keep their bones from becoming brittle as they grow older.

1 lb. (500 g) dry beef tendon, soaked, or fresh beef gristle from the shin

5 oz. (150 g) lean pork

⅔ cup (150 ml) vegetable oil or melted lard

6½ tablespoons thick broad-bean sauce (made in Sichuan)

2 cups (500 ml) clear chicken stock

4 scallions cut into 1-inch (2.5 cm) lengths

2 -inch piece (¾ oz. / 25 g) peeled fresh ginger, sliced into 15 pieces

3 tablespoons rice wine

½ teaspoon salt

(Pinch of Gourmet Powder)

2 tablespoons cornstarch, dissolved in 2 tablespoons water

Sweet red pepper and cucumber, for garnish

1. Cut the beef into 2-inch (5-cm) strips. Plunge the beef tendon into rapidly boiling water for 1 minute. Drain and wash in cold water. Simmer in water to cover for about 2 hours.

2. Cut the pork into cubes. In a wok, heat half the oil, add the pork cubes, and stir-fry until lightly browned. Set aside.

3. Heat the remaining oil in a wok, add the broad-bean sauce, and stir-fry until the oil turns red, about 2 minutes. Add chicken stock and scoop out any soybean pieces from the sauce that may have sunk to the bottom of the wok. Add the beef tendon strips, pork, scallions, ginger, rice wine, salt, (and Gourmet Powder) and simmer over a low flame for 1 hour or longer, until the beef tendon is tender. Discard the scallions and ginger. The gravy may already be as thick as you like; if not, add the dissolved cornstarch, a bit at a time, and stir until the gravy thickens to the consistency you like. Serve garnished with slices of sweet red pepper and unpeeled cucumber sticks.

A plate of three beef shins showing the tendon, and a bowl of raw pork cubes and tendon strips.

Fish-Flavored Shredded Pork
Yuxiang rousi 鱼香肉丝

Soaked dried bamboo shoots and black fungus, along with other seasonings, give this dish the distinctive flavor for which it is named. If pickled hot pepper is not available, chili pepper may be substituted (do not soak the chili pepper). The ingredients should be cut into thin slices to facilitate quick frying, but keep the pepper pieces large enough to remove easily before serving if you want to avoid eating these fiery hot vegetables. The entire frying time should be less than two minutes.

- 5 oz. (150 g) lean pork
- 2 oz. (60 g) soaked dried black fungi
- 1 oz. (30 g) soaked dried bamboo shoot
- 2 tablespoons cornstarch, dissolved in 4 tablespoons water
- ¼ teaspoon salt
- 1 tablespoon chopped peeled fresh ginger
- 4 cloves garlic, chopped
- 2 scallions, chopped
- 1½ teaspoons sugar
- 1½ tablespoons soy sauce
- 2 teaspoons vinegar
  (Pinch of Gourmet Powder)
- ¼ cup (60 ml) clear chicken stock
- ½ cup (125 ml) vegetable oil
- 1 pickled hot pepper, soaked and chopped, or 2 dried chili peppers, chopped

1. Slice the pork, then cut into matchstick-thin strips 2½ inches (6 cm) long. Slice the black fungi and bamboo shoots into equally thin strips. In a small bowl, mix the pork with ⅔ of the dissolved cornstarch and half of the salt, and turn to coat well.

2. Place the ginger, garlic, and scallions in a bowl; stir in the sugar, soy sauce, vinegar, (Gourmet Powder), chicken stock, and the remaining salt and dissolved cornstarch. Set this fish-flavored seasoning mixture aside.

3. Heat the oil in a wok over an intense flame. Add the pork and stir-fry until the pork turns white, about 30 seconds. Add the pickled hot pepper and continue to fry until the oil turns red, about 15 seconds more. Stir in the black fungi and the bamboo shoots and fry for an additional 30 seconds. Add the seasoning mixture and stir vigorously for a few seconds, then transfer to a platter and serve.

1. Some of the ingredients: black fungus, bamboo shoots, scallions, cucumber, ginger, garlic, and pork.

2. Slice pork and cut into matchstick-thin strips. Chop scallions and ginger.

3. Add hot pepper to wok when pork turns white.

4. Pour fish-flavored sauce over pork mixture.

Sunflower Pork
Kuihua rou　葵花肉

2 lbs. (1 kg) thick bacon

3 medium carrots, peeled

14 dried black mushrooms
1 inch (2.5 cm) in diameter,
soaked

1 cup (250 ml) clear chicken
stock

¼ cup (70 ml) soy sauce

2 teaspoons salt

2 teaspoons sugar

(1 tablespoon MSG)

1 teaspoon rice wine

¼ teaspoon ground black
pepper

2½ teaspoons sliced scallion
(½-inch / 1.25 cm pieces)

1 teaspoon sliced fresh ginger

1½ tablespoons cornstarch
paste

12 scallions, halved and
slivered, for garnish (with
bulbs intact)

Bacon, carrots, and mushrooms are arranged to resemble the center of a sunflower. The ingredients, carefully assembled on a plate, are steamed in a flavorful broth and then inverted onto a serving platter. The stock is then thickened and poured over the dish and steamed split scallions are arranged radiating from the center to complete the flower. For this amount of food you will need a steamer long enough to hold a large plate. You can improvise a steamer by placing the plate on top of a heatproof glass or jar inside a large covered pot with enough water to prevent boiling away during steaming.

1. Simmer the bacon in water 30 minutes. Drain and allow to cool. When cold, cut into 2-by-1-by-1¾-inch (5 x 2.5 x 4-cm) pieces.

2. Cut the carrots into pieces the same size as the pork. Remove and discard the mushroom stems. Dip the mushroom caps into boiling water, then cool in cold water.

3. On a heatproof plate, stack mushroom caps, bacon and carrot pieces, arranged in circular pattern to resemble a sunflower center. Mound any leftover pieces on top, following the pattern.

4. In a bowl, combine the chicken stock, soy sauce, salt, sugar, (MSG), rice wine, and pepper; pour over the meat and vegetables. Add the scallion and ginger, and steam the dish over an intense flame for 30 to 40 minutes.

5. Discard the scallion and ginger. Carefully drain off the liquid from this steamed mixture into a wok; invert the meat and vegetables onto a serving platter. (Rearrange as necessary to reassemble the sunflower.) Heat the liquid in a wok over a medium flame; stir in the cornstarch paste and cook until the gravy is thickened. Pour the gravy over the sunflower, garnish with the scallions, and serve.

Stir-Fried Pork Tenderloin With Coriander
Yuan bao liji 芫爆里脊

This savory dish is easy to prepare. The aromatic coriander scents the air as it cooks, and its flavor, along with the flavors of the garlic and scallion, complements that of the succulent deep-fried pork tenderloin. Coriander grown in the autumn has the richest fragrance.

6½ oz. (200 g) pork tenderloin
2½ oz. (75 g) coriander leaves
1 medium egg white
2½ teaspoons cornstarch paste
¼ teaspoon salt
(½ teaspoon MSG)
1 scallion, chopped
1 tablespoon chopped peeled

fresh ginger
2 medium cloves garlic, sliced
1½ teaspoons rice wine
5 teaspoons clear chicken stock
Dash of rice wine vinegar
2 cups (500 ml) vegetable oil
Dash of sesame oil

1. Cut the pork into 1½-by-1-by-⅛-inch (4-cm-by-2-cm-by-2-mm) slices. Cut the coriander leaves into 1¼-inch-long (3-cm-long) pieces.

2. In a medium-size bowl, combine the egg white, cornstarch paste, half of the salt, (and ¼ teaspoon MSG) to make a batter. Add the pork, gently turning the slices in the batter to coat thoroughly; set aside.

3. Combine the scallion, ginger, garlic, and coriander in a bowl and add the remaining salt, the rice wine, (remaining MSG), the chicken broth, and vinegar and mix; set aside.

4. Heat the vegetable oil in a wok over an intense flame. When the oil is moderately hot, add the pork and cook for 1 minute, stirring gently with chopsticks to keep the pieces from sticking together, then scoop out.

5. Empty the wok of all but 2½ tablespoons oil, return the fried pork to the wok, and add the reserved seasoning mixture. Sprinkle a few drops of sesame oil over the mixture and toss the wok for a few seconds. Transfer to a platter and serve.

Slab bacon with Fermented Bean Curd
Nanru kourou　　　　南乳扣肉

Four cooking methods—boiling, frying, stir-frying, and steaming—are used to cook the pork in this dish. Generous amounts of garlic, ginger, and scallions add robust flavors to the strong cheesy odor of fermented bean curd. Fermented bean curd (or *tofu*) is sold cubed in bottles filled with brine. It is sometimes labeled "bean cake."

3 cubes fermented bean curd

3¼ cups (810 ml) clear chicken stock

3 medium potatoes (13 oz./410 g)

1¼ lb. (625 g) streaky pork (slab bacon) with the skin

1½ teaspoons soy sauce

4 cups (1 L) peanut oil

2 scallions, minced

4 teaspoons minced peeled fresh ginger

10 medium-size cloves garlic, minced

2 teaspoons rice wine

2 teaspoons sugar

1 teaspoon salt

1 tablespoon cornstarch paste

1. Mash the bean curd, along with 2 tablespoons of the chicken stock, into a pulp. Wash and peel the potatoes and cut into pieces 1½-inch (4-cm) thick.

2. Place the thick bacon in a wok in enough water to cover and bring to a boil over a medium flame. Boil for 5 minutes. Remove, pat dry, and brush with the soy sauce. Heat 3 tablespoons of oil in the wok over an intense flame. When the oil is very hot, carefully slide the pork, skin side down, into the wok, and cook until the skin is browned, about 2 minutes. Remove the pork and soak in cold water, to cover, until it softens, about 10 minutes. Remove from the water, pat dry, and slice into 1½-inch-wide (4-cm) strips.

3. Heat 3 tablespoons of the oil in a clean wok over an intense flame. Add the scallions, ginger, and garlic, and stir-fry briefly. Add the bean curd mixture and stir several times. Add the bacon strips and stir-fry for 10 seconds more. Add the remaining chicken stock, rice wine, sugar, and salt and heat to a boil. Reduce flame to low and simmer over low heat for 5 minutes.

4. Meanwhile, in a clean wok, fry the potatoes in the remaining oil until browned, about 20 minutes.

5. Transfer the bacon and its sauce to a heatproof bowl and steam over an intense flame for 10 minutes. Remove the pork slices from the wok with a long-handled strainer and place them in the center of a serving platter. Surround the pork with the fried potatoes.

6. Heat the remaining sauce in the wok over a medium flame until hot and stir in the cornstarch paste. When the sauce has thickened slightly, pour over the pork and serve.

Pork 113

Mongolian Hot Pot
Shuan yangrou 涮羊肉

Mongolian Hot Pot is a full meal in itself. Lamb is sliced paper-thin and cooked at the table by swirling it through a simmering pot of shrimp-and-mushroom flavored broth. Each diner then dips his or her cooked meat into individual bowls of sauces and condiments. The second step is to add Chinese cabbage, noodles and dumplings to the pot and eat them with a bowl of the broth.

The meat must be tender and thinly sliced so it cooks in a few seconds. The breed of sheep raised in Mongolia for this dish produce lean, mildly-flavored meat. The lambs are slaughtered when they reach about 50 pounds (25 kilos).

The meat dumplings, sesame seed cakes, and preserved garlic are traditional delicacies among the nomadic Mongol tribesmen but are not essential to the preparation or service of this dish. Sesame paste (or tahina), pickled chive flowers, chili oil, and shrimp sauce are sold in cans or bottles. If using frozen lamb, do not thaw and refreeze, but slice before thawing takes place.

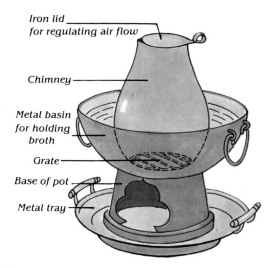

Iron lid
for regulating air flow

Chimney

Metal basin
for holding
broth

Grate

Base of pot

Metal tray

The Mongolian Hot Pot, a brass vessel, is used for cooking lamb in the style of the Northern herdsmen.

MONGOLIAN HOT POT

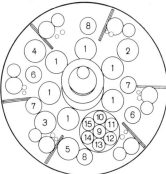

1. sliced lamb
2. stuffed dumplings
3. wheat noodles
4. vermicelli
5. Chinese cabbage
6. preserved garlic
7. sesame seed cake
8. minced scallion and coriander
9. dissolved fermented bean curd
10. pickled chive flowers
11. chili oil
12. sesame paste
13. soy sauce
14. shrimp sauce
15. rice wine

⅓ cup (85 ml) rice wine
7 tablespoons sesame paste
3¼ oz. (100 g) fermented bean curd, mashed
3¼ oz. (100 g) pickled chive flowers
⅓ cup (85 ml) soy sauce
⅓ cup (85 ml) chili oil
⅓ cup (85 ml) shrimp sauce
½ cup (50 g) finely chopped coriander leaves
½ cup (1¾ oz./50 g) finely chopped scallions
8 oz. (250 g) Chinese cabbage leaves
3¼ oz. (100 g) cellophane noodles
3¼ (100 g) wheat noodles
2 tablespoons vegetable oil
4 cups (1 L) clear chicken stock
2½ lb. (1.25 kg) fresh lean lamb, boned
¾ oz. (25 g) dried shrimp
¾ oz. (25 g) dried mushrooms

14 meat dumplings
5 sesame seed cakes
5 cloves sweetened preserved garlic

1. Place the rice wine, sesame paste, bean curd, chive flowers, soy sauce, chili oil, and shrimp sauce in individual bowls. Place the coriander and scallions on individual plates.
2. Chop the Chinese cabbage leaves into pieces 1¼ inches (3 cm) square. Soak the cellophane noodles in cold water. Place the cabbage leaves and cellophane noodles in separate bowls.
3. Briefly dip the meat dumplings and wheat noodles in boiling water; drain. Coat them with vegetable oil to prevent their sticking together. Place on individual plates.
4. Heat the chicken stock in a wok over a medium flame. Add the dried shrimp and mushrooms and cook for several minutes.
5. Place the hot pot on a metal tray. Light the charcoal in the chamber and fill the pot with the mushroom and shrimp broth. Place the hot pot in the center of the table and surround with the platters of lamb, sauces, condiments, cabbage leaves, cellophane noodles, dumplings, and wheat noodles.

To eat, each person mixes the sauces and condiments in his or her own bowl. When the broth boils, each diner picks up two or three slices of meat at a time with chopsticks and swirls them this way and that in the boiling broth for a few seconds. When the slice begins to curl and lose its pinkness, dip it into the sauce and condiments before eating. The sesame cakes and preserved garlic are eaten along with the meat. After the meat is finished, add the cabbage and cellophane noodles to the remaining broth; heat and add more water if necessary. Next add the dumplings and wheat noodles and cook for 1 minute; these are eaten last. Top off the meal with a bowl of the very savory broth that remains.

Preparing the meat. Cut the boned lamb, along the grain, into pieces 6½ inches (16 cm) square and 1¼ inches (3 cm) thick. Place these in a metal container, pressing them together; put in freezer for twelve hours, until completely frozen. (The frozen meat will be far easier to slice thin.) Place the frozen meat on a chopping block and trim the sides smooth for appearance. Cover part of the meat with a cloth to provide a better grasp for slicing. Hold the cloth-covered end firmly, and thinly slice the meat with a cleaver. Each square should yield about 100 slices. Fold each slice in half as you cut it; place the slices neatly on a platter.

Lamb   115

Braised Lamb Slices
Pa yangroutiao 扒羊肉条

This tender lamb dish is flavored with star anise and ginger. If younger lamb is substituted for mutton, the cooking time can be cut in half. The shape and smoothness of the lamb slices is important. Trim the raw loin into a smooth-sided rectangular slab. Immerse it in cold water to firm it and scrape away any stains or roughness before slicing.

1 lb. (500 g) lean loin of lamb, trimmed
2½ tablespoons sesame oil
1 teaspoon chopped scallion, white part only
1 teaspoon thinly sliced peeled fresh ginger
2 whole star anise
1½ tablespoons rice wine
1½ tablespoons soy sauce
(Pinch of Gourmet Powder)
1 tablespoon cornstarch
1 each cucumber and tomato, plus 2 radishes, unpeeled and carved into decorative shapes for garnish, as shown in the photograph.

1. In a large pot, submerge the lamb in enough cold water to cover. Bring to a boil, uncover, and simmer over a low flame for 1½ hours. Remove the lamb, reserving the cooking broth.

2. Trim the meat so it is smooth and the slices are uniform in size. Slice across the grain, into pieces that are ⅜-inch thick by 4 inches long (1 x 10 cm). Do not slice completely through the meat. Leave about ⅛ inch (0.5 cm) uncut at the bottom. Set the meat in a heatproof bowl with the smooth, unsliced side down.

3. Heat 1 tablespoon sesame oil in a wok over a medium flame. When the oil is moderately hot, add the scallion, ginger, and star anise. Stir-fry long enough to release the sweet aroma of the anise. Stir in the rice wine, 2 teaspoons soy sauce, and ½ cup (125 ml) of the reserved lamb cooking liquid and bring to boiling.

4. Pour the hot broth over the lamb and place the bowl in a steamer. Steam over an intense flame for 20 minutes. Scoop out and discard the scallion pieces, ginger, and anise stars. Transfer the meat, with the slices held tightly together, to a wok and place over a medium flame. Add the hot broth, bring it to boiling and stir in the remaining soy sauce. Dissolve the cornstarch in two tablespoons of the broth and stir it into the broth in the wok.

5. As soon as the liquid boils quickly turn the meat upside down on a serving platter so the smooth, uncut surface is facing up. Pour the remaining sesame oil over the meat and quickly slice down through the uncut surface to release each slice. Garnish with the carved vegetables and serve.

Shashlik

Kao yangrouchuan   烤羊肉串

Pieces of lamb tenderloin, a most tender cut of meat, are marinated in an aromatic and delicate sauce of Sichuan peppercorns, sesame paste, pepper, tomato, scallion, and egg. They are roasted over a hot charcoal fire very briefly to allow the outside to become crisp, while the inside remains tender and pink. The finest cuts are taken from Mongolian lamb weighing 50 pounds (25 kilos). Use five stainless steel skewers 14 inches (35 cm) long.

1½ lb. (750 g) tenderloin of lamb

1 teaspoon Sichuan peppercorns

¼ teaspoon salt

(¼ teaspoon Gourmet Powder)

2 tablespoons finely chopped tomato

1 scallion, finely chopped

2 eggs

5 teaspoons ground black pepper

½ cup (50 g) flour

3 tablespoons sesame paste

1. Prepare a charcoal fire for broiling the lamb. Cut the meat into 1¾-by-1¼-by-¾-inch (4-cm x 3-cm x 2-cm) pieces and place in a large bowl. In a small bowl, add 5 teaspoons boiling water to the Sichuan peppercorns and steep for 2 minutes. Strain the peppercorns from the "tea;" set the "tea" aside.
2. Add the salt, (Gourmet Powder), tomato, scallion, and Sichuan peppercorn "tea" to the meat and stir to mix. Add the eggs, ground black pepper, flour, and sesame paste to the seasoned meat and stir to coat the meat thoroughly with the mixture. Let stand for 15 minutes.
3. Place 5 or 6 pieces of lamb close together on a stainless steel skewer, leaving about 1 inch (2.5 cm) of the pointed end exposed. Broil the lamb over a very hot charcoal fire for 3 minutes until the meat is browned. Turn the skewer over and broil the other side until browned—the lamb should still be pink on the inside. Serve the lamb still on the skewers, to keep the lamb warm. Diners will slide the pieces off onto their plates.

1. Cut lamb into rectangular slices.

2. Add eggs, black pepper, flour and sesame paste to lamb.

3. Mix to coat lamb thoroughly with seasonings.

4. Place lamb on skewers, leaving tip of skewer exposed.

5. Broil lamb on one side until browned, then turn skewer.

Grilled Lamb
Kao yangrou 烤羊肉

Because of its assertive odor, lamb has usually been a historic favorite of only the nomadic, sheep-herding peoples of northern China. Of late, it occasionally appears even in banquets and restaurant cuisine. Fresh coriander leaves and scallions are grilled with the wafer-thin slices of lamb. Fresh coriander, too, has a strong presence, so be sparing with it if the lamb is young. Preparing this dish is more fun if diners grill their own individual portions, preferably at the table. This also allows each diner to season the meat to taste.

It is essential to use a grill with rods or mesh close enough together (⅛ inch/0.5 cm apart) so that the thin pieces of meat and scallion do not fall through into the fire. As traditionally served by the Mongol nomads, this dish comes with preserved, pickled garlic cloves, and both sesame-seed and ox-tongue cakes. See recipe for the preserved garlic in Section Five.

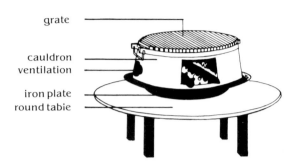

Diagram of Iron Grill. An iron cauldron sits in center of an iron-covered round table. Square grate, made of iron rods, rests on iron ring.

6 tablespoons minced peeled fresh ginger

1 lb. (500 g) lamb-leg meat, with a thin layer of fat

2 scallions

1¾ oz. (50 g) fresh coriander leaves

5 tablespoons soy sauce

2 teaspoons rice wine

5 teaspoons sugar

1 teaspoon sesame oil

(1 teaspoon MSG)

1. Place the ginger in a twist of fine-mesh cheesecloth or a garlic press and squeeze tightly to extract the juice. Pour 3 tablespoons water over the ginger and squeeze again, to yield a total of 3 tablespoons juice. Discard the pulp and set the juice aside.

2. Cut the meat against the grain into about 50 thin slices 6 inches (15 cm) long and 1¼ inches (3 cm) wide. Cut the slices crosswise into three sections each. Carving wafer-thin slices will be easier if the lamb is frozen first.

3. Slice the scallions into 2-inch (5-cm) strips and chop the coriander leaves into ¾-inch (2-cm) sections. Set them aside. Combine the soy sauce, ginger juice, rice wine, sugar, sesame oil, (and MSG) in a bowl.

4. Prepare a grill using pine, pine cones, or other aromatic wood. Dip the slices of lamb in the sauce for a few seconds. Spread the scallions, then the lamb, on the grill and stir with long-handled chopsticks until they sizzle and begin to smoke. Sprinkle the coriander leaves over them. Scoop and flip the pieces with chopsticks on a spatula, so all sides cook evenly. When the slices curl and the strong bouquet of the coriander is released (2 to 3 minutes), scoop each serving onto a plate and eat it while it is hot. Beer makes a hearty companion for this dish.

Sweeter Than Honey
Tasai mi　它赛密

Sweet, tender, and reddish-brown in color, this dish was a favorite in the Qing Palace. It was originally prepared with venison. In the autumn of 1772, when the Qian Long emperor made an inspection tour of the region outside the Great Wall, he shot three deer. The imperial kitchen then concocted a dish from the venison that the emperor lauded as "sweeter than honey."

5 oz. (150 g) tenderloin of lamb or mutton
1 -inch section of peeled fresh ginger
1 teaspoon soy sauce
2 teaspoons cornstarch paste
1 egg yolk, beaten
2½ cups (625 ml) vegetable oil
1½ tablespoons sugar
½ teaspoon vinegar
½ teaspoon rice wine
1 teaspoon peanut oil

Cut the lamb into ¾-inch (2-cm) thick strips. Coat the strips with a batter of egg yolk and

cornstarch. Deep fry the batter-dipped meat. Quick-fry to thicken the sauce before serving.

1. Cut the mutton diagonally into pieces 1-inch by ¾-inch by ¾-inch (3-cm x 2-cm x 2-cm); it is easier to cut if the mutton is frozen.

2. In a medium-size bowl, mix ½ teaspoon of the soy sauce, ½ teaspoon of the cornstarch paste, and the beaten egg yolk. Add the meat and coat thoroughly with this mixture.

3. Heat the wok over an intense flame. Add all but two tablespoons of the vegetable oil and heat it until moderately hot. Add the meat, stirring quickly with iron chopsticks (to keep the meat from sticking together). When the meat starts to curl and turn greyish-white, after about

1 minute, remove and drain.

4. In another bowl, squeeze the ginger in a garlic press to extract about ⅛ teaspoon of juice. Combine it with the sugar, remaining soy sauce, vinegar, rice wine, the remaining cornstarch paste, and 2 tablespoons water to make a sauce.

5. Clean the wok and place over a high flame. Add 2 tablespoons of vegetable oil. Then add the meat and the sauce from the bowl. Quick-fry for 5 to 6 seconds only. As the liquid begins to thicken sprinkle with the peanut oil and toss the wok 2 or 3 times. Transfer to a platter and serve.

Sautéed Chicken Breasts in White Sauce
Liu jipu　　　　　　熘 鸡 脯

This White Sauce is actually a delicious soup. A paste made of mashed chicken meat, cornstarch, wine, and egg whites magically separates into pea-sized pellets when deep-fried in melted lard. Chinese dried "scallops," which are really *conpoy*, a close relative in the shellfish family, are sold in dried form. They are very, very costly but delicious, and the quantity required is small. See recipe following Ingredients Guide for clear stock.

3½ oz. (110 g) Chinese dried scallops

3½ oz. (110 g) fresh peas

3½ oz. (110 g) chicken breast meat

5 egg whites

1 tablespoon cornstarch

2 teaspoons rice wine

(Pinch of MSG)

½ teaspoon salt

2 cups (500 ml) melted lard or vegetable oil

5 cups (1.25 L) clear chicken stock

1 tablespoon chicken fat, melted

1. Soak the scallops in hot water for 2 to 3 hours, steam them briefly over a medium flame, then crumble apart. Steam the fresh peas until just cooked, about 3 minutes. Mince the chicken, then mash it with a wooden mallet or the back of a cleaver.
2. Beat the egg whites until frothy and combine with the chicken, 1 teaspoon of the cornstarch, 1 teaspoon of the rice wine, (pinch of MSG), and ¼ teaspoon salt. Mix thoroughly to form a paste.
3. Heat the lard or oil in a wok over an intense flame. When the oil is hot, add the chicken paste and deep-fry for about 1 minute, until the mixture forms white pellets the size of peas. When that happens, scoop them out with a wire strainer spoon and set them aside. Ladle the melted lard carefully out of the wok.
4. Add the chicken stock to the wok and bring to boiling over a medium flame. Add the remaining wine, salt, (and a pinch of MSG). Combine the remaining cornstarch with twice the amount of water and stir it into the chicken stock mixture. Stir in the peas, scallops, and chicken pellets. Sprinkle with the melted chicken fat, transfer to a tureen and serve.

1. Mash chicken breasts with back of a cleaver or wooden mallet.

2. Mix beaten egg white mixture into mashed chicken.

3. Gently pour chicken paste into hot oil in wok.

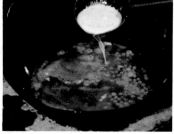

4. Pour cornstarch solution into chicken stock.

Beautiful Lady Marries Gifted Scholar

Yunü pei cailang　　　玉女配才郎

It is said that this special dish was ordered by Zhu Yuanzhang, the first emperor of Ming Dynasty (1368–1644). When he was young, he had been a page boy in the Ma family. He fell in love with the daughter of the household and when they parted, he told her that he would marry her one day. On his coronation day, to show his commitment to her, he ordered his chef to make this "Beautiful Lady Marries Gifted Scholar" dish. The dish consists of asparagus spears and lengths of mustard greens aligned in rows; mandarin duck-shaped dumplings are placed in pairs between the rows of vegetables. Since pairs of mandarin ducks are believed to be eternally faithful, they are a Chinese symbol for married love. If mustard greens are unavailable, substitute collard greens or Italian broccoli.

1 tablespoon peeled minced fresh ginger

8 oz. (250 g) asparagus

8 oz. (250 g) lengths of mustard greens

1¾ oz. (50 g) green soybeans

5 oz. (150 g) chicken breast meat

3¼ oz. (100 g) white-fleshed fish fillet

(1 teaspoon MSG)

1 teaspoon salt

4 egg whites

24 rape leaves

5 teaspoons minced cooked ham

⅓ cup (85 ml) peanut oil

⅓ cup (60 ml) clear chicken stock

2 teaspoons rice wine

5 teaspoons melted chicken fat

2 teaspoons cornstarch paste

1. Squeeze the ginger in a twist of fine-mesh cheesecloth, or a garlic press, into a bowl. Pour two teaspoons of water into the squeezed pulp and squeeze it again. Peel the asparagus and remove the outer leaves from the mustard greens. Place the asparagus on a plate; set aside. Cut the mustard lengthwise into pieces the same size as the asparagus spears. In boiling water to cover, cook the beans until tender. Remove the bean skins and mash the soybeans.
2. Cut the chicken and fish into small pieces and mash together. In a bowl, mix ½ teaspoon ginger juice, (½ teaspoon MSG), and ½ teaspoon salt. Add the chicken and fish mixture and mix well. Beat the egg whites until frothy and add to mixture; mix well to make a batter. Divide the batter into two equal parts. Mix one half with the mashed beans to make a light green batter.
3. Wash the rape leaves. To soften them for easy rolling, dip them in boiling water for 5 seconds, then place immediately in cold water. Place a little of the batter from each bowl in each rape leaf, the green batter on one side and the white on the other. Sprinkle the minced ham on the white batter on each leaf, and roll up the leaf to resemble a mandarin duck. Pile these rolls on a plate and steam for five minutes. Unroll and discard the leaves.
4. Stack them on the plate alongside the asparagus. Heat 4 teaspoons of the chicken broth, the remaining salt, (MSG), and the rice wine in a wok over a medium heat. Add the lengths of mustard and the asparagus, keeping them separate, and cook for 3 minutes. Add the chicken fat and half the cornstarch paste. Toss the wok and flip the dish onto a serving platter.
5. Heat the remaining chicken stock over a low flame. Add the mandarin-duck dumplings and cook for 15 seconds. Stir in the remaining cornstarch paste until it is thickened. Place the dumplings in pairs on the platter and serve.

Moon and Flowers
Huayue sanbao 花月三宝

This soup got its name from the bamboo shoots carved into rhomboid, flower-like shapes. The prawns add a wonderful flavor contrast to the soup's other ingredients, which include crisp asparagus.

- 2 prawns
- 2 rape leaves
- ½ oz. (15 g) cooked ham
- 10 asparagus spears
- ½ lb. (250 g) poached chicken breast
- ½ oz. (15 g) soaked dried bamboo shoots
- 4 slices fresh bamboo shoots, each 1-by-½-by-⅛ inch (2.5 cm x 1.25 cm x 0.3 cm)
- 2½ tablespoons cornstarch
- 2 teaspoons salt
- (2 teaspoons MSG)
- 1 teaspoon rice wine
- 1 medium egg white
- 5 cups (1.25 L) clear chicken stock

1. Remove and discard the prawn heads, shells, and veins then mash them. Shred one of the rape leaves and cut the other one into small pieces. Mince one third of the ham and cut the remaining ham into small diamond shapes. Cut the asparagus spears into 1-inch (2.5-cm) pieces. Slice the chicken breast. Carve the soaked dried bamboo shoots into floral shapes.

2. Dip the fresh bamboo shoot slices in water, then roll them in the cornstarch. Mix the mashed prawns with the salt, (MSG), rice wine, and egg white. Spread this mixture over the bamboo shoot slices and place the slices on a small plate. Sprinkle them with the shredded rape leaf and the minced ham, then steam these bamboo "flowers" for 3 minutes.

3. In a wok over a medium flame, heat the chicken stock, asparagus, sliced chicken, ham diamonds, small pieces of rape leaf, and the dried bamboo shoot "flowers" just until heated through. Transfer to a serving tureen, add the steamed bamboo "flowers," and serve.

Jade-Like Velvet Chicken with Water Chestnuts
Feicui furong jipian   翡翠芙蓉鸡片

Minced chicken and water chestnuts, blended with a batter, become white flakes when dropped into hot oil. After frying the mixture, a reduction of chicken stock and wine intensifies the flavor. The addition of jewel-like cucumber chips turns the smooth, soft, aromatic chicken flakes the color of jade.

- 2 oz. (60 g) chicken breast meat, skin and fat removed
- 2 water chestnuts, cooked and peeled
- 6 egg whites
- 2 teaspoons cornstarch paste (Pinch of MSG)
- 1½ teaspoons chopped scallion
- 1 teaspoon chopped peeled fresh ginger
- 5 cups (1.25 L) vegetable oil
- ½ cup (125 ml) clear chicken stock
- 1 tablespoon rice wine Pinch of salt
- 1 tablespoon finely chopped peeled cucumber
- ¼ teaspoon melted chicken fat
- 1 each cucumber and carrot, peeled and decoratively carved into flower shapes, for garnish

1. Mince the chicken and the water chestnuts and mix them.
2. Stir the egg whites slowly in a bowl while adding the minced chicken and water chestnut mixture. When they are blended, gradually stir in the cornstarch paste, (MSG), scallion, and ginger.
3. Heat the oil in a wok over a medium flame, until hot. Drop the batter into the hot oil, a spoonful at a time. When the batter fluffs into white flakes, turn the flakes over, then scoop out with a slotted spoon and drain.
4. Remove the oil from the wok and add the chicken stock, rice wine, salt, and the

1. *Peel and chop cucumber into small pieces. They supply jade-green color.*

chicken "flakes." Bring to boiling over an intense flame and continue to cook until the liquid has evaporated. Add the cucumber and combine thoroughly. Sprinkle with the warm, melted chicken fat; transfer to a platter; and serve, garnished with the cucumber and carrot flowers as shown in the photograph.

2. *Separate whites of six eggs; set aside in a bowl.*

4. *Stir egg whites and add minced chicken and water chestnuts mixture.*

3. *Mince breast meat from a very young chicken and two water chestnuts.*

5. *Drop spoonfuls of mixture into hot oil. It will separate into white flakes.*

Velvet Chicken with White Fungi
Jirong yiner　　　　鸡茸银耳

Velvet chicken is one of the few Chinese dishes made with milk. Chicken is mashed very thoroughly, mixed with egg whites and white fungus (sometimes called tremella), and formed into small ovals. These are first cooked briefly in boiling-hot water, then added to a milk and chicken broth-based sauce. Scallions and ginger juice subtly flavor this delicate dish. Make the ginger juice by squeezing about 1 tablespoon minced peeled fresh ginger, in a twist of fine-mesh cheesecloth or in a garlic press, into a bowl. Pour 1 teaspoon water over the squeezed pulp and squeeze it again.

¼ oz. (7.5 g) soaked white fungi

2 teaspoons rice wine

½ teaspoon ginger juice

2½ oz. (75 g) chicken breast

5 oz. (150 ml) milk

2 medium egg whites

3 tablespoons melted chicken fat

1½ tablespoons chopped scallions

5 oz. (150 ml) clear chicken stock

¼ teaspoon salt

(½ teaspoon Gourmet Powder)

2 teaspoons cornstarch dissolved in 1 tablespoon water

Radishes and cucumbers, for garnish

1. Reserve one piece of white fungus about ½ inch (1.5 cm) in diameter; chop the remaining fungi into ⅓-inch-square (1-cm) pieces. Combine 1 teaspoon rice wine with ¼ teaspoon ginger juice and soak the chopped white fungus pieces for 2 minutes; drain.

2. Pound the chicken meat with a cleaver. Add 2 teaspoons milk, a few drops at a time, and continue pounding the meat until it is as smooth as velvet. Place the chicken in a bowl with the marinated white fungus. Beat the egg whites in a bowl until frothy and mix gradually with the chicken and white fungus until mixture becomes a smooth purée.

3. Heat 10 cups water in a wok to boiling, then turn down the heat. Form the chicken mixture into oval pieces about 2 inches (5 cm) long, 1¼ inches (3 cm) wide, and ⅓ inch (1 cm) thick, and drop them one by one into the hot water. Turn up the heat until the water boils again. Then lower the heat, turn the pieces over, and raise the heat again until the water boils again. Scoop out the ovals and drain.

4. Heat 1 tablespoon chicken fat in a wok over an intense flame. Before the fat gets too hot, add the chopped scallions, and stir-fry briefly until they give off a sweet aroma. Add 1 teaspoon rice wine and the chicken stock. With a slotted spoon, remove the scallions and place the chicken ovals in the wok, along with the salt. Heat to boiling, then cook 1 minute more.

5. Remove two thirds of the stock. While still heating it, add the remaining milk, (Gourmet Powder), and ginger juice to the remaining broth. When the mixture is about to boil, add the dissolved cornstarch and stir until the mixture thickens. Sprinkle with 1 tablespoon chicken fat, toss the wok, then sprinkle with the remaining fat. Place the chicken in its sauce on a serving platter, top with the single large piece of white fungus, and surround it with radish and cucumber pieces.

Walnut Chicken

Jiangbao jiding taoren 酱爆鸡丁桃仁

Chicken and walnuts are stir-fried separately and combined in a sauce made from soy paste and ginger, then served on a bed of stir-fried spinach. The success of this dish depends largely on proper stir-frying of the soy paste. After the sugar and other ingredients are added, the paste should become dark in color. When this occurs, immediately add the chicken cubes and walnuts before the paste becomes too thick and bitter. If the chicken cubes and walnuts are added too early, the paste will be too thin and the chicken cubes colorless. Soybean paste is made from fresh fermented black soybeans ground fine. It is deep brown and has a briny taste. In some stores it is labeled "ground bean sauce."

- 5 oz. (150 g) chicken breast meat
- 8 leaves (1¾ oz. / 50 g) fresh spinach
- ⅔ cup (1¾ oz. / 50 g) shelled walnut halves
- 2½ tablespoons sugar
- 3½ tablespoons rice wine
- 2 teaspoons finely minced peeled fresh ginger
- 3 tablespoons soybean paste
- 1 egg white
- 4 teaspoons cornstarch paste (Pinch of MSG)
- 4 cups (1 L) vegetable oil
- 5 teaspoons sesame oil

1. *After soaking walnuts, remove their skins.*

2. *Fillet breast meat from bones.*

3. *Dice meat into large bite-sized cubes.*

1. Fillet the meat from the chicken breasts and dice it into ¾-inch (2-cm) cubes. Thoroughly wash the spinach leaves to remove sand and grit, and pat dry. Cut it into strips about 1-inch (2.5-cm) wide. Place the shelled walnuts in a bowl and pour boiling water over them; soak for 1 hour and remove the skins.
2. In a small bowl, combine the sugar, rice wine, and ginger. Set this seasoning mixture aside.
3. In a separate bowl, beat the egg white thoroughly, and gradually beat in the cornstarch, (and MSG). Dip the chicken cubes in this batter, turn to coat well, and let stand while frying the spinach and walnuts.
4. Heat a wok over a medium flame until hot, pour in 2 tablespoons of the vegetable oil, and swirl to coat the wok. Add the spinach strips and gently stir-fry until they have lost their crispness, 1 to 2 minutes. Turn the spinach out onto a warm serving platter. Arrange it as a bed for the other ingredients and keep it warm.
5. Wipe the wok and return it to a medium flame. When the wok is hot, pour in ¼ cup (50 ml) of vegetable oil, swirl to coat the wok, then add remaining vegetable oil. Add the walnuts before the oil becomes very hot. Scoop them out when they are crisp, not more than 5 minutes. (Adjust the heat to crisp the walnuts completely through before they scorch.) Scoop them from the oil and put aside nearby in a warm bowl.
6. Add the chicken cubes to the oil and quickly stir-fry until the meat turns white and tender, 1 to 2 minutes. Scoop out the chicken with a strainer spoon and put them in the bowl with the walnuts.
7. Empty and wipe the wok. Return it to the flame and add the sesame oil. When the oil is hot, add the soybean paste and stir-fry quickly until it changes color (being careful not to let it burn). Pour in the seasoning mixture of sugar, wine, and ginger. As soon as it darkens, immediately stir in the chicken pieces and walnuts and stir-fry for about 5 minutes, coating them well with the soy paste sauce.
8. Turn the chicken and walnuts, with their sauce, onto the bed of spinach on the platter and serve.

4. *Coat cubes with egg white and cornstarch paste.*

5. *Deep-fry walnuts until crisp, then chicken until tender.*

6. *Remove chicken cubes and drain off oil.*

7. *Stir-fry soybean paste in sesame oil; add wine, sugar, and ginger.*

Shandong Roast Chicken Legs

Shandong shaojitui　山东烧鸡腿

Chicken legs are marinated, deep fried, and then steamed with a variety of seasonings. Though the marinating and steaming take a few hours, this dish is easy to prepare and the resulting chicken is tender and intensely flavored with ginger, cassia bark, and aniseed.

¼ cup (60 ml) soy sauce

2 teaspoons rice wine

½ teaspoon salt

12 chicken legs

4 cups (1 L) peanut oil

2 scallions, coarsely chopped

2 tablespoons chopped peeled fresh ginger

¾ oz. (25 g) cassia bark

¾ oz. (25 g) aniseed (about ¼ cup)

1. Combine the soy sauce, rice wine, and salt in a bowl. Marinate the chicken legs in this mixture for 2 hours, turning occasionally.

2. Heat the oil in a wok over an intense flame until hot; add the chicken. Stir until the chicken turns golden, about 10 minutes. Remove the legs; drain and place in a heat-proof bowl.

3. Add the scallions, ginger, cassia bark, and aniseed to the bowl with the chicken legs, and steam for 3 hours. Remove the large pieces of the seasonings and serve the chicken legs.

Braised Chicken Drumsticks on Romaine Lettuce
Shengcai pa jitui　　　　生菜扒鸡腿

A rice wine and soy sauce marinade lends these chicken drumsticks a hearty flavor; frying, then simmering, makes them golden brown on the outside and meltingly tender on the inside. They are served around a mound of deep-green, stir-fried romaine leaves.

5 teaspoons rice wine
3 tablespoons soy sauce
10 chicken drumsticks
4 cups (1 L) clear chicken stock
2 teaspoons vinegar
½ teaspoon salt
(1 teaspoon MSG)
2 scallions, cut into pieces 1½ inches (4 cm) long

1-inch (2.5-cm) cube peeled fresh ginger, mashed
4 cups (1 L) vegetable oil
5 teaspoons sugar
2 teaspoons cornstarch paste, diluted with 3 teaspoons water
3¼ oz. (100 g) romaine lettuce, cut into strips

1. In a large bowl, combine 2 teaspoons of the rice wine with the soy sauce and marinate the drumsticks in this mixture for 30 minutes. Remove the drumsticks and drain; discard the marinade. In a separate bowl, combine the chicken stock, remaining rice wine, vinegar, salt, (MSG), scallions, and ginger. Set aside.

2. Heat the oil in a wok over a medium flame until hot. Add the drumsticks and fry until golden brown, about 10 minutes. Remove the drumsticks and drain.

3. Empty all but 2½ tablespoons of the oil into a bowl and set aside. Heat the remaining oil in the wok over a medium flame just until warm. Add the sugar and stir constantly until the mixture turns golden. Add the seasoning mixture and the drumsticks. Bring to boiling, then reduce the flame to low and simmer for 30 minutes.

4. Remove the scallion and ginger pieces. Stir in the diluted cornstarch paste. Raise the flame to medium and cook, stirring constantly, until the sauce thickens and coats the drumsticks.

5. In a separate wok, heat the reserved oil over an intense flame until hot. Add the lettuce strips and deep fry until they darken, about 5 seconds. Remove from oil, drain, and heap in the center of a serving platter. Arrange the drumsticks in a circle around the lettuce with the small-end "handles" pointing out; pour the remaining sauce over the drumsticks and serve.

Chicken　127

Steam-Pot Chicken
Qiguo ji   汽锅鸡

This dish, served as a soup or as a main course, is popular in Yunnan Province. Made of reddish clay, the steam pot is about 8 inches (20 cm) in diameter. Its height, including the lid, is about 6 inches (16 cm). Chinese stores often stock steam pots in a larger size. A steam channel rises in the center. The steam enters the "belly" of the pot through this channel. This creates a combination of heating techniques: that of a double-boiler and that of a steamer; the result is a delicious soup and a moist, tender chicken.

¾ oz. (25 g) ham
6 soaked dried black mushrooms (½ oz. / 15 g)
1½ lb. (750 g) chicken, with head
½ oz. (15 g) bamboo shoots

Pinch of salt
¼ teaspoon sugar
(½ teaspoon MSG)
3 tablespoons rice wine
2 slices peeled fresh ginger

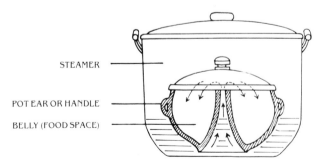

STEAMER

POT EAR OR HANDLE

BELLY (FOOD SPACE)

This pot-bellied earthen steamer has a funnel that rises in the center, with a cover. Steam rises through center funnel from bottom, and into food placed in belly.

1. Cut two thin slices from the ham; set aside. Use remaining ham to make ⅓-inch (1-cm) squares. After soaking the mushrooms for 30 minutes, cut off and discard the stems. Set aside two small round mushrooms and cut the rest into ⅓-inch (1-cm) squares. Make horizontal slashes, halfway, along one side of each of two bamboo shoots, like a fan. These will make the "wings" of the finished chicken (see photo). Dice the remainder of the bamboo shoots.

2. To prepare the chicken, cut it open through the breastbones. Clean and rinse. Cut off the lower tips of the legs. Cut off the head at the upper end of the neck, the legs near the hip joint, and the wings near the shoulder joint. (Break the bones by making cuts from the underside of the legs and wings without detaching the skin.)

Make a perpendicular cut on the lower side of the head without cutting it through entirely. Cut the remainder of the chicken into 1¼-inch (3-cm) chunks.

3. Place the chicken and ham chunks, diced mushrooms and bamboo shoots in a steam pot (see illustration). Set the legs and wings symmetrically on top, skin facing upward. Stand the head upright in front. Place the reserved ham slices, bamboo shoot "wings," reserved mushroom caps, salt, sugar, (MSG), rice wine, and ginger on the chicken chunks (see picture).

4. In a large pot, heat water to boiling. Reduce heat but keep the water boiling gently. Put in the steam pot; the boiling water should remain below the handles. Steam the chicken for 3 to 4 hours, then serve.

Chicken in Oyster Sauce
Haoyou quji　蠔油焗鸡

Chicken in Oyster Sauce is a famous dish from the Guang-dong region. The whole chicken is coated with rice wine and soy sauce to give it a deep, rich color when it is deep fried. After frying it is cut into pieces small enough to eat with chopsticks and served with a very flavorful sauce made with scallions, dates, oyster sauce, bamboo shoots, ginger, and black mushrooms. Pickled rutabaga from Yunnan Province is also used as a flavoring in the sauce.

3 soaked dried black mushrooms (¾ oz./25 g)

1¾ oz. (50 g) bamboo shoots, sliced

1 chicken (3 lb./1.5 kg)

2 teaspoons rice wine

2 teaspoons soy sauce

6 cups (1.5 L) peanut oil

4 scallions, cut into 1-inch (2.5-cm) pieces

2 tablespoons sliced peeled fresh ginger

1¾ oz. (50 g) pickled rutabaga from Yunnan Province, sliced into 1-inch-long (2.5-cm) pieces

5 dates, pitted and rinsed

2½ cups (625 ml) clear chicken stock

3 tablespoons oyster sauce

1½ teaspoons sugar

1 teaspoon salt

¼ teaspoon pepper

(2 teaspoons MSG)

1 tablespoon cornstarch paste

⅓ teaspoon sesame oil

1. Dip the black mushrooms and bamboo shoots into boiling water for 5 seconds; drain.

2. Coat the chicken with a mixture of 1 teaspoon rice wine and 1 teaspoon soy sauce. Heat all but ⅓ cup (85 ml) of the peanut oil in a wok over a medium flame until hot. Add the chicken and deep fry for 30 minutes.

3. Meanwhile heat the remaining peanut oil in a separate wok over a medium flame. Add the scallions, ginger, and remaining teaspoon of rice wine and stir. Add the mushrooms, bamboo shoots, rutabaga, and dates. Add the chicken stock, remaining soy sauce, the oyster sauce, sugar, salt, and pepper; heat just to boiling, then lower the heat and simmer.

4. (When the chicken is almost finished deep frying, add the MSG to the sauce.) Remove the chicken from the oil, drain, and cut into small pieces.

5. Remove the rutabaga pieces from the sauce; discard. Remove the mushrooms, bamboo shoots, and dates from the sauce and place on a platter; arrange the chicken on top.

6. Stir the cornstarch paste into the remaining sauce; cook until the sauce is thickened. Sprinkle the sesame oil over the dish, then pour on the sauce and serve.

Chicken with Straw Mushrooms
Caogu zhengji   草菇蒸鸡

This easy-to-prepare dish is steamed over an intense flame for 20 minutes, leaving the chicken juicy and tender. A young chicken is used—in China, old fowl are used only for soup. Roosters are considered nutritious, but *only* if killed before they start to crow. Straw mushrooms may be purchased canned in brine, but they have so much more flavor in dried form, the extra soaking step required is well worth the effort.

1. Soak the dried mushrooms, in enough warm water to cover, until softened. The skins will come off easily;

- 6 dried straw mushrooms
- 1¼ lb. (625 g) chicken breast meat, skin attached
- 1 scallion, cut in 1-inch (2.5-cm) lengths
- 2 teaspoons thickly sliced peeled fresh ginger
- 1½ tablespoons soy sauce
- 1 tablespoon rice wine
- 1½ teaspoons salt
- Pinch of sugar
- (1½ teaspoons MSG)
- ½ cup (125 ml) melted chicken fat
- 1 tablespoon cornstarch paste

discard the skins and stems. Rinse mushrooms and return them to their soaking water. If using straw mushrooms canned in brine, substitute brine for soaking liquid, and omit salt in recipe. Cut the chicken into 1½-inch (4-cm) cubes.

2. In a large shallow bowl, combine the chicken with the mushrooms and soaking liquid. Add the scallions, ginger, soy sauce, rice wine, salt, sugar, (MSG), melted chicken fat, and the cornstarch paste.

3. Steam over an intense flame for 20 minutes. Remove from the wok, discarding the scallions and ginger; place the chicken and mushrooms on a platter and serve.

The ingredients are assembled in bowls before cooking.

Dongan Chicken
Dongan ziji　东安子鸡

Named after Hunan's Dongan County, this well-known dish is spicy, hot, and slightly sour. A young chicken is first parboiled and then stir-fried with a wonderful combination of spices, including ginger, garlic, and Sichuan pepper.

1 chicken (about 2 lbs. / 1 kg)
⅓ cup (85 ml) melted lard
2 tablespoons finely shredded peeled fresh ginger
1 teaspoon Sichuan peppercorns
4 cloves garlic, chopped
2 dried chili peppers, soaked and chopped
¼ teaspoon rice wine vinegar
2 teaspoons rice wine
½ teaspoon salt

(¼ teaspoon MSG)
½ cup (125 ml) clear chicken stock
½ sweet green pepper, shredded
½ sweet red pepper, shredded
2 scallions, chopped
4 teaspoons cornstarch paste
½ teaspoon sesame oil
Cucumbers and other colorful raw vegetables cut into decorative shapes, for garnish

1. In a large pot, simmer the chicken in water to cover for 10 minutes, or until nearly tender. Remove from pot; remove skin and bones and cut meat along the grain into strips measuring about ¾-by-2 inches (1.5-by-5-cm). Set aside.
2. Heat the lard in a wok over an intense flame. Stir-fry the ginger, Sichuan pepper, garlic, chili peppers, and chicken for 1 minute. Add the vinegar, rice wine, salt, (and (MSG) and stir briefly.
3. Add the chicken stock and simmer over a low flame for about 4 minutes. Add the green and red peppers and the scallions. Add the cornstarch paste and toss the wok several times. Sprinkle the mixture with the sesame oil and serve garnished with raw vegetables.

Curry Chicken
Naiyou gali jikuai　奶油咖喱鸡块

In Guangdong, where this dish originated, the chicken is served with a starchy sauce called "oily flour." Curry and chili peppers make this a very spicy dish, but a subtle touch is added by the fresh coconut juice. (Canned coconut milk can be substituted, yielding a slightly different taste.) Curry-flavored oil is a semi-liquid imported in cans (usually 15 oz.) or bottles with narrow necks like ketchup bottles.

7 oz. (200 g) coconut meat (about ½ coconut)

1 chicken (1½ lb. / 750 g)

5 cups (1.25 L) peanut oil

½ lb. (250 g) potatoes, cut into "rolling knife" pieces

2½ cups (625 ml) clear chicken stock

2 teaspoons rice wine

1½ teaspoons sugar

1 teaspoon salt

(Pinch of MSG)

3 dried chili peppers, chopped

⅔ cup (3¼ oz. / 100 g) minced onion

1½ tablespoons minced, peeled fresh ginger

2 tablespoons curry-flavored oil

3 tablespoons flour

½ cup (125 ml) milk

1. Shred the coconut meat and squeeze to extract the juice; set the juice aside. Remove the skin and bones from the chicken and cut the meat into 1½-inch (4-cm) cubes. Heat 4 cups (1 L) of the peanut oil in a wok over a medium flame until hot and fry the chicken pieces just until cooked through, but not browned, about 2 minutes. Remove the chicken pieces and drain. Add the potato pieces to the hot oil and fry over a medium flame until softened slightly but not browned, about 5 minutes.

2. Empty the wok of all but 2½ tablespoons of the peanut oil and begin to re-heat over a medium flame. When the oil is just warm, stir in the chicken stock, rice wine, sugar, salt, (MSG), and the chicken pieces. Heat, but do not let it boil.

3. Meanwhile, heat ⅓ cup (85 ml) peanut oil in a pan over an intense flame. When the oil is hot, add the peppers, onion, ginger, and curry-flavored oil and stir to combine. Add this mixture to the chicken in the wok and bring to boiling.

4. Empty the wok into a heatproof medium-size bowl and steam for 15 minutes. Add the potato pieces and steam for 5 minutes more.

5. Meanwhile, clean the wok, heat the remaining peanut oil over a low flame and stir in the flour. Keeping the flame low so the flour does not burn or stick, stir until the mixture is just warmed through, then pour the "oily flour" into a bowl; set aside.

6. With a slotted spoon or Chinese strainer on a handle, remove the potatoes and chicken from the steaming bowl, place on a serving platter, and cover to keep warm while finishing the sauce. Scrape any bits of potato and chicken out of the wok. Pour in the steaming chicken broth mixture from the bowl. Return the wok to the flame, stir in the milk and the coconut juice and bring to boiling. Add the "oily flour" and stir to combine thoroughly. Pour the mixture over the chicken and serve.

Frog-Shaped Chicken
Hama ji 蛤蟆鸡

Chicken is arranged to resemble a frog floating on a pond, partly hidden in a clump of reeds. The chicken wings are raised, the legs stretched back, and the wrinkled skin is dotted with soybeans. Gluten cubes, slivers of bamboo shoots, and cucumber slices are the "reeds" surrounding the "frog." The gluten can be found in Chinese grocery stores prepared and sometimes frozen, in large cubes. An unusually large quantity of fresh ginger is used, but the long cooking time gentles its bite, giving the chicken an exquisite, subtle flavor. If you cannot find a chicken young enough, use a Cornish game hen. Cut notches into the cucumber before slicing so the slices look like gears.

1¾ oz. (50 g) gluten

1 chicken (1 lb. / 500 g)

2 tablespoons soy sauce

5 cups (1.25 L) vegetable oil

1 tablespoon rice wine

1½ teaspoons sugar

4 scallions, cut into 1-inch (2.5-cm) pieces

½ cup (110 g) crushed peeled fresh ginger

⅓ cup (50 g) thinly sliced bamboo shoots

2½ cups (625 ml) clear chicken stock

(1 teaspoon Gourmet Powder)

1 -inch (2.5-cm) section thinly sliced unpeeled cucumber

½ cup (125 g) soybeans, cooked

1½ tablespoons sesame oil

1. Steam the gluten over an intense flame until its texture starts to resemble that of a honeycomb. Soak it briefly in cold water to eliminate the sticky substance on its surface. Remove from the water and squeeze out the excess liquid. Cut the gluten into ½-inch (2.5-cm) cubes. Boil the cubes in water for 3 minutes; remove, drain, and squeeze out the excess water by gently pressing the cubes with the flat side of a cleaver. Set aside.

2. Lay the chicken on its breast and make 1½-inch (4-cm) cuts along each rib, being careful not to detach the skin from the meat. Break the shoulder joints so that the wings can be extended, then strike the back of the bird with the side of a cleaver to flatten it out. Place the chicken in a medium-size bowl, pour the soy sauce over it, and let it soak for about 10 minutes. Pour off the soy sauce and reserve.

3. Heat the vegetable oil in a wok over an intense flame. When the oil is hot, add the chicken and fry until the skin becomes golden brown and crisp, about 15 minutes. Remove from the wok and drain.

4. Place the chicken, breast down, in a medium-size clay pot. Add the reserved soy sauce, the gluten cubes, rice wine, sugar, scallions, ginger, bamboo shoots, and chicken stock. Bring to boiling, then reduce the flame to low, cover, and simmer for 30 minutes. Turn the chicken over and continue to simmer until the meat is tender, but not falling off the bone, about 10 minutes more.

5. Remove and discard the scallions and ginger. (Stir in the Gourmet Powder.) Arrange the soybeans on the chicken breast and sprinkle with sesame oil. Float the cucumber slices on the surface of the broth. Simmer 3 minutes more and serve in the clay pot or on a platter.

Fried Chicken Shish Kabob
Zha jirouchuan　炸鸡肉串

Small portions of chicken breast on skewers make this Northern-style treat appropriate as a hot appetizer for a Western meal. Ten chunks of chicken breast are first coated in a peppery ginger batter, then deep-fried to make them crisp. Soaking the chicken meat in salted water before cooking is the secret to keeping the flesh firm. (Use five 7-inch/18 cm stainless steel skewers.)

½ lb. (250 g) chicken breast meat

2 eggs

(½ teaspoon MSG)

1½ tablespoons rice wine

½ teaspoon ground white pepper

½ cup (55 g) flour

3 tablespoons sesame seeds

1 teaspoon chopped scallion

1 teaspoon tomato paste

½ teaspoon salt

¼ teaspoon minced peeled fresh ginger

2½ cups (625 ml) vegetable oil

1 cucumber, peeled and decoratively sliced, for garnish

2 red peppers, decoratively cut, for garnish

1. Cut the chicken breast diagonally into 1-by-¾-by-1-inch (2.5 x 2 x 2.5-cm) cubes and soak them in salted water for a few minutes.

2. In a medium-size bowl, combine the eggs, (MSG), rice wine, white pepper, flour, sesame seeds, scallion, tomato paste, salt, and ginger and mix thoroughly. Coat the chicken cubes with this mixture, then stick them onto the skewers, leaving a small space between each piece of meat.

3. Heat the oil in a wok over a gentle flame until it reaches a moderate temperature. Slide the kabobs into the oil and fry until the chicken meat turns a golden yellow, about 3 to 4 minutes. Remove the kabobs from the oil and drain. Place on a platter, garnish with the cucumber and red peppers and serve.

Daokou Fried Chicken

Daokou shaoji 道口烧鸡

This uniquely-flavored chicken dish comes from the town of Daokou, in Hua County, Henan Province. The special flavor comes from the stock and spices. Save the stock, so you can add water and more spices next time you make Daokou Chicken.

If you want the chicken to look like the Chinese version (see photo), butcher the whole plucked chicken as follows: cut off the claws. Jerk loose the windpipe and esophagus through a slit made under the neck. Make a 2¾-inch (7-cm) cut under the breast and pull out the viscera. Cut the rib bones on both sides and break the spine. Brace the abdominal cavity open with a short length of sorghum stem or bamboo. Bend the neck backwards until it touches the back. Cross the wings over the neck and shove them up through the slit in the neck and into the mouth. Wash and dry the trussed chicken.

Hard is the case of him who will stuff himself with food the whole day without applying his mind to anything. Confucius

2 small broiling chickens, cleaned

5 oz. (150 ml) honey

10 cups (2.5 L) melted chicken fat or peanut oil

10 cups (2.5 L) clear stock

Pinch of salt

Pinch each of cardamom, lilac, cassia, Dahurian angelica root, galingale (a kind of ginger), and dried tangerine peel, all tied tightly into a cloth bag

1. Mix ½ cup (125 ml) water with the honey and brush the chickens with the mixture; let stand for a few minutes. Heat the chicken fat or oil to cover the chickens in a wok until hot. Deep fry the chickens until they turn a dull red, 1 to 2 minutes. Remove and drain.

2. Place the chickens in a cauldron with stock to cover. Add the salt and condiments in the cloth bag. Submerge the chickens and hold them in place with bamboo combs or wooden forks so they cannot float. Bring the stock to boiling over an intense flame, then reduce to a low flame and simmer for 4 hours. Remove the chickens by gripping each one between two porcelain plates to keep the skins intact; transfer them to a platter and serve. Beer goes well with Daokou Chicken.

Pickled Chicken Cubes
Hongzao jiding 红糟鸡丁

Cubes of chicken are mixed with red distiller's mash, an ingredient used in the making of wine—hence the term "pickled" in the dish's name. This ingredient turns the chicken red during deep frying. The chicken cubes are then stir-fried in a slightly sweet sauce containing cucumber, scallion, garlic, and ginger. To keep the chicken tender, be sure not to overcook it during either of the two frying steps.

7 oz. (200 g) chicken breasts

2 -inch (1¾ oz./50 g) section unpeeled cucumber

3 tablespoons red distiller's mash

1 egg white

1 tablespoon cornstarch paste

(¼ teaspoon MSG)

2 cups (500 ml) vegetable oil

1 teaspoon minced scallion

½ teaspoon minced garlic

½ teaspoon minced peeled fresh ginger

5 teaspoons rice wine

3 tablespoons sugar

¼ teaspoon salt

5 teaspoons clear chicken stock

½ teaspoon melted chicken fat

1. Cut the chicken breasts and the cucumber into ½-inch (1.25 cm) cubes.

2. In a bowl, combine the distiller's mash, the egg white, 2 teaspoons of the cornstarch paste, (and half of the MSG). Add the chicken and coat thoroughly with the batter.

3. Heat the oil in a wok over a medium flame. Drop in the coated chicken cubes and stir to separate until they turn red, about 2 minutes. Remove the cubes; drain.

4. Pour off all but 3 tablespoons of the oil and heat over a medium flame. Add the cucumber, scallion, garlic, and ginger and stir for a few seconds. Add the rice wine, (remaining MSG), the sugar, salt, and chicken stock and stir. Add the chicken cubes; then add the remaining teaspoon of cornstarch paste and stir until the mixture thickens. Sprinkle with the chicken fat and serve.

Stress has to be placed not only on "color, fragrance, taste, and shape, but also on the nourishment of the dish."

Gansu Duck
Gansu ya 甘肃鸭

This flavorful dish, which originated in the northwest of China, was traditionally served in large pieces and eaten with the hands. Today it is prepared in small, bite-size pieces and eaten with chopsticks. The duck is fried and then simmered with scallions, ginger, garlic, chili, and star anise. The anise adds a subtle, distinctive flavor.

1 lb. (500 g) duck meat, on the bone

½ cup (125 ml) vegetable oil

1 scallion, chopped

2 teaspoons crushed and mashed peeled fresh ginger

2 cloves garlic, sliced

2 whole anise stars

4 cups (1 L) clear chicken stock

½ cup (125 ml) soy sauce

1½ tablespoons rice wine

½ teaspoon sugar

(1 teaspoon MSG)

2 dried chili peppers, chopped

1 sweet green pepper, sliced

1 sweet red pepper, sliced

1. With a cleaver, chop the duck meat into 1-inch (2.5-cm) pieces, leaving the meat on the bone.

2. Heat the oil in a wok, gradually, until moderately hot; add the duck pieces and cook slowly until both sides turn golden.

3. Add the scallion, ginger, garlic, and star anise. Then add the chicken broth, rice wine, soy sauce, sugar, (and MSG). Heat over an intense flame until boiling.

4. Add the chili peppers and lower heat. Simmer for about 1 hour, or until the duck meat pulls away from the bone easily.

5. Remove from heat, drain off liquid, and discard the scallions, ginger, garlic, anise, and chili. Reserving a few slices of red pepper for garnish, add the remaining red and green peppers to the wok and toss a few times. Transfer to a serving platter, garnish, and serve.

Duck 137

Beijing Roast Duck
Beijing kaoya 北京烤鸭

The master chefs at the Quanjude restaurant in China's capital city of Beijing are the final authority on the world-famous delicacy known as "Peking Duck." For literally hundreds of years—long before the spelling of the city's name was changed from Peking to Beijing—the secrets of creating the unique color, texture, flavor, and fragrance of Peking Duck have been handed down from master to apprentice. The instructions that follow provide a rare, privileged glimpse into those zealously guarded procedures. Anyone planning to construct a domed brick oven after reading this description to replicate the taste of the duck as it was in China should realize that part of the secret of this recipe's original success lies in the conditions under which the ducks are raised. Accordingly, a recipe designed for Western home kitchens follows this one. Long may the meat be moist, the skin crisp, and the fragrance savory!

4½ -5 lb. (2-2.5 kg) Beijing duck

2 tablespoons malt sugar (or honey) dissolved in ½ cup (125 ml) water

12 scallion brushes (see recipe following for Beijing Duck—Western Style)

24 thin pancakes for duck (see recipe that follows)

½ cup (125 ml) sweet-bean sauce (see recipe that follows)

1. Pluck and clean the bird. Cut off the feet. Sever the esophagus and windpipe with a small incision in the neck. Pull out the tongue and cut it off. Pump air in between the skin and the duck flesh from the incision in the neck. (Restaurants use compressed air. At home, use a bicycle pump, sports-ball inflator, or blow hard through a rubber tube.) Make a slit about 2 inches (5 cm) long under the right wing. Pull out the inner organs, wash the inside thoroughly and hang the duck up to dry. Pour about 4 cups (1 L) boiling water over it to seal the pores. This should make the skin airtight, preventing the fat from escaping while the duck is being roasted, and allow the air pumped between the skin and flesh to swell to the maximum when heated. Brush the entire bird with the malt-sugar or honey solution to enrich its mellow, golden sheen and make the skin crisper and tastier.

2. Hang the duck in a cool, shadey well-ventilated place for about 4 hours until it is dry. Wedge a piece of sorghum stalk about 3 inches (8 cm) long into the duck anus and pour boiling water into the empty cavity until it is about 80 percent filled. When the duck roasts, the water inside will keep on boiling. This will not only keep the meat tender and succulent but will also shorten the roasting time.

3. The oven for roasting ducks in authentic Beijing style is built with bricks in the shape of a tall box with a domed ceiling. Parallel rows of bars are fixed into the sides for hanging the ducks while they roast. A small iron door in the front of the oven gives access to the inside.

Heat from the oven's wood-burning fire-pit radiates outward to the walls and up to the roof of the oven. The ducks are roasted by this radiated heat, not by direct heat from the fire. Usually, only wood from fruit trees is used to fire the oven, because it yields an aroma that permeates the meat with the proper heady fragrance and sweetness. The heat in the oven should be kept at 450-480 F (230-250 C) degrees. The roasting time varies with the weather and the weight of the duck. Generally, a 4½ lb (2 kg) duck needs 45 minutes of roasting in the winter. The color of the skin tells the chef when to remove the duck from the oven. When it is ready to serve, it should have a shiny golden-brown color and weigh about a third less than it did at the start.

4. Both the dark, crackly skin and the meat are sliced into thin pieces, about 2½ inches square (6 cm), immediately before serving. These slices are then dipped into a sweet bean-paste sauce, topped with scallion brushes—made by slivering one end of 2-inch (5-cm) sections of scallion—and rolled up inside very delicate pancakes (see recipe that follows), producing a tidy packet to eat with the fingers. In the summer, thin-sliced cucumbers and radishes are also included, and those with a sweet tooth like to add raw sugar to their packet of princely finger-food. Since no part of the duck need go to waste, the duck bones with Chinese cabbage and winter melon make a fine, light soup, served toward the end of the meal. Cold slices of duck meat can also be served with fiery Maotai liquor, wine, or beer before a banquet begins.

Beijing Roast Duck—Western Style
Beijing kaoya—Xishi

This recipe for the famous "Peking Duck" has been developed by the American editors for Western home kitchens. The process of creating this masterpiece begins the day before you serve the duck.

1 duck (5 lb./2.5 kg)
1 tablespoon salt
1 tablespoon rice wine
¼ cup (60 ml) honey or maple syrup

½ cup hoisin sauce (or sweet bean-paste sauce; see recipe that follows)
4 scallions
Parsley, for garnish

1. Hang ducks to dry in cool place after sealing pores of skin.

2. Duck hanging in authentic Beijing roasting oven.

3. Slice duck skin and meat into bite-sized squares before serving.

4. Dip slices into sauce, add slivered scallion, and roll or fold up in thin pancake.

1. Early the day before you will serve the duck, rinse it under lukewarm running water and drain. Pour 5 quarts (5 L) boiling water slowly in a fine stream over both sides of the duck, so that its skin becomes almost white. Drain well, pat skin and body cavity dry, and rub the body cavity with the salt and rice wine.

2. Place the duck, breast side down, on a wire rack on top of a roasting pan; refrigerate, uncovered, for several hours.

3. Meanwhile make the thin pancakes (see recipe that follows). Refrigerate pancakes until 15 minutes before serving the duck.

4. To make scallion brushes, peel the tough outside layers from the white ends of raw scallions; cut that part into 1½-inch (4-cm) lengths. Sliver it down most of its length, leaving one end attached—or from both ends leaving a bit at the middle solid. Soak the scallions in water and refrigerate for half an hour or more before serving so they curl.

5. Brush the duck skin with the honey or maple syrup. Refrigerate again, breast side up and uncovered, overnight, until 5 hours before serving the next day.

6. Heat the oven to 175 F (80 C) degrees. Place the duck

on a rack in a roasting pan and roast for 1½ hours. Increase the oven heat to 325 F (160 C) degrees and roast the duck, breast side down, for 1½ hours; then turn it breast side up and roast until it is golden and the skin is crisp, 1 to 1½ hours more.

7. About 15 minutes before the duck is done, steam the pancakes over a medium flame until they are soft and heated through, about 10 minutes. Remove the pancakes from the plate, fold in quarters, and set aside.

8. Place the duck on a large serving platter. Garnish with parsley and a few thin pancakes. Place the hoisin sauce in a small bowl; place the scallions on one plate and the remaining pancakes on another.

9. Serve the duck at the table. Slice most of it, including the skin, into 2-by-1-inch (5 × 2.5 cm) rectangles, placing these on a smaller plate. Pass the pancakes, the cut-up duck, the bowl of hoisin sauce, and the dish of raw scallion brushes. Each diner places one or two pieces of duck at the center of a pancake, dabs on some hoisin sauce, adds a scallion brush, then rolls or folds the laden pancake into a neat package to pick up and bite into.

Duck   139

Thin Pancakes for Duck
Baobing

These pancakes are always served with Peking Duck (Beijing Roast Duck) and with many other recipes that call for eating slices of a whole roast duck served hot. Because the pancakes are rolled out very thin, a high-gluten flour will make them hold together more reliably than regular white flour.

2½ cups (275 g) flour
½ teaspoon salt
Flour, for dusting
Oil, for brushing.

1. In a large bowl, combine the flour and salt, then gradually add 1 cup (250 ml) boiling water, blending until the mixture pelletizes into the size of peas. Press the mixture into a ball, turn onto a lightly floured board, and knead to form a soft, smooth dough. Shape the dough into a roll about 16-inches (40-cm) long and 2½-inches (6-cm) wide. Cut the roll crosswise into eight pieces, then cut each piece in half. Cover with a damp cloth and set aside.
2. Lightly dust a pastry board with flour. Place two slices of the dough on the board; with fingers, flatten each into a circle about 3-inches (8-cm) across and ¼-inch (0.7-cm) thick. Brush the tops generously with oil, then place one on top of the other, oiled sides together. Lightly dust a rolling pin with flour, then roll the circle from the center to form a thin pancake 7 inches (17 cm) in diameter, turning it over several times to roll both sides evenly.
3. In an ungreased wok over a medium flame, cook each circle on one side unti light brown, 2 to 3 minutes. Turn over and cook the other side, then remove to a large plate.

Carefully separate the two layers, making two thin pancakes. Stack these, one on top of the other, browned side up. Repeat with the rest of the dough, stacking the pancakes on the plate as they are done, then refrigerate until needed. (There should be 16 pancakes in all.)

Sweet Bean-Paste Sauce
Tiendoujiang

This sauce is served to enhance the flavor of roast duck. The slices of meat or skin are dipped into the sauce, or the sauce is dabbed on top of the duck pieces before they are wrapped, with scallions, into their pancake envelope. The essential ingredient is sweet bean paste, which is made from fermented black soybeans. Bottled hoisin sauce is an acceptable substitute if the paste is not available. This recipe makes enough for at least one meal of Beijing Roast Duck.

4 tablespoons sweet bean paste (or hoisin sauce)
4 tablespoons sugar
½ cup (125 ml) water
2 tablespoons sesame oil

1. Mix the bean paste, sugar, and water in a small bowl.
2. Heat a small wok and add the oil. Continue to heat until the oil is moderately hot. Add the bean-paste mixture and, over intense flame, stir until it has thickened and the sugar is completely dissolved. Serve cold, in a small bowl.

140   Duck

Beijing Duck Rolls

Beijing yajuan 北京鴨卷

This very rich and delicate dish is made with duck skins, which are stuffed with duck meat flavored with a variety of seasonings, then breaded and deep fried in duck fat. (If duck fat is unavailable, chicken fat or lard may be substituted.) The duck must first be boiled, to make it easier to remove the skin. The longer it is boiled, the easier it is to get the skin off—but if it is boiled for too long, the skin will fall apart.

1 5 lb. (2 kg) duck, cleaned

¼ teaspoon ground black pepper

¼ teaspoon salt

½ teaspoon chopped scallion

½ teaspoon chopped peeled fresh ginger

½ teaspoon chopped water chestnuts

½ teaspoon soy sauce

½ teaspoon sesame oil

½ teaspoon rice wine

(½ teaspoon Gourmet Powder)

3 tablespoons cornstarch

3 eggs, beaten

1 cup (3½ oz. / 110 g) dried bread crumbs

3 cups (750 ml) melted duck fat

Spread duck meat mixture on pieces of duck skin, then roll them up and deep-fry them.

1. Remove as much of the solid fat as possible, render it and set it aside. Put the duck in a pot with enough water to cover and simmer for about 30 minutes or until the skin becomes loosened from the flesh but is still firm and resilient enough so it does not tear.
2. Remove the skin in large sheets and cut it into 2¼-by-1¾-inch (6 × 4.5-cm) pieces. Slice the meat from the legs and thighs. Mash it and mix in a bowl with the pepper, salt, scallion, ginger, water chestnuts, soy sauce, sesame oil, rice wine, (and Gourmet Powder) to make a paste.
3. Spread a little of this mixture on one end of each duck skin piece, then roll up into a 1¾-inch (4.5-cm) roll, ½ inch (1.5 cm) in diameter. Dust the rolls with the cornstarch, roll in the beaten eggs, then roll in the bread crumbs to coat thoroughly.
4. Heat the duck fat in a wok over a medium flame. Just before the fat begins to smoke, turn off the heat. Drop the rolls into the fat and stir gently two or three times with a spatula. Turn the heat back on and deep fry the rolls until they float to the surface. Lower the heat and continue to fry until the duck rolls begin to turn golden brown, 2 to 3 minutes. Then turn the heat back up and fry the rolls for a few seconds more. Scoop out the rolls, drain, place on a platter, and serve.

Duck Smoked with Camphor Leaves and Tea
Zhangcha yazi   樟茶鸭子

This is a rare and highly honored recipe. The cleaned duck is first marinated, then smoked with camphor fragrance, steamed for tenderness, and finally deep fried to make the skin crispy. The smoking is not difficult; it is a common practice in Chinese home kitchens. The liquor called for in this recipe is a clear spirit distilled from sorghum or corn. Substitute corn whiskey or vodka. The flour sauce is sold in China commercially bottled. The camphor and cypress may be omitted, especially if the sawdust has a pungent fragrance, as cedar or pitch pine do.

1 duck (4 lb./2 kg)
8 teaspoons salt
2 tablespoons clear liquor
15 Sichuan peppercorns
1 teaspoon ground black pepper
   (Pinch of Gourmet Powder)
4 cups (1 L) vegetable oil
1 tablespoon sesame oil
8 scallions, chopped
10 teaspoons sweet fermented flour sauce (or hoisin sauce)
16 thin pancakes (see recipe for Beijing Roast Duck)

Smoking ingredients
3¼ oz. (100 g) camphor leaves or chips
1 lb. (500 g) cypress leaves or chips
¾ oz. (25 g) jasmine tea leaves
8 oz. (250 g) pine sawdust
2 teaspoons sugar

Editor's note:

If you do not have a smoking oven use a large, old, heavy pot or wok with a high-domed lid. Line both pot and lid with double layers of heavy aluminum foil, leaving extra overhang around the rims. Scatter the dry smoking ingredients evenly over the bottom. (Sprinkling with a little sugar will make them smoke more quickly.)

Wipe a rack with oil and suspend it firmly, 2 inches (5 cm) above the smoking ingredients. Place the duck on the rack. It should be no closer than 1 inch (2.5 cm) to the sides of the pot or lid.

Place the pot over an intense flame until the smoke starts to rise in steady puffs, 6 to 10 minutes. Cover and seal in the smoke by crimping the overhanging foil. Leave a small "spout" open through which you can keep checking the density of the smoke without uncrimping the foil and lifting the lid.

Color is the best indicator of doneness. After 30 minutes, unseal, lift the lid, and disperse the smoke. If the duck is golden brown or darker, it is done. The maximum smoking time is 1½ hours; the minimum is ¼ hour. Steam the duck a little longer if the smoking time is under 1 hour. After you remove the duck and rack, gather up and seal the smoking material inside the aluminum foil; discard immediately to reduce house odors. This smoking procedure is explained in detail in Barbara Tropp's excellent book, *The Modern Art of Chinese Cooking.*

1. Wash the duck inside and out and set in a bowl. Combine the salt, clear liquor, Sichuan peppercorns, ground black pepper, (and Gourmet Powder). Brush the duck, inside and out, with this mixture. Marinate it, covered, for 12 hours, then drain off the marinade.

2. Place the duck in a smoking pot and smoke with the ingredients listed, until the duck turns a golden brown, 30 minutes to 1½ hours. Lift the smoked duck into a steamer and steam over an intense flame for 40 minutes.

3. Heat the oil in a wok over an intense flame. Deep fry the duck for 3 minutes, basting with the hot oil if it is not completely submerged. Remove the duck from the oil, drain briefly, and brush with the sesame oil. Slice the skin and meat into 2½-inch (6-cm) square pieces and place on a serving platter.

4. Chop the scallions into small pieces, or make scallion brushes, and place them on a small serving plate. Pour the fermented flour sauce (or hoisin sauce) into a small serving bowl. Dip the duck pieces in the sauce and eat them, together with the scallions, wrapped in thin pancakes.

Succulent Duck

Xiangsuya 香酥鸭

A whole duck is marinated in a magical mix of spices and seasonings for four hours and then steamed for four hours more. The tender, flavorful duck is then briefly deep-fried to make the flesh succulent and the skin crispy brown. In Beijing this dish is usually served with pancakes stuffed with fresh scallions along with a sweet brown sauce (made with fermented flour) for which hoisin sauce is a close substitute. See the recipe for "Beijing Duck" for instructions for making the pancakes and sauce.

1. Duck with its array of exotic seasonings and spices for marinade.

2. Spoon marinade over duck and let steep for 4 hours, turning it occasionally.

5 -lb. (2.5 kg) duck, cleaned and washed
6 tablespoons soy sauce
3 tablespoons rice wine
¼ cup (¾ oz. / 25 g) chopped scallions
1 tablespoon Sichuan peppercorns
5 teaspoons sweet brown sauce
4 teaspoons peeled fresh ginger, sliced
1 teaspoon whole cloves
½ teaspoon salt
4 anise stars
1 stick cinnamon
10 cups (2.5 L) peanut oil

1. Wash duck inside and out; drain well. Combine remaining ingredients except the duck and the oil. Place the duck in a large bowl and spoon marinade over it. Marinate the duck for 4 hours, turning it occasionally.
2. Remove the duck from the sauce and steam over a medium flame for 4 hours, adding more water as needed. Remove the duck and allow to drain.
3. Heat half the oil in a large wok to 400 F (200 C) degrees. Deep-fry the duck, breast first, until browned, about 5 minutes. Add the remaining oil; deep-fry the back until browned, about 5 minutes. Remove from the oil and drain. Place the whole duck on a platter and serve. Cut the duck into small pieces at the table, and eat with chopsticks.

3. Place duck in steamer and steam for 4 hours, then deep-fry to a crispy brown.

Bundled Duck
Chaiba yazi 柴把鸭子

For this dish a whole duck is steamed. The duck meat and skin, bamboo shoots, pieces of ham, and mushrooms are cut into strips and tied with sea grass to look like bundles of sticks. These bundles are steamed and served with a thickened chicken-stock gravy. Dried sea grass is sold in Chinese groceries. If it is unavailable to you, use dried seaweed sold in sheets and cut into strips after soaking.

1 duck (5 lb./2.5 kg)
15 large soaked black mushrooms (5 oz./150 g), stemmed
8 oz. (250 g) bamboo shoots
8 oz. (250 g) ham
2½ oz. (75 g) dried sea grass
1¼ cup (315 ml) clear chicken stock
3 tablespoons melted chicken fat
4 teaspoons salt
4 teaspoons sugar
1 tablespoon rice wine
(2 teaspoons MSG)
5 teaspoons soy sauce
5 teaspoons cornstarch paste

1. Cut the duck open along the back; clean and rinse. Place in a bowl and steam over a medium flame until partially cooked, about 30 minutes. Drain and allow to cool. Carefully remove the bones, keeping the skin attached to the meat. Place on a cutting board and cut lengthwise into three broad slices, then cut each slice into strips ½ inch (1.5 cm) wide.
2. Cut the soaked mushrooms, bamboo shoots, and ham into strips half the width of the duck strips. Soak the sea grass in warm water until soft, about 1 minute, then rinse. Dip the mushrooms and bamboo shoot strips in boiling water, then into cold water, and drain.
3. On one side of each strip of duck meat, placed skin side down, lay a piece of mushroom, then cover with a piece of bamboo shoot. On the other side of the strip of duck, place a strip of ham; continue until all the bamboo shoots, mushrooms, and ham strips are used up. There will be leftover duck; set it aside. Tie up the bundles of "sticks" with a piece of sea grass.
4. Pile the "bound sticks," skin side down, on a large deep plate. Place the reserved duck meat on top. Add 1 cup (250 ml) chicken stock, the chicken fat, 2 teaspoons salt, 2 teaspoons sugar, the rice wine, (and 1 teaspoon MSG), and steam for 10 minutes over a medium flame.
5. Pour off the liquid to use later, but without disturbing the meat and bundles on the plate. Invert a serving platter on top of them. Carefully turn the wok upside down so the bundles remain neatly piled on the platter, but are now facing up.
6. Return the liquid to the wok and add the remaining chicken stock, salt, sugar, (MSG), and the soy sauce, and heat over a medium flame. When it is hot, add the cornstarch paste and stir until thickened. Pour over the bundled duck on the platter and serve.

Golden Fish Duck Webs
Jinyu yazhang 金鱼鸭掌

Chinese chefs enjoy shaping the ingredients of their creations into the forms of nature. In this case, the main ingredient is the webbing from ducks' feet, and the form is exotic tropical fish. Webs are considered a delicacy because their gelatin protein is thought to keep aging bones supple and to fuel the body's systems. The ducks' feet are stewed whole to soften the skin and cartilage around the bones so they can be removed from the back, leaving the shape of the web intact.

In this dish the webs become platforms for a spread of mashed chicken meat bound with egg whites and cornstarch. After they have been decorated they are steamed so they plump up into fat little fish.

Facai, a thread-like, purple moss which is packaged dried, is used only as a garnish, so it is not essential. Fish maw is the stomach, usually deep-fried, dried, and sold in bulk (sometimes floating from the ceiling like white clouds) in Chinese grocery stores.

2 medium egg whites, well-beaten
1 tablespoon rice wine
(¾ teaspoon MSG)
1 teaspoon salt
1 teaspoon cornstarch
2 teaspoons melted lard
7 oz. (200 g) chicken breast meat
14 duck feet
4 canned maraschino cherries
¼ oz. (7.5 g) *facai* (hair-fine, dark purple sea moss)

2 oz. (55 g) ham, minced
5 teaspoons minced rape leaves
¾ oz. (25 g) soaked black mushrooms, stemmed
¾ oz. (25 g) soaked bamboo shoots
1¾ oz. (50 g) soaked fish maw
2 cups (500 ml) clear stock
2 teaspoons cornstarch, dissolved in 4 teaspoons water
1 tablespoon chicken fat

1. Combine the egg whites with 2 teaspoons rice wine, (½ teaspoon MSG), the salt, cornstarch, and lard. Mash the chicken breast meat with the back of a cleaver and blend into the egg white mixture.

2. Boil the duck feet in water to cover over a low flame for 45 minutes. Remove from water and allow to cool. Extract the bones without tearing the web; pull them out through the bottom. If they do not come out easily, boil them a bit longer. Turn the feet upside down and place on a heatproof plate. Mound the chicken paste over them. They will plump, when steamed, to look like goldfish.

3. Cut each cherry into eight pieces. Place one on each side of the fatter end to make the eyes of each goldfish. Decorate each "fish" with the threadlike moss, ¼ oz. (7.5 g) of the minced ham, and the chopped rape leaves as shown in the photograph. Steam for 3 to 4 minutes.

4. Mince the black mushrooms, bamboo shoots, and fish maw. Blanch in boiling water for 2 minutes, then drain. Place in a wok and add 1¼ cups (315 ml) clear stock and ½ teaspoon rice wine. Cover and simmer for 3 minutes; drain and pile on a serving platter. Arrange the "goldfish" on top of this mixture.

5. Heat the remaining clear stock to a boil. Combine the remaining rice wine, (MSG), and dissolved cornstarch. Stir into the boiling stock until it thickens. Sprinkle this sauce with the chicken fat, pour over the "goldfish," and serve.

Fried Duck Gizzard and Liver
Zha yazhengan　炸鸭胗肝

Duck gizzards and livers, parboiled and deep fried, are accompanied by prawn crackers. This dish is usually served as an appetizer course at a banquet dinner. To eat it in the traditional fashion, dip each piece into prickly ash (spiced salt), a condiment made of table salt and Sichuan peppercorns (see recipe following Ingredients Guide).

8 oz. (250 g) duck gizzards
8 oz. (250 g) duck livers
4 cups (1 L) melted duck fat
20 prawn crackers (1 oz. / 30 g)
Prickly ash (spiced salt)

One characteristic of the Chinese cuisine is the correct proportion between the five flavors—sweet, sour, bitter, pungent, and salty.

Zhou Ruchang, The China Art Institute

1. Remove the yellow lining from the duck gizzards; cut each gizzard crosswise into 4 pieces. Remove the ducts from duck livers and cut each liver into 4 pieces.
2. Heat about 2 cups water to a boil in a pot. Add the gizzards and cook for 1 minute; scoop out. In the same water, cook the livers for 1 minute. Skim the froth from the surface of the water; remove the pot from the heat, set aside.
3. In a wok, heat the duck fat over an intense flame. When hot, drop in the prawn crackers. Scoop the crackers out as soon as they turn whitish and float to the surface, about 10 seconds. Arrange the crackers around the edge of a serving platter.
4. In the same fat, over an intense flame, deep fry the gizzards for 30 seconds; scoop out and drain. Remove the livers from the water and drain; deep fry for 30 seconds. Add the deep-fried gizzards and fry the gizzards and livers together until they become crisp and brown outside, but are still soft inside.
5. Remove them from the fat and place in the center of the serving platter surrounded by the prawn crackers. The prickly ash is served in a small bowl to accompany the duck pieces; each piece is dipped in the prickly ash before it is eaten.

Duck Hearts Maotai

Huoliao yaxin 火燎鸭心

Duck hearts are mixed with a sweet and flavorful marinade and then deep-fried. Scoring the duck hearts creates an attractive pattern as they cook, gives them a pleasantly crisp texture, and enhances their flavor because the marinade is more thoroughly absorbed.

If duck fat is not available for deep-frying, chicken fat, lard, or vegetable oil will do as well. It is important to drain the duck hearts of their marinade before frying, to prevent the oil from splattering—keep a lid on hand in case splattering does occur.

If Maotai liquor (a ferocious, clear Chinese spirit from the northern town of Kweichow) is unavailable, gin or vodka may be used, but the aromas differ. The scallion and coriander-leaf garnish provides a lively contrast to the rich flavor of the duck.

1 lb. (500 g) duck hearts (about 23)

1 tablespoon Maotai liquor

1 teaspoon sugar

½ teaspoon soy sauce

½ teaspoon salt

½ teaspoon sesame oil

¼ teaspoon ground black pepper

4 cups (1 L) duck fat

Scallions cut in thin strips, for garnish

Coriander leaves, for garnish

1. Wash the duck hearts, removing excess fat. Cut into halves and score the inside surfaces crosswise.

2. In a bowl, combine the Maotai liquor, sugar, soy sauce, salt, sesame oil, and pepper. Add the duck hearts and mix well. Remove the hearts from the marinade and drain thoroughly; gently pat dry and set aside.

3. Heat the duck fat in a wok over a medium flame until it bubbles. Carefully add the duck hearts (take precautions against splattering oil). Stir gently two or three times with a spatula until cooked through (the inside will no longer be pink), no more than 3 seconds. Scoop out from the fat and drain. Place on a platter, garnish with the scallion strips and coriander leaves, and serve.

1. Score inside of duck hearts crosswise.

2. Scoop out duck hearts from bubbling fat.

Duck 147

Skillet-Baked Soufflé
Tieguo dan 铁锅蛋

The blended dominant flavors of seafood, sesame oil, lard, and rice wine give this generously laden soufflé a haunting fragrance. Make sure the oven is preheated and a constant temperature maintained (peek fast and gently or not at all) to ensure that the mixture rises like a soufflé. If dried sea cucumber is unavailable, substitute fresh squid. If dried shrimp are unavailable, substitute fresh or canned—if canned do not parboil. Smithfield smoked ham approximates Chinese ham in flavor and texture.

⅓ cup (¾ oz. / 25 gm) of the
  following ingredients, diced:
  soaked dried sea cucumber,
  scallops, ham, chicken
  meat, pork, duck meat,
  bamboo shoots, soaked
  dried shrimp
7 medium eggs
5 oz. (150 ml) clear
  chicken stock

2 teaspoons melted lard
5 teaspoons soy sauce
2 teaspoons rice wine
  (Pinch of MSG)
  Pinch of salt
1 teaspoon sesame oil

sistency as a soufflé mixture.
3. Place the skillet in the preheated oven and bake until the eggs rise and turn

golden brown, about 10 minutes. Remove from the oven, sprinkle with sesame oil, and serve in the skillet.

1. Dice first group of ingredients before parboiling.

2. Add eggs to chicken stock, melted lard, soy sauce, rice wine and salt.

1. Parboil or steam the first group of ingredients until they are about half-cooked. (You may want to cook the pork completely.)
2. Preheat the oven to 350 F (180 C) degrees. Place the partially precooked ingre-

dients in a deep heavy iron skillet or soufflé dish. Break the eggs into the skillet and stir to combine thoroughly. Add the chicken stock, lard, soy sauce, rice wine, (MSG), and salt; stir well. The result should be the same con-

3. Stir mixture thoroughly in high-sided, cast-iron skillet or soufflé dish.

4. Keep oven, whether Chinese brick or Western electric, at even temperature.

Walnut Pigeon Eggs
Hetao gedan 核桃鸽蛋

Ingredients with different textures make up this delicious dish, which would be perfect as a hot appetizer for a Western meal. The walnuts add a wonderful crunchy contrast to the pigeon eggs; the puréed pork, chicken, and fried bread squares add still other textures. If pigeon eggs are unavailable fresh, use small chicken or pullet eggs. Collard greens or broccoli leaves may be substituted for rape leaves.

6 pigeon eggs

5 oz. (150 g) boneless chicken breast, minced

1¾ oz. (50 g) pork fat, minced

2 egg whites

3 tablespoons cornstarch

(1 teaspoon MSG)

5 teaspoons rice wine

½ teaspoon salt

½ teaspoon chopped peeled fresh ginger

12 slices of bread, each ¼ inch (0.8 cm) thick and 2¾ inches (6.5 cm) square

6 walnuts, each meat broken into 4 pieces

4 cups (1 L) peanut oil

Deep-fried rape leaves or potato shreds

6 maraschino cherries

3 decorative leaves, for garnish

1. Place the pigeon eggs in a pot and cover with cold water. Heat over a low flame until the water comes to a boil, and simmer gently for 5 to 6 minutes after the water boils. Cool eggs in cold water, then remove the shells and cut each egg in half lengthwise.
2. Mash the chicken meat and pork fat with the back of a cleaver. Put in a bowl and mix in the egg whites, cornstarch, (MSG), rice wine, salt and ginger. Spread this mixture on the bread slices. Place an egg half, flat side down, and 2 walnut pieces atop mixture on each slice.
3. Heat the oil in a wok over a medium flame until hot. Deep-fry the egg-and-bread slices until golden brown, about 4 minutes. Remove and drain. Place the deep-fried rape leaves or potato shreds in the center. Arrange the eggs in three lines to form a triangle, each garnished at the center with a leaf and two cherries as shown in the photograph.

Pigeon Egg "Elephant Eyes"
Xiangyan gedan　象眼鸽蛋

Minced pork and prawns are marinated in rice wine, ginger, and scallions. Pigeon eggs are surrounded with this mixture on pieces of bread sprinkled with ham to resemble elephant eyes, and deep-fried. The Chinese believe the elephant to be a lucky animal. Therefore, this dish—in addition to being delicious—is thought to bring good fortune. The picture shows a double recipe suitable for a large dinner party or banquet.

5 pigeon eggs, hard boiled and shelled

5 oz. (150 g) bread—not salt-free

1¾ oz. (50 g) prawns

1¾ oz. (50 g) pork

1 teaspoon rice wine

(½ teaspoon MSG)

¼ teaspoon salt

¼ teaspoon sugar

1 teaspoon sesame oil

1 egg white

1 tablespoon cornstarch paste

½ teaspoon minced scallion

½ teaspoon minced peeled fresh ginger

1 tablespoon minced ham

4 cups (1 L) vegetable oil

Cucumber, carved into flower shapes, for garnish

1. Cut the pigeon eggs in half lengthwise. Cut the bread into slices 2 inches (5 cm) square and ⅛ inch (0.3 cm) thick. Place an egg half, flat side down, on each slice of bread.

2. Finely mince together the prawns and pork. Mix in the rice wine, (MSG), salt, sugar, sesame oil, egg white, cornstarch paste, scallions, and ginger. Set aside for 30 minutes.

3. Spread the prawn and pork mixture onto the slices of bread around each egg half, sloping from the height of the egg to the edge of the slice to resemble elephant eyes. Place the minced ham at the corners of the "eyes" to resemble furrows.

4. Heat the oil in a wok over a medium flame. When hot, slide in the bread slices, eye side up, one by one. Scoop out when they are crisp—after about 2 minutes. Arrange on a serving platter and garnish with flowers made from cucumber slices.

Pigeon Eggs in White Sauce
Yunpian gedan   云片鸽蛋

Small Chinese wine cups, used to steam pigeon eggs in this dish, give the eggs a distinctive shape. The eggs are served with a simple but distinctive white sauce. Substitute small chicken eggs if pigeon eggs are not available. The cooking technique resembles coddled eggs. The wine cups should be heatproof; use small ceramic cups if heatproof glass cups are not available.

1 cucumber
1 tablespoon melted chicken fat
18 pigeon eggs
18 large-leafed bean sprouts
¾ cup (200 ml) clear chicken stock

2 teaspoons rice wine
Pinch of salt
(Pinch of MSG)
1 teaspoon cornstarch, dissolved in 2 teaspoons water

1. Cut the unpeeled cucumber into long, thin spiral strips for garnish. Brush a little chicken fat inside each of the 18 small wine cups. Break a pigeon egg into each cup, keeping the yolk unbroken. Wash the bean sprout leaves and place one over each cup. Place the cups in a steamer and steam for 5 minutes. Remove the eggs to a shallow serving bowl and surround with the cucumber-peel spirals.
2. Heat the chicken stock to boiling in a wok. Add the rice wine, salt, (and MSG). Pour in the dissolved cornstarch and stir until thickened. Pour this sauce over the pigeon eggs and serve.

Stir-Fried Fish Fillets
Zhuachao yupian 抓炒鱼片

In this easy-to-prepare dish, fish strips are coated with a cornstarch batter, deep fried, and then stir-fried briefly in a delicious sweet and sour sauce flavored with scallions and ginger.

Fillet black carp and cut it into chunks.

7 oz. (200 g) white-fleshed fish fillets

1 cup (250 ml) cornstarch, dissolved in 1 cup (250 ml) water

2 cups (500 ml) peanut oil

5 teaspoons sugar

2 teaspoons rice wine

2 teaspoons soy sauce

2 teaspoons vinegar

1½ scallions, chopped

4 teaspoons chopped peeled fresh ginger

(Pinch of MSG)

2½ tablespoons lard

1. Cut the fish fillets into 2-by-1½-by-½-inch (5 x 3.5 x 1-cm) strips. Reserve ⅓ cup (85 ml) of the cornstarch mixture. Dip the fish strips in the remaining cornstarch mixture and turn to coat well.

2. Heat the peanut oil in a wok over an intense flame. When the oil begins to smoke, slide the fish strips into the wok, one by one. When they turn golden brown, after about 2 minutes, scoop them out. (Do not overcook or they will fall apart when stir-fried.)

3. In a small bowl, combine the sugar, rice wine, soy sauce, vinegar, scallions, ginger, (MSG), and the reserved cornstarch paste. Heat the lard in a wok over an intense flame. When the lard is hot, pour in the seasoning mixture and stir until thickened.

4. Add the deep-fried fish strips and stir-fry quickly for 30 seconds. Place on a platter and serve piping hot.

Palace Gate Fish
Gongmen xianyu 宫门献鱼

It is said that during one of his inspection trips, the Kang Xi emperor of the Qing Dynasty visited Yunnan Province, coming one day into a humble tavern to rest. Since the emperor was also hungry the cook served him his specialty—flowery fish. The head and the tail were set at either end of a platter and the space between filled with the boned meat and covered with colorful, quick-fried vegetables. The emperor, greatly delighted, praised the cook for his delicious dish. Since then it has been called Palace Gate Fish because it was worthy of entering into the favor of the emperor.

1 carp (3 lb./1.5 kg)
1 carrot
1/3 oz. (10 g) bamboo shoots
1/2 cucumber
2 1/3 cups (600 ml) peanut oil
1/2 oz. (15 g) hot pickled mustard tuber, minced
1 soaked dried black mushroom, stemmed and chopped
3 tablespoons rice wine
(2 teaspoons MSG)
1 teaspoon salt
3 tablespoons sugar

3 tablespoons vinegar
5 teaspoons clear chicken stock
6 tablespoons sesame oil
2 cloves garlic, minced
1/2 oz. (15 g) sweet red pepper, minced
1 egg white
1 teaspoon minced, peeled fresh ginger
1/2 oz. (15 g) pork, chopped
1/2 teaspoon melted chicken fat
5 teaspoons cornstarch paste

1. Clean the carp; cut off the head and tail and set them aside. Fillet the skin and bones away from the meat and cut the meat into slices. Cut the carrot, bamboo shoots, and cucumber into small rounds and slices.

2. Heat 3 1/4 oz. (100 ml) peanut oil in a wok over a medium flame until hot. Fry the fish head and tail for a few minutes, then add the minced pickled mustard, mushroom, 4 teaspoons rice wine, (1 teaspoon MSG), 1/2 teaspoon salt, 4 teaspoons sugar, 4 teaspoons vinegar, and the chicken stock. Heat this mixture to boiling, then lower the heat and cook, stirring, until the sauce thickens, 20 to 30 minutes. Remove the fish head and tail and place them on opposite sides of a platter. Discard the sauce. Sprinkle the sesame oil, garlic, and peppers over the head and tail.

3. In a bowl, combine 1/4 teaspoon salt, 3 teaspoons rice wine, and the egg white. Add the fish slices and mix well to coat. Heat 2 cups (500 ml) peanut oil over a low flame until hot. Drop in the fish slices one by one. Scoop them out when they begin to turn white, about 1 minute. Pour out all but 2 tablespoons of the oil.

4. Turn up the heat to an intense flame and stir-fry the ginger, carrot, bamboo shoots, cucumber and pork, stirring until the pork is cooked, about 2 minutes. Add the remaining rice wine, (MSG), salt, sugar, vinegar, and 1/4 teaspoon chicken fat. Stir to mix well, then add the fish slices and the cornstarch paste. Toss the wok, then sprinkle with the remaining chicken fat. Arrange the sauce-covered slices side by side on the platter. Place this mixture between the head and tail, to form the body of the fish.

Stuffed Mandarin Fish
Huaitai guiyu 怀胎桂鱼

A mandarin fish (or porgy or other white-fleshed fish) is cleaned through the gills to keep it intact. It is stuffed with fish, black mushrooms, bamboo shoots, sea cucumbers, and water chestnuts, then steamed and served with a clear sauce.

There is nobody who does not eat and drink, but there are few who can distinguish flavors.

Mencius

1 mandarin fish (3 lb. / 1.5 kg)
5 oz. (150 g) fish fillet
1¾ oz. (50 g) bamboo shoots
6 soaked dried black mushrooms (1¾ oz. / 50 g)
1¾ oz. (50 g) soaked dried sea cucumbers
4 water chestnuts (1¾ oz. / 50 g)
2 egg whites
3 teaspoons rice wine
2 teaspoons salt
(¾ teaspoon MSG)

2½ tablespoons melted lard
4 scallions, chopped
4 tablespoons chopped peeled fresh ginger
1¾ oz. (50 g) boiled ham, sliced
1 cup (250 ml) clear stock
1½ tablespoons cornstarch, dissolved in 2 tablespoons water
1 tablespoon melted chicken fat

1. Scale and gill the fish, leaving no visible cut. Scald fish in boiling water and scrape away surface body secretion. Score both sides of the fish diagonally.

2. Mash the fish fillet. Cut 5 thin circular slices from bamboo shoots; cut remaining bamboo shoots, 2 mushrooms, sea cucumbers, and the water chestnuts into cubes.

3. In a bowl, combine the cubes with the mashed fish, egg whites, 1½ teaspoons rice wine, 1 teaspoon salt, (½ teaspoon MSG), and the lard; mix into a batter. Stuff the mandarin fish through the gills with the batter and place on a platter. Sprinkle

the fish with ¾ teaspoon rice wine, (¼ teaspoon MSG), ¾ teaspoon salt, mushrooms, bamboo shoot slices, scallions, and ginger. Steam over intense flame for 40 minutes.

4. Drain the liquid and discard the scallions and ginger. Rearrange the mushrooms and bamboo slices in a line atop the fish and add the ham at the tail as shown in the photograph. Pour the stock into a wok and heat to boiling. Mix in the remaining salt, rice wine, (and MSG). Add the dissolved cornstarch and stir until thickened. Sprinkle with the melted chicken fat, pour over the mandarin fish and serve.

Steamed Mandarin Fish

Wuliu guiyu 五柳桂鱼

This recipe calls for a mandarin fish to be cleaned through a tiny slit. Freshwater bass is the best substitute, or use any firm, white-fleshed fish. The fish is parboiled, then boiled, and then steamed in a sprightly sauce flavored with ginger and scallion. It is covered with fresh, matchstick slices of sweet green and red pepper, ginger, bamboo shoots, and mushrooms, and served with a thickened sauce made from the seasoned fish-steaming liquid.

1 sweet green pepper

1 sweet red pepper

¾ oz. (25 g) winter bamboo shoots

¾ oz. (25 g) soaked mushrooms, stemmed

1 mandarin fish (1½ lb. / 750 g)

¼ teaspoon rice wine

¼ teaspoon salt, dissolved in 1 teaspoon water

3 -inch (7.5 cm) piece of peeled fresh ginger root

1 teaspoon shredded scallion

¼ teaspoon cornstarch, dissolved in ½ teaspoon water

6 tablespoons clear chicken stock

(¼ teaspoon Gourmet Powder)

1 teaspoon melted chicken fat

Cucumber and radish cut in decorative shapes, for garnish

1. Wash and seed the peppers. Cut peppers, ginger, winter bamboo shoots, and mushrooms into matchstick-sized slices, 2½ inches (6.5 cm) long. Keep these ingredients in separate neat bundles. Arrange the separate piles on a plate.

2. Scale the fish and remove the gills. Make a small slit at the anus and pull out the inner organs at either end of the fish, through the gill opening and the slit. (Handle the fish with care so that it remains intact, with the head, tail, and fins still on.) Soak the fish in hot water for 1 minute. Scrape off its skin with a cleaver, then soak the fish in cold water until it turns a grayish-white,

2 to 3 minutes. Lay it on a cutting board and score crosswise on both sides to make rhomboid-shaped cuts with sides ¾ inch (2 cm) long. In a large pot, with boiling water to cover, cook until almost done, about 1 minute. Drain and place in a heat-proof bowl.

3. In a small bowl, combine the rice wine, dissolved salt, ¼ teaspoon ginger juice (squeeze a ½-inch/1.3-cm slice in a garlic press), and scallion, and pour over the fish. Place the fish in a steamer over a medium flame for 15 minutes. Remove the

scallion; drain off the liquid and set aside. Transfer the fish to a serving platter. Arrange the bundles of green and red peppers, ginger, bamboo shoots, and mushrooms side by side along the length of the fish.

4. Heat a wok over an intense flame; before it gets hot, add the fish-cooking liquid, then stir in the dissolved cornstarch, chicken stock (and Gourmet Powder), and stir until it thickens. Sprinkle with the chicken fat and pour over the fish. Garnish with the decorative cucumber and radish and serve.

Stuffed Crucian Carp
Hebao jiyu　荷包鲫鱼

Two crucian carp are stuffed with a delicious mixture of bacon, prawns, mushrooms, bamboo shoots, ham, scallions, ginger, and garlic, then sealed with cornstarch and egg white, and deep-fried until golden. Finally, they are simmered in a flavorful sauce and served with slices of ham, bamboo shoots, and black mushrooms. The stuffing remains a surprise to diners until the last minute.

2¾ lb. (375 g each) crucian carp

1¾ oz. (50 g) soaked black mushrooms

1¾ oz. (50 g) winter bamboo shoots

1 oz. (30 g) ham

1½ scallions

½ oz. (15 g) peeled fresh ginger

4 cloves garlic

7 oz. (200 g) slab bacon

3¼ oz. (100 g) prawns, shelled and deveined

2 egg whites

5 teaspoons soy sauce

1 tablespoon rice wine

(1 teaspoon MSG)

1 teaspoon salt

1 teaspoon sesame oil

3 tablespoons cornstarch paste

2 cups (500 ml) peanut oil

1⅓ cup (350 ml) clear chicken stock

1 tablespoon sugar

1. *Some of the ingredients: Crucian carp, bacon, bamboo shoots, black mushrooms, and eggs.*

1. Scale and gill the fish. Leave the heads and tails on. Clean each fish through a 3¾-inch (9-cm) cut along the belly and wash. Dice half the black mushrooms, winter bamboo shoots, and ham, chop half the scallions, ginger, and garlic. Place in a bowl.

2. Mince the bacon and prawns; place in the bowl with the mushroom mixture. Add 1 egg white, 3 teaspoons soy sauce, 2 teaspoons rice wine, (½ teaspoon MSG), the salt, and the sesame oil; mix well. Stuff the fish with this mixture through the cut. Beat the remaining egg white until frothy and mix with 1½ tablespoons of the cornstarch paste; use this batter to seal the cut.

3. Heat the peanut oil in a wok over a medium flame. When the oil is hot, slide the fish in carefully and fry until both sides of each fish are golden; about 3 minutes per side. Remove to a plate.

4. Slice the remaining black mushrooms, bamboo shoots, ham, scallions, ginger, and garlic. Pour off all but 3 tablespoons of the oil and heat the wok over an intense flame. Stir-fry the scallions, ginger, and garlic slices until their aroma is released, about 10 seconds. Pour in the chicken stock and add the sliced black mushrooms and bamboo shoots, the sugar, the remaining soy sauce, rice wine, (and MSG). Lower the heat, add the fish, and simmer for 10 minutes.

5. Transfer the fish to a platter; add the ham slices to the sauce and continue cooking for 1 minute. Remove the ham and mushroom and bamboo shoot slices and place them in neat rows over the fish. Add the remaining cornstarch paste to the sauce and stir until it thickens. Pour the sauce over the fish and serve.

2. *Stuff crucian carp with bacon and prawn mixture.*

3. *Seal cut in fish with batter, then carefully slide fish into hot oil.*

Pine Cone Carp
Songta huoyu 松塔活鱼

This diverting and taste-tempting dish is made of carp fillets butterfly-carved to resemble pine cones and served with a garlicky sweet-and-sour sauce. Although this dish uses a large quantity of oil for deep frying (to cover the "cones"), less than 10 percent of the oil is absorbed in cooking.

1 carp (1½ lb. / 750 g)

3 eggs, well beaten

⅔ cup (150 g) cornstarch

6 cups (1.5 L) peanut oil

¾ cup (200 ml) clear stock

5 teaspoons soy sauce

5 teaspoons vinegar

½ cup (110 g) sugar

2 medium cloves garlic, sliced

5 teaspoons cornstarch, dissolved in 3 tablespoons water

1. Clean and scale the fish and remove the head. Cut the fish in half lengthwise; remove the bones and skin. Score each fillet diagonaly at ½-inch (1.5-cm) intervals to form a diamond pattern, but do not cut all the way through the fish.
2. Brush the fillets with the beaten eggs. Sprinkle with the dry cornstarch, using your fingers to separate the fish segments so as to coat them evenly. Roll up the fillets so that the individual segments separate to look like pine cones.
3. Heat the oil in a wok over a medium flame until fairly hot. Slip the fish cones in carefully so they do not unroll. Deep fry until the fish turns slightly golden, about 15 minutes, keeping the temperature of the oil constant. Carefully remove the fish cones from the wok, drain, and set upright on a platter. Pour off all but 2½ tablespoons of oil from the wok.
4. In a bowl, mix the clear stock, soy sauce, vinegar, sugar, garlic, and dissolved cornstarch.
5. Heat the reserved oil in the wok and pour in the clear stock mixture. Stir constantly with a spatula until it boils and thickens. Pour over the "pine cones" and serve.

Fried Fish Slices
Zha guazao 炸瓜枣

In this Fujian-style dish, a yellow croaker is filleted, and slices of the fish are covered with a thick batter and deep-fried. The batter, made from water, yeast, and flour, should not be so thick that it fails to cling to the fish. The fish slices are served with fried Chinese cabbage leaf strips, which add color counterpoint and a novel texture.

1 yellow croaker (1 lb./500 g)
1 tablespoon rice wine
1 teaspoon mashed peeled fresh ginger
(½ teaspoon MSG)
¼ teaspoon salt
¼ teaspoon sugar

1¼ cups (140 g) flour
1 teaspoon powdered yeast
3 cups (750 ml) vegetable oil
1⅓ oz. (40 g) Chinese cabbage leaves, sliced into very thin strips

1. Fillet the fish and cut the fillets into ½-by-1¼-inch (1 × 3-cm) slices. In a large bowl, combine the rice wine, ginger, (MSG), salt, and sugar. Add the fish pieces and stir, then let the fish marinate for 1 hour.
2. Make a batter with the flour, ¾ cup (200 ml) warm water, and the yeast. Add a few drops more water if the batter is unmanageably thick and sticky. Allow to rise, about 30 minutes.
3. When the batter has doubled in bulk, coat the fish slices generously. Heat the oil in a wok until about half-heated. Turn off the heat and quickly slip in the fish slices. Keep separating them with chopsticks or they will stick together. Turn the heat back up to an intense flame and fry until the batter swells and turns brown, about 1 minute. Scoop out the fish; drain well. Fry the Chinese cabbage strips in the oil for less than 1 minute; scoop out and drain. Serve the fish on a platter, surrounded with the fried Chinese cabbage.

Deep-Fried Mandarin Fish
Songshu guiyu 松鼠桂鱼

A deep-fried mandarin fish or other white-fleshed fish (porgy is the best shape) is served with diced vegetables in a delicious sweet-and-sour sauce. This is a lushly colorful dish, with the reds of the pepper, tomato sauce, and ham blending with the green, white, and black of scallion, cucumber, bamboo shoots, and mushrooms.

1. Dice mushrooms, bamboo shoots, cucumber, and sweet red pepper.

2. Score two fillets joined at tail, placed skin-side down.

3. Slice lengthwise once, then diagonally from center cut. Do not cut all the way through.

4. Fish, dusted with cornstarch, hangs from the skin like kernels on an ear of wheat.

1 mandarin fish (1 lb. / 500 g)
Pinch of salt
1 teaspoon rice wine
1 cup (220 g) cornstarch
6 cups (1.5 L) peanut oil
¼ cup (60 ml) clear stock
5 tablespoons sugar
2 tablespoons vinegar
2 teaspoons soy sauce
2 teaspoons tomato sauce
2 tablespoons chopped scallion
1 tablespoon chopped peeled fresh ginger

2 cloves garlic, minced
1 teaspoon cornstarch, dissolved in 2 teaspoons water
¾ oz. (25 g) soaked black mushrooms, diced
¾ oz. (25 g) winter bamboo shoots
3 tablespoons diced cucumber
3 tablespoons (¾ oz. / 25 g) diced sweet red pepper
1½ tablespoons (½ oz. / 15 g) diced cooked ham

1. Clean the fish. Cut off the head and reserve. Slice off the two boneless fillets leaving the skin on and keeping the two fillets connected at the tail. Separate the bones completely from the meat and discard them, but leave the tail on.

2. Place the two fillets, still joined at the tail, skin-side down. Slice each lengthwise down almost to the skin but not through it. Then make a series of parallel cuts diagonally away from both sides of the center-line slice. Again, cut each slice only partway through (as shown in second photograph). Press the pieces open slightly (as in third photograph).

3. Roll the fish in the dry cornstarch. Heat all but 3 tablespoons of the oil in a wok over an intense flame. When the oil is hot, fry the fish until it turns golden, about 2 minutes. Drain and place on a serving platter. Fry the fish head for 2 minutes; drain and place on the same platter.

4. In a bowl, mix the clear stock with the sugar, vinegar, soy sauce, tomato sauce, remaining rice wine, chopped scallion, ginger, garlic, a pinch of salt, and the dissolved cornstarch.

5. Heat the remaining peanut oil in a clean wok over an intense flame. Add the black mushrooms, bamboo shoots, cucumber, pepper, and ham; stir-fry for 15 seconds. Pour in the sauce mixture. Cook, stirring, until the sauce thickens, about 10 seconds. Pour the sauce over the fish and serve.

Stir-Fried Fish

Wuchai chao yusi 五彩炒鱼丝

Fish pieces coated in an egg-white batter, then fried with a variety of vegetables—mushrooms, carrots, sweet red pepper, and bean sprouts—and served in a slightly sweet sauce make a temptingly colorful dish. A quick blanching of the mushrooms and carrots assures uniform cooking.

1 lb. (500 g) fresh white-fleshed fish

3 oz./100 g (about 10) soaked dried black mushrooms

¼ lb. (125 g) carrots

½ sweet red pepper

3¼ oz. (100 g) mung bean sprouts

2½ tablespoons cornstarch

¼ teaspoon salt

½ teaspoon pepper

(½ teaspoon MSG)

2 teaspoons rice wine

2 egg whites

¼ cup (60 ml) sesame oil

2 cups (500 ml) peanut oil

1½ tablespoons clear chicken stock

1 teaspoon cornstarch paste

½ teaspoon sugar

1 scallion, minced

1 tablespoon minced peeled fresh ginger

1. Clean, skin, and bone the fish; cut into ¾-by-2-inch (2-by-5-cm) pieces.

2. Cut the mushrooms, carrots, and red pepper into ¾-by-2-inch (2-by-5-cm) pieces. Dip the mushroom and carrot pieces into boiling water for about 30 seconds, then plunge immediately into cold water; drain. Cut off the ends of the mung bean sprouts.

3. Combine the cornstarch, salt, pepper, (MSG), rice wine, egg whites, and sesame oil in a large bowl. Add the fish pieces and coat them thoroughly with the mixture.

4. Heat the peanut oil in a wok over an intense flame and, when hot, add the fish pieces. Deep fry them briefly, until cooked through, using chopsticks to keep the fish pieces from sticking together. Remove the fish from the oil with a spatula and drain.

5. In a separate pot, combine the chicken broth, cornstarch paste, and sugar, and heat over a low flame until thickened; keep warm.

6. Pour off all but ½ cup of oil from the wok, return to the fire, and heat until the oil is hot. Stir-fry the mushrooms, carrots, red pepper, bean

sprouts, scallion, and ginger.

7. Add the fish and the cornstarch mixture to the vegeta-

Some of the ingredients: Bean sprouts, fish pieces, vegetables.

bles in the wok. Toss the wok to mix well, transfer to a serving platter, and serve.

Deep fry fish pieces, using chopsticks to keep them from sticking together.

Sweet and Sour Fish "Tiles" and Baked Noodles

Tangcu wakuaiyu 糖醋瓦块鱼

This dish is a two-part adventure: a fish in a sweet and sour sauce, and deep-fried noodles that are dipped into the sauce after the fish is eaten. The fish is cut into rectangular pieces, then dipped into a savory batter, and deep fried. They curl when cooked so they resemble roof tiles. Traditionally the noodles are baked in an earthen oven for a long time at a low temperature, rather than deep fried.

2 medium eggs
1 cup (220 g) flour
1 carp (1½ lb./750 g)
5 pieces (¼ oz./8 g) dried black mushroom, soaked
¾ oz. (25 g) bamboo shoots
2 scallions
1 tablespoon peeled fresh ginger
3 cloves garlic, coarsely chopped

1 cup (250 ml) clear chicken stock
¼ cup (55 g) sugar
¼ cup (60 ml) vinegar
1½ tablespoons soy sauce
1½ tablespoons cornstarch, dissolved in 1½ tablespoons water
¾ cup (about 175 g) cornstarch
7 cups (1.75 L) vegetable oil

1. Combine 1 egg with the flour and knead into a fairly hard dough, cover, and set aside.

2. Clean the fish, removing gills and viscera. Cut off the two fillets and remove the skin. Cut fillets into 1-inch (2.5-cm) diamonds. Diagonal cuts 1-inch (2.5-cm) apart, followed by 1-inch (2.5-cm) diagonal cuts in the opposite direction, achieve the desired shape.

3. Slice the black mushrooms, bamboo shoots, scallions, and ginger into 1-inch-long (2.5-cm) pieces and combine them in a bowl with the garlic, chicken stock, sugar, vinegar, soy sauce, and the dissolved cornstarch.

4. Roll out the dough as thin as you can, not more than ¹/₁₆-inch (2-mm) thick. Fold it back and forth, accordion-like, into 3-inch (7.5-cm) stacked layers. Trim from one end with a sharp cleaver, cutting down through the full stack of layers. Make the cuts as thin as possible to produce hair-fine noodles.

5. Beat the remaining egg and combine with the dry cornstarch, adding enough water to make a thin batter. Dip the fish pieces into the batter and turn to coat well. Heat all except 2 tablespoons of the oil in a wok over a medium flame and gently slide the fish pieces into the hot oil one by one. Deep fry for about 10 minutes, or until the fish turns a light golden brown and the edges curl slightly. Carefully remove the fish and drain. Dip fish skeleton, with the head and tail attached, into the batter, drop into the hot oil and fry for about 5 minutes. Remove and drain. Keep the oil hot for frying the noodles just before serving.

6. Place the fish skeleton on a platter, with the head at one end and the tail at the other. Arrange the deep-fried fish "tiles" to cover the skeleton between the head and the tail. Heat the remaining 2 tablespoons of oil in a saucepan over a medium flame until hot and stir in the sweet and sour seasoning mixture. Bring mixture to a boil, stirring constantly, and pour over the fish. Keep the fish warm while preparing the noodles.

7. Drop the noodles into the hot oil and fry for 10 seconds. Remove them with a slotted spoon or Chinese strainer on a wooden handle, drain, place in a large shallow serving bowl, and serve along with the fish, or tuck them in billows under the chin and fins of the fish. After the fish "tiles" have been served, mix the noodles into the sweet and sour sauce and serve.

1. Cut the fish into squares.

2. Dip the fish in the batter and lower into the wok.

3. Sprinkle with the sweet-sour sauce.

4. Pie up the dough pieces, cut into noodles and deep fry.

Green and White Fish Balls

Liangse yuwan 两色鱼丸

Ginger and scallions flavor the delicate fish balls cooked in a light broth. If possible, use fish stock for the broth. Substitute fish for the pork in the recipe for clear stock following the Ingredients Guide. Cucumber slices provide extra zest as well as ornamental value. Be sure to dry the rape leaves thoroughly; their juice (when they are squeezed) is used to tint some of the fish-ball mixture, and if the leaves are wet, too much liquid will be added and the fish balls will fall apart during cooking. If the fish mixture seems too loose, add a sprinkling of cornstarch to bind it. Any firm-fleshed, fresh-water fish may be used if carp is not available.

2 scallions

2 tablespoons peeled fresh ginger, sliced

5 oz. (150 g) rape leaves

8 black mushrooms, each 1 inch (2.5 cm) in diameter, soaked

1¾ oz. (50 g) winter bamboo shoots

2 -inch (5-cm) section (1¾ oz./50 g) cucumber

7 oz. (200 g) boneless fish fillets (black carp or mandarin)

1 egg white

5 teaspoons rice wine

(2 teaspoons MSG)

1 teaspoon salt

3 cups (750 ml) clear fish stock

¾ oz. (25 g) boiled ham, chopped

1. Cut the scallions into 1-inch (2.5-cm) pieces; add the sliced ginger and ½ cup water. Let stand 2 hours to extract the flavors, then strain and reserve the liquid; discard scallions and ginger.

2. Wash rape leaves, drain, then dry thoroughly. Slice black mushrooms and bamboo shoots. Peel and slice cucumber. Finely mash fish with the back of a cleaver.

3. For fish batter: in a bowl, combine the fish, egg white, 1 tablespoon of rice wine, (½ teaspoon of MSG), ¼ teaspoon of salt, and the liquid from the scallion-and-ginger mixture. Divide the batter in half and place each half in a separate bowl.

4. Wrap the chopped rape leaves in a piece of cheesecloth and squeeze a few drops of juice into one of the bowls of fish batter to tint it green; mix well.

5. Place a wok over a low flame. Pour in 5 cups of cold water and slowly bring to a boil. As the water boils, form the green and the white fish mixtures (separately) into small balls. To shape the balls, put some of the fish mixture into your palm. Close your fist around the mixture and squeeze a little of it out the top, through the circle formed by your thumb and index finger. Scoop it up with a spoon; it is now ready to drop into the water. Drop the balls into the boiling water one by one. (Wait until the water comes back to boil before adding the next ball.) As each cooked ball rises to the surface, scoop it out with a wire mesh spoon and place it in a tureen. Place the white balls on one side and the green ones on the other to form the interlocking pattern of the "yin" and "yang" symbols.

6. Pour off the water from the wok and pour in the stock. As it heats add the remaining rice wine, (MSG), salt, as well as the mushrooms, bamboo shoots, and ham. Heat to boiling. Add the sliced cucumber. Pour the broth over the fish balls and serve.

Fish Balls in Fruit Sauce
Guozhi yuqiu　果汁鱼球

This delectable, colorful fish dish is flavored with garlic, onion, pineapple, and pungent sauce (which is similar to Worcestershire sauce). Tomato sauce gives the dish its red color. The pieces of fish, still attached to the skin, curl into balls when they are deep-fried. The trick is to deep-fry the fish pieces so they do not turn brown, yet stay crispy under the sauce. The head and tail, though deep-fried, are not eaten.

- 1 mandarin fish or other white-fleshed fish (3 lb./1.5 kg)
- 1 scallion, cut in two
- 2 slices peeled fresh ginger root
- 1 teaspoon rice wine
- (1 teaspoon MSG)
- 5 teaspoons salt
- ¼ teaspoon ground black pepper
- 2 teaspoons sesame oil
- 1½ tablespoons cornstarch, dissolved in 3 tablespoons water
- ½ cup (125 g) cornstarch
- 3 tablespoons tomato sauce
- 4 teaspoons pungent sauce
- 7 teaspoons sugar
- 5 oz. (150 ml) clear chicken stock
- 4 cups (1 L) peanut oil
- 5 to 6 cloves garlic, peeled and mashed
- 5 teaspoons onion, diced
- ¾ oz. (25 g) pineapple, diced
- ⅓ cup (25 g) green soy beans
- ¾ oz. (25 g) carrot, diced (three-fourths small carrot)

1. Clean the fish; chop off the head and tail and set them aside. Cut the fish lengthwise in half and fillet the meat from the bones (without removing the skin). Place the fish on a chopping board, skin side down. Make two parallel slices lengthwise, dividing the fillet into thirds. Then cut parallel slices across each piece ½ inch (4 cm) apart. Cut almost to the skin but not through it, so those pieces remain attached to the skin when you pick up the fillet.
2. In a bowl, combine the scallion pieces, 2 slices ginger, the rice wine, (½ teaspoon MSG), 1 teaspoon salt, the pepper, and 1 teaspoon sesame oil. Add the fish chunks and marinate for at least 10 minutes.
3. Brush the chunks and the head and tail of the fish with 3 teaspoons diluted cornstarch paste. Dip the pieces in the dry cornstarch and set aside.
4. In a small bowl mix the tomato sauce, pungent sauce, (remaining MSG), 1 teaspoon salt, the sugar, the remaining sesame oil, the chicken stock, and the remaining cornstarch paste; set this sauce aside.
5. Heat 3½ cups peanut oil in a wok over a medium flame until it is hot. Add the fish head and tail and deep-fry for 2 minutes. Drain and place at opposite ends of a platter. Add the fish chunks to the wok and deep-fry for 2 minutes. Drain and arrange between the head and tail.
6. Pour off the oil and clean the wok. Heat 3 tablespoons peanut oil over an intense flame until it is hot. Add the garlic and the onion and stir-fry for a few seconds. Stir in the pineapple, green soy beans, carrot, and the reserved sauce. When the mixture boils, add the remaining oil and stir for 1 minute. Pour over the fish and serve.

1. After marinating, brush pieces of fish with cornstarch paste and cover with dry cornstarch.

2. Deep-fry head and tail in hot oil. Remove them and fry chunks of fish until just crispy, not browned.

3. Arrange on serving platter, reconstructing fish, and garnish with tangerine or orange sections, parsley, and cherries.

4. Thicken red sauce made with tomato sauce, chicken broth, and flavorings in hot wok; pour over fish and serve immediately.

Grape-Cluster Fish
Putaoyu 葡萄鱼

The chef who invented this recipe wished to create a fish dish that would resemble a cluster of grapes. She succeeded, after several attempts, by developing the following technique. First she cut fish fillets (still in their skins) crosswise and lengthwise and coated them in bread crumbs, so that when the fish was cooked it separated into rounded pieces that still clung to the skin. Then the chef mixed a purplish-red sweet-and-sour sauce to pour over the fish, making it look and taste like grapes. Her recipe results in this delicious food sculpture, crisp on the outside and tender on the inside, prepared in the style of the southern province of Anhui.

2 fillets cut from a 2½-lb. (1.25-kg) black carp, with skin attached

¼ teaspoon rice wine

(Pinch of MSG)

1 teaspoon minced scallion

½ teaspoon minced fresh ginger root

½ cup (55 g) flour

1 egg, beaten

1 cup (150 g) bread crumbs

4 cups (1 L) vegetable oil

4 green vegetable leaves, rinsed, dried, and cut to resemble grape leaves

¾ cup (200 ml) clear chicken stock

3 tablespoons dry red wine

½ teaspoon vinegar

5 teaspoons sugar

Pinch of salt

1 tablespoon cornstarch dissolved in 2 tablespoons water

1. Trim the fillets so they are wider at one end. Make evenly spaced parallel crosswise slices ¾ inch (2 cm) apart along the flesh side of the fillet. Cut about halfway through to the skin, then slant the cut toward the previous cut. *Do not cut the skin*—stop cutting before you reach the skin. Turn the fillet 90 degrees and slice crosswise in the same manner, making the cuts about ⅓ inch (1 cm) apart. The fillets should now have rectangular cubes all still attached to the skin.

2. In a medium-size bowl, combine the rice wine, (pinch of MSG), scallion, and ginger. Soak the fillets for 30 minutes in this marinade.

3. Dredge the fillets in the flour, making sure that every cube is thoroughly covered. Dip the fillets in the beaten egg, then coat well with the bread crumbs.

4. Heat the oil in a wok over a medium flame until hot. Fry the vegetable leaves until they are crisp, less than 1 minute. Arrange them on a platter and keep them warm.

5. Reheat the oil in the wok over an intense flame. When the oil is moderately hot, add the fillets carefully. As the skin becomes crisp, lower the heat and continue frying until all sides of the cubes have turned brown. Then raise the heat and cook until the skin starts to curl and the cubes begin to separate and stand out. Remove the fillets from the wok, drain them, and place on the bed of warm vegetable leaves on the platter.

6. In a clean wok, combine the chicken stock, red wine, vinegar, sugar, salt, (remaining MSG), and the dissolved cornstarch. Taste and adjust the amount of vinegar or sugar, if necessary, to achieve the sweet-sour flavor of ripe red grapes. Bring the mixture to boiling over a medium flame. When it thickens to the consistency of a light syrup, pour it over only the fish, not the leaves, and serve.

1. Slice fish into cubes that are undercut and still attached to skin.

2. Cut fillet is ready to soak for 30 minutes in marinade of rice wine, scallion, and ginger.

3. After dredging fish cubes on all sides with flour, coat with bread crumbs.

4. Slide fillet into moderately hot oil over intense flame. Be gentle so cubes do not fall off.

Braised Fish Maw With Ham and Bamboo Shoots
Huosun pa guangdu   火笋扒广肚

Maw is the stomach lining of the fish and is available raw or dried. In this dish, bamboo shoots, black mushrooms, ham, and scallions are used to flavor the fish maw cooked in chicken stock. Do not overcook the maw, as it will lose its texture.

1¾ oz. (50 g) bamboo shoots

¼ lb. (125 g) dried fish maw

2½ oz. (75 g) cooked ham

1 medium dried black mushroom (⅓ oz./10 g)

1 scallion

1 tablespoon rice wine

¼ cup (60 ml) vegetable oil

2 cups (500 ml) clear chicken stock

1 teaspoon salt

5 teaspoons Gourmet Powder)

5 teaspoons cornstarch, dissolved in 3 teaspoons water

1 tablespoon melted chicken fat

1. Cut the bamboo shoots into 1¾-by-1¾-by-¹⁄₁₆-inch (4-cm x 2-cm x 2-mm) slices and place in a large bowl. (There should be 10 to 15 slices.) Pour boiling water over the bamboo shoots and let stand for 2 to 3 minutes; drain. Soak the fish maw in hot water for 10 minutes. Drain, rinse, and cut into pieces the same size as the bamboo shoots. Cut the ham into the same size pieces and steam for 2 minutes. Soak the mushrooms in hot water until they are soft. Remove and discard the stems and cut the caps in half. Cut the scallion into ¾-inch (2-cm) pieces.

2. In a large pot, heat 3½ cups (825 ml) of water to boiling and add 1 teaspoon rice wine. Add the fish maw and boil for 3 minutes; remove and drain.
3. Heat the oil in a wok over a low flame. When just warm, add half of the scallion pieces, let them simmer for about 30 seconds to release their flavor into the oil, then remove and discard. Making sure that the oil is still just warm, stir in the remaining rice wine, and the chicken stock. (If oil is too hot, it will splatter when the wine is added.) Add the fish maw, bamboo shoots, ham, mush-

room pieces, and salt, and heat to boiling.
4. Add the remaining scallion (and the Gourmet Powder). Skim off the foam and continue to simmer until most of the liquid has evaporated.
5. Remove the fish maw, bamboo shoots, and mushroom pieces with a strainer-spoon and place on a serving platter. Stir the dissolved cornstarch into the liquid remaining in the wok and heat to boiling. Pour the sauce over the fish maw and vegetables, sprinkle with the chicken fat, and serve.

Fried Eel Strips
Chao shanhu 炒鳝糊

When you put the live eel into the pot of boiling water, be sure to clamp the cover onto the pot quickly and hold it firmly, or the eel may jump out.

The eel slices in this dish are tender and rich, and are best eaten piping hot. If fresh bamboo shoots are used, scald them in boiling water first to remove the bitter taste. Prepare a serving dish in advance with a mound of minced garlic, which will later be mixed with the cooked and seasoned eel, ham, bamboo shoots, and coriander.

4 cloves garlic

4 scallions

¾ oz. (25 g) peeled fresh ginger

¾ oz. (25 g) ham

2½ tablespoons sliced bamboo shoots

⅓ oz. (10 g) fresh coriander leaves

4 teaspoons vinegar

5 teaspoons rice wine

5 teaspoons salt

1½ lb. (750 g) live eel

5 teaspoons soy sauce

½ teaspoon sugar

3¼ oz. (100 ml) clear chicken stock

(½ teaspoon Gourmet Powder)

¼ cup (60 ml) vegetable oil

5 teaspoons cornstarch, dissolved in 5 teaspoons water

Pinch of ground black pepper

5 teaspoons sesame oil

1. Finely mince the garlic. Mound it in the center of a serving platter. Cut two scallions into 1¾-inch (4-cm) pieces; chop the remaining scallions. Mince one third of the ginger and crush the rest. Cut the ham into thin strips 2 inches (5 cm) long, ¼ inch (0.5 cm) wide and ⅛ inch (0.3 cm) thick. Cut the bamboo shoots into strips the same size as the ham and scald in boiling water. Cut the coriander leaves into ¾-inch (2-cm) sections.
2. Heat 8 cups (2 L) water in a pot, add 1½ tablespoons vinegar, ½ tablespoon rice wine, the salt, scallion pieces, and crushed ginger and heat to boiling. Add the live eel, holding the pot lid very tightly. Heat to boiling again, then reduce heat to a low flame for about 6 minutes. When the eel becomes soft, remove and place in cold water. Use a small knife with a thin blade to cut the eel from belly to head; remove the entrails. Cut off the two pieces of meat along the backbone and discard the head and bones. Cut the eel into 2-inch (5-cm) slices. Plunge slices into hot boiled water for a while. Drain.
3. Mix together 2 teaspoons rice wine, ½ teaspoon vinegar, the soy sauce, sugar, chicken stock (and Gourmet Powder). Heat the vegetable oil in a wok over an intense flame. Add the chopped scallion and minced ginger, and stir until they give off a strong aroma. Immediately add the eel and chicken stock mixture and stir a few times. Add the dissolved cornstarch, then heat to boiling and sprinkle with the black pepper. Remove the eel.
4. Place the eel slices on the serving platter, around the mound of garlic. Surround the eel with the ham, bamboo shoots, and coriander.
5. Heat the sesame oil over an intense flame until it is very hot. Splash it on the minced garlic, which will sizzle and give off an aroma. Thoroughly mix the minced garlic with the eel, ham, bamboo shoots, and coriander; serve piping hot.

Fried Eels with Sauce

Ganshao shanyuduan 干烧鳝鱼段

Many people consider eels a delicacy. Live eels are very slippery and hard to work with, but some fishmongers will be happy to clean them. The garlic, ginger, and scallions with which the eel is cooked take away its fishy taste. Be sure to serve this dish piping hot.

1 lb. (500 g) live eel
2½ cups (625 ml) peanut oil
2 scallions
4 tablespoons peeled fresh ginger
6 cloves garlic
¾ oz. (25 g) pork fat, diced
1 tablespoon soybean paste with chili
3 tablespoons diced soaked black mushrooms
2½ tablespoons diced winter bamboo shoots
2 tablespoons clear chicken stock
3 tablespoons sugar
5 teaspoons rice wine
2 tablespoons soy sauce
(½ teaspoon MSG)
Pinch of salt

1. Cut the head and tail off the eel and discard; remove the entrails. Rinse the eel and chop crosswise into 2-inch (5-cm) pieces. Cut the scallions, ginger, and garlic into small slices.

2. Heat 2 cups (500 ml) oil in a wok over a medium flame. Add the eel and stir-fry for 30 seconds; scoop out.

3. Empty the wok, then heat ½ cup (125 ml) oil until it is very hot. Stir-fry the scallions, ginger, and garlic. Add the diced pork fat and soybean paste and stir until the fat melts and blends with the soybean paste. Add the mushrooms and bamboo shoots and stir-fry for 1 minute. Add the chicken stock, fried eel, sugar, rice wine, soy sauce, (MSG), and salt. Cover and simmer over a low flame until the sauce thickens, about 10 minutes. Place the eel on a serving platter, pour the sauce over it, and serve.

Crispy Prawns
Yousu daxia 油酥大虾

These prawns, coated with an egg-white batter and then deep fried, are a festive orange color. They are braised with ginger and scallion, and chili sauce gives them a peppery flavor.

½ lb. (250 g) shelled prawns

1 teaspoon cornstarch paste, diluted with 1 tablespoon water

½ egg white

¼ teaspoon salt

(¼ teaspoon MSG)

4 cups (1 L) vegetable oil

1 scallion, sliced

2 teaspoons chopped peeled fresh ginger

2 teaspoons rice wine

½ teaspoon sugar

1½ tablespoons clear chicken stock

½-inch section unpeeled cucumber, sliced

2 medium-size black mushrooms, soaked, stemmed, and sliced

¼ teaspoon chili sauce

1. Remove the prawn heads, devein and wash out the back. Cut partway through the underside and press flat. In a large bowl, mix the diluted cornstarch paste, egg white, salt (and MSG); add the prawns and turn them in the batter until evenly coated.

2. Heat the oil in a wok over an intense flame. Lower the prawns into the hot oil (setting aside remaining prawn batter) and fry until they float to the surface. Scoop out and drain.

3. Remove all but 2 tablespoons of the oil from the wok and heat over a low flame. Add the scallion, ginger, wine, sugar, chicken stock, and fried prawns. Add the reserved batter and stir. Add the cucumber, black mushrooms, and chili sauce and toss the wok two or three times. Transfer to a platter and serve.

Maid Marrying Herself Off
Hongniang zipei 红娘自配

This dish is said to have been created by Liang Lingting, a celebrated chef in the Imperial kitchen and uncle of a young maid-in-waiting for the Empress Dowager Ci Xi. Because the chef's niece, Liang Hongping, was getting older, he was anxious for her to leave the imperial service and marry.

To convey his wish to Ci Xi, Liang Lingting prepared for her a dish called "maid marrying herself off" that had been inspired by an episode in the romantic tale *The Western Chamber*. This famous Chinese story quotes an old proverb, "When a girl is grown up, it is unwise to keep her long at home." The literary reference so angered the Empress Dowager that she threw the dish out. Some time later, however, Ci Xi remembered an edict that had been issued by her deceased husband, Emperor Guang Xu, proclaiming that all of the older maids in his court should be allowed to return home. She summoned Liang Lingting and asked him to prepare "maid marrying herself off" again, whereupon she released all of the older maids. As a result, this exotic and beautiful dish became famous with the common people.

Traditionally, the "maid," sculpted from a simple flour and water dough, is placed in the center of the dish. Prawns are filled with a stuffing of pork tenderloin and served with deep-fried bread cubes and tomato sauce. To duplicate it successfully, make sure that the prawn backs are sliced to prevent them from curling and losing their stuffing. Even without the "maid," this delightful dish is worth the effort.

2¼ cups (250 g) flour

¾ oz. (25 g) dried sea cucumber

4 dried black mushrooms (each about 1 inch (2.5 cm) in diameter)

12 prawns

5 oz. (150 g) pork tenderloin, finely minced

2 medium egg whites

4 cups (1 L) peanut oil

3½ oz. (105 g) rape leaves

4 to 5 slices (3½ oz./105 g) bread, cut in ½-inch (1.25-cm) cubes

2 to 3 tablespoons bamboo shoots, sliced

1 teaspoon chopped cooked ham

½ cup (110 g) loosely packed, stemmed parsley leaves

1 tablespoon rice wine

1 scallion, chopped

Pinch of ground black pepper

(1 teaspoon MSG)

1 teaspoon minced peeled fresh ginger

1 teaspoon tomato sauce

2 teaspoons salt

1. Combine 2 cups (220 gm) flour with about a cup (250 ml) water to make a stiff paste that will hold its shape. Form the dough into the figure of a "maid." Let it dry hard (paint it, if you like, as shown). Place in the center of a serving platter.

2: After soaking the sea cucumber for about 24 hours, clean, rinse, pat dry, and chop. Remove the stems from the mushrooms and soak caps in hot water.

3. Remove and discard the heads and shells of the prawns, leaving tails intact. Make a lengthwise cut down the back of each prawn, cutting almost, but not quite all the way through. Rinse away the black vein under water, pat dry, and press prawns open with the flat side of a cleaver.

4. Combine the minced pork with the egg whites and stuff a small amount of this mixture into the back of each prawn. Press the prawns firmly around the stuffing and roll in flour to coat.

5. Heat the peanut oil in a wok over an intense flame until hot. Slip stuffed prawns carefully into the oil, one by one. (Hold the tail tips as they fry, keeping them out of the oil.) Fry until golden brown. Remove prawns and drain, keeping oil hot. Drop the bread cubes into the hot oil and fry until golden. Remove and drain.

6. Pile rape leaves around the maid on the serving platter and arrange fried prawns in a circle around them. Pile the bread cubes on top of the rape leaves.

7. Empty wok of all except 2 tablespoons of the oil and stir-fry the bamboo shoots, sea cucumber, mushrooms, ham, and parsley leaves for 30 seconds. Add the rice wine, scallion, pepper, (MSG), ginger, tomato sauce, and salt. Pour the sauce over the bread cubes and serve.

Ruyi Prawns
Ruyi daxia 如意大虾

It takes only a few simple ingredients to make this appealing dish of tender shrimp coated in a crisp, light egg-white batter. The tails of the shrimp and the colorful vegetables add a festive touch.

6 large shrimp
  Pinch of salt
(½ teaspoon MSG)
1 teaspoon rice wine
4 medium egg whites
1 teaspoon flour
1 teaspoon cornstarch
2 cups (500 ml) vegetable oil
  Cucumber and red and green peppers cut into decorative shapes, for garnish

1. Remove the heads and shells from the shrimp, leaving the tails intact. Make a small slit along the back, then rinse under cold running water to remove the vein. Make small slits across the back to keep the shrimp from curling as they cook. Cut the shrimp open from the underside, being careful not to cut all the way through. Flatten slightly with the side of a cleaver.

2. Sprinkle the shrimp with the salt, (MSG), and rice wine, and let stand for a minute. In a medium-size bowl, beat the egg whites until frothy, then beat in the flour and cornstarch until well mixed. Roll the shrimp in the mixture, leaving the tails uncoated.

3. Heat the oil in a wok over a medium flame. When the oil is warm (before it reaches the maximum heat), carefully slide the shrimp into the wok, using chopsticks to prevent them from sticking. When the shrimp puff up and turn a pale golden color, about 30 seconds, scoop out and drain.

4. Serve on a platter garnished with the cucumber and red and green peppers.

Phoenix-Tail Prawns
Fengwei daxia 凤尾大虾

Prawns are marinated with scallion, ginger, and rice wine, resulting in a wonderfully subtle flavor. They are then breaded and deep fried and served on a platter garnished with fried rape leaves.

2 oz. (60 g) rape leaves
6 prawns (1 lb./500 g)
2 cups (500 ml) vegetable oil
1 cherry
1 teaspoon chopped scallion
½ teaspoon crushed and minced peeled fresh ginger

2 teaspoons rice wine
(¼ teaspoon MSG)
Pinch of salt
½ cup (50 g) flour
2 eggs, beaten
1½ cups (150 g) bread crumbs

1. Slice the rape leaves into very thin strips. Shell the prawns, leaving the tails intact; devein. Cut each prawn lengthwise, almost—but not quite—through; spread the prawn open. Make 2 horizontal cuts to sever the cartilage; make 2 perpendicular cuts so the prawns will not curl when fried.

2. Heat the oil in a wok over a medium flame and fry the rape briefly. Drain and place in the center of a platter. Place the cherry on top.

3. Combine the scallion, ginger, rice wine, (MSG), and salt in a bowl. Add the prawns and marinate in the mixture for at least 10 minutes.

4. Roll the prawns in flour, shaking off the excess; dip them in the eggs, then roll them in the bread crumbs, leaving the tails uncoated.

5. Reheat the oil over an intense flame. Cook the prawns one by one by dropping them into the hot oil, turning them with chopsticks. Scoop them out when they begin to turn golden, about 1 minute.

6. When all the prawns have been deep fried, reheat the oil and drop all the prawns back into the hot oil together. Fry until they turn a golden brown, 1 to 2 minutes. Remove from oil, drain, and cut each into 3 pieces; arrange them around the rape leaves on the platter.

Buddhist Prawns
Luohan daxia　罗汉大虾

Prawns, with heads and bodies separated and each prepared in a different manner, are served with stir-fried rape leaves and two sauces: a sweet, gingery brown sauce and a thickened chicken stock. If rape leaves are unavailable substitute sliced cucumber.

12 prawns
⅓ cup (85 ml) melted lard
5 teaspoons sugar
 (Pinch of MSG)
1½ cups (375 ml) clear chicken stock
4 teaspoons rice wine
4 teaspoons shredded peeled fresh ginger
7 oz. (200 g) fillet of white-fleshed fish, mashed
1 medium egg white
 Pinch of salt

1 teaspoon cornstarch
1½ teaspoons minced ham
2 tablespoons chopped rape leaves
12 soybean sprouts
2 teaspoons cornstarch, dissolved in 4 teaspoons water
1 tablespoon melted chicken fat
8 oz. (250 g) rape leaves, finely shredded

1. Cut the prawns in half at the base of the head and set heads aside. Leaving the tails intact, remove the shells. Without cutting all the way through, split each prawn down the center of the inside curve. Slit very lightly along the back and rinse out the vein under cold running water. Flatten them and set aside, on an ovenproof dish, on a platter.

2. Heat all but 2½ tablespoons of the lard in a wok over a medium flame. When hot, add the heads of the prawns and stir-fry. Add the sugar, (pinch of MSG), 1½ tablespoons chicken stock, 2 teaspoons rice wine, and the ginger. Reduce the flame to low and simmer, being careful not to let the sugar burn, for about 10 minutes. The sauce should turn brown. Remove from heat and keep warm.

3. In a medium-size bowl, combine the mashed fish, egg white, 1 teaspoon rice wine, a pinch of salt, (pinch of MSG), and the cornstarch to make a batter. Lay the prawns flat, back-side down on the ovenproof dish and spread the fish batter on them. Sprinkle with the minced ham and chopped rape leaves. Place 1 bean sprout on the tail of each and steam the prawns for 10 minutes.

4. Heat the remaining chicken stock in a pot over a medium flame until boiling. Add the remaining rice wine, a pinch of salt, (and a pinch of MSG); stir in the dissolved cornstarch until the sauce is thickened. Sprinkle with the chicken fat, remove from heat, and set aside.

5. Quickly stir-fry the shredded rape leaves in the remaining lard in a wok over an intense flame. Pile the rape leaves in the middle of a serving platter; arrange the prawn heads in brown sauce on one side of the platter and the steamed prawns on the other side. Pour the chicken stock sauce over the steamed prawns and serve quickly before the hot lard cools.

1. Shell prawns; cut in half at base of head.

2. Stir-fry prawn heads in lard.

3. Spread prawn bodies with fish batter.

4. Steam decorated prawn bodies.

Orchid Prawns
Lanhua daxia 兰花大虾

For this recipe, some of the prawns are left whole with head and tails intact, and some are mashed and combined with a seasoning mixture to stuff whole black mushrooms. The bright orange color of the cooked prawns contrasts nicely with the white fungus "orchids." The prawns are tender, the mushrooms soft, and the white fungi translucent and slightly crunchy.

7 prawns

10 large soaked black mushrooms (each 1¾ inches in diameter)

10 whole white or snow fungi

¾ oz. (25 g) fatty pork, minced

2 water chestnuts, peeled and minced

¼ teaspoon cornstarch, dissolved in ¾ teaspoon water

¼ teaspoon minced scallion

¼ teaspoon minced peeled fresh ginger

5 teaspoons rice wine

¼ teaspoon salt

(5 teaspoons MSG)

2 medium egg whites

½ cup (125 ml) plus 1 teaspoon vegetable oil

¼ teaspoon minced garlic

¼ teaspoon sugar

1 cup (250 ml) clear chicken stock

1 -inch (2.5-cm) section unpeeled cucumber, sliced and arranged to resemble flower petals, for garnish

1. Remove the heads, tails, and shells from 2 of the prawns. Devein, mince, and set aside. Leaving the heads on and the tails intact, shell and devein the remaining 5 prawns. Set aside.

2. Remove and discard the stems from the black mushrooms, steam caps for 3 minutes, and drain. Soak the white fungi, drain, and remove discolored parts.

3. In a medium-size bowl, combine the minced prawns with the pork and water chestnuts. Add ⅓ of the dissolved cornstarch, half of the scallion, half of the ginger, 2 teaspoons rice wine, half of the salt, (half of the MSG), and one of the egg whites. Blend well to make a smooth mixture.

4. Place the black mushrooms on a plate, top down, and stuff with the shrimp mixture, leaving a small hollow in the center. Steam over a low flame for 5 minutes.

5. Turn off the flame and drop a small amount of the second egg white into the hollow in the center of each mushroom, topping each with a white fungus. Steam for 2 minutes more over a low flame.

6. In a wok over a medium flame, heat ½ cup (125 ml) oil. When it is moderately hot, fry the whole prawns until they turn orange, about 1 minute. Add the remaining rice wine, scallion, ginger, salt, (and MSG). Add the garlic, sugar, and chicken stock and bring to boiling. Add the remaining dissolved cornstarch and cook until the sauce thickens. Sprinkle the remaining oil over the prawns and transfer to a serving platter. Surround the prawns with the mushrooms and the cucumber flowers and serve.

Braised Prawns in Shells
Ganshao daipi daxia 干烧带皮大虾

Prawns are braised in hot, spicy Sichuan bean sauce with an abundance of garlic, ginger, and scallions. It is traditional to cook the prawns without removing the shells.

1½ lb. (750 g) prawns
1 cup (250 ml) vegetable oil
3 tablespoons cubed pork fat
3½ tablespoons Sichuan bean sauce
2 tablespoons chopped peeled fresh ginger
8 cloves garlic, chopped
5 teaspoons rice wine
¾ teaspoon salt
½ teaspoon sugar
(Pinch of Gourmet Powder)
1 cup (250 ml) clear chicken stock
1 teaspoon rice wine vinegar
8 scallions, chopped

Some of the ingredients: prawns, scallions, flavorings.

1. With kitchen shears, cut each prawn along its back to expose the black vein, but leave the shell intact. Rinse out the black vein with cold running water.
2. Heat ⅓ cup vegetable oil in a wok over an intense flame. Add the prawns and stir-fry until both sides turn orange, about 2 minutes. Remove the prawns to a bowl.
3. Remove the oil from the wok, then heat the remaining oil over a medium flame. When hot, add the pork fat cubes. After 15 seconds, turn the cubes, cook for 15 seconds more, then add the bean sauce. Stir until the mixture yields a distinctive aroma.
4. Add the prawns, ginger, garlic, rice wine, salt, sugar, (Gourmet Powder), and chicken stock. Cook over an intense flame for 5 minutes. Stir in the vinegar; when most of the liquid has evaporated, add the scallions. Remove to a platter and serve.

Braised Shrimp
Ganshao daxia 干烧大虾

1 lb. (500 g) large whole shrimp

⅓ cup (85 ml) vegetable oil

1 cup (250 ml) clear chicken stock

1 tablespoon rice wine

4 teaspoons sugar

2 teaspoons tomato paste

¼ teaspoon salt

(¼ teaspoon Gourmet Powder)

1 tablespoon minced hot-pickled vegetable

1 scallion, minced

2 teaspoons minced peeled fresh ginger

2 cloves garlic, minced

¾ teaspoon sesame oil

1½ tablespoons chopped coriander leaves

Shrimp are fried and then braised in a sauce of chicken stock, tomato paste, hot-pickled vegetable, and other flavorings. They are then tossed lightly in sesame oil and garnished with wonderfully fragrant coriander leaves.

1. Shell and devein the shrimp; cut each in two at the base of the head.

2. Heat the vegetable oil in a wok over an intense flame until hot. Add the shrimp bodies and heads and stir vigorously, pressing the heads of the shrimp gently against the side of the wok with a spoon to release the juices.

3. After about 5 seconds add the chicken stock, rice wine, sugar, tomato paste, salt, (and Gourmet Powder) and mix thoroughly. Stir in the hot-pickled vegetable, scallion, ginger, and garlic.

4. Reduce the heat slightly and simmer until most of the liquid has evaporated and the shrimp have expanded and turned red, about 4 minutes. Sprinkle the shrimp with the sesame oil and toss the wok to coat them lightly in the oil. Arrange the shrimp on a platter, sprinkle with the coriander, and serve.

Two-in-One Shrimp
Liangchi daxia 两吃大虾

Two kinds of shrimp, dried and fresh, give this dish a distinctive flavor. It is also very decorative, with balls of savory chicken atop the fresh shrimp. The chicken balls may at first seem too soft to hold their shape, but when rolled in a mixture of minced ham, mushrooms, and dried shrimp, they will form neat, small balls with which to decorate the shrimp.

10 large whole shrimp

5 teaspoons rice wine

1 teaspoon salt

(½ teaspoon MSG)

1 tablespoon minced cooked ham

1 tablespoon minced soaked dried black mushrooms

2 tablespoons minced dried shelled shrimp

3 tablespoons minced pounded chicken breast

1 egg white

1 cup (250 ml) clear chicken stock

⅓ cup (85 ml) peanut oil

1 tablespoon (⅓ oz. / 10 g) peeled fresh ginger cut in thin strips

1 scallion, cut in thin strips

3 tablespoons sugar

1. Cut the shrimp in half at the base of the head and set the heads aside. Shell and devein the shrimp, leaving the tails intact, then cut each shrimp open lengthwise down the back, being careful not to cut all the way through.

2. Place the opened shrimp on a platter and sprinkle over them 1 teaspoon rice wine, ¼ teaspoon salt, (and ¼ teaspoon MSG).

3. Combine the ham, mushrooms, and dried shrimp in a bowl. In a separate medium-size bowl, combine the chicken, egg white, 2 teaspoons rice wine, ¼ teaspoon salt, (and a pinch of MSG); mix well. Form the mixture into balls to fit in the curve of the opened shrimp and roll each ball in the ham, mushroom, and shrimp mix-

ture; place on top of the shrimp on the platter. Pour 3 tablespoons chicken stock over the shrimp and the chicken balls and steam for 10 minutes.

4. Heat the oil in a wok over an intense flame. Add the shrimp heads and stir-fry for 30 seconds. Lower the heat, then add the ginger and scallion strips, the remaining rice wine, salt, (MSG), and chicken stock and stir briefly. Simmer for 10 minutes.

5. When the liquid thickens, remove the shrimp heads and place them in the center of a serving platter. Arrange the opened shrimp and chicken balls around the heads, pour the remaining cooking liquid from the heads over the platter, and serve.

Goldfish Prawns

Jinyu daxia 金鱼大虾

These prawns are cut open and marinated, then shaped like goldfish, with heads made of a minced-chicken mixture and cherry halves for the eyes. The prawns are steamed and served with a chicken-flavored sauce.

6 prawns
2 tablespoons rice wine
1 teaspoon salt
(½ teaspoon Gourmet Powder)
2½ oz. (75 g) chicken breast meat
2 medium egg whites
¼ cup (60 ml) peanut oil
1 tablespoon cornstarch paste
3 tablespoons flour
6 cherries, pitted and cut in half
6 pieces white fungus (each 1 inch / 2.5 cm in diameter)
5 teaspoons clear chicken and duck stock
½ teaspoon melted chicken fat

1 -inch (2.5-cm) section unpeeled cucumber cut into fan-shaped slivers, for garnish

1. Remove and discard the heads and shells of the prawns, but leave the tails intact. Without cutting all the way through, split each prawn down the center of the back and rinse out the vein under cold water. Spread the prawns open and lightly score the inside surface crosswise. In a large bowl, combine 1 tablespoon rice wine, ½ teaspoon salt, (and ¼ teaspoon Gourmet Powder). Let the prawns stand in this mixture for 10 minutes.

2. Mince the chicken breast. In a large bowl, combine the minced chicken, the egg whites, ¼ teaspoon salt, the peanut oil, and half the cornstarch paste.

3. Remove the prawns from the rice-wine mixture, spread them flat, dust both sides of each with the flour, and lay them out on a large plate. To make the goldfish shape, form a head for each prawn out of a ball of the chicken mixture, and attach by pressing it gently to the head end of the prawn body. Place a cherry half on either side of each "goldfish" head for eyes. Place a piece of white fungus on each head. Steam the goldfish for 10 minutes over an intense flame. Set the goldfish aside and cover to keep warm.

4. Remove the steamer and water from the wok. Add the stock to the wok and heat to boiling. Add the remaining salt, (Gourmet Powder), and rice wine. Skim off the foam, add the remaining cornstarch paste, and stir until the mixture thickens. Pour the sauce over the "goldfish," sprinkle with the melted chicken fat, garnish with the cucumber fans, and serve.

Fried Prawn Balls
Zha xiaqiu 炸虾球

A mixture of prawns, pork, and water chestnuts is rolled in bread crumbs and then deep fried. The crumbs give the balls a crisp golden coating. The trick is to watch the color while they are deep frying. When they are half-cooked they will begin to turn golden. Turn the heat down and back up again to make them golden *brown* and crispy.

7 oz. (200 g) prawns, minced
1¾ oz. (50 g) fatty pork, minced
3 water chestnuts, minced
1 egg white
Pinch of salt
1 tablespoon sesame oil
1 teaspoon rice wine
¼ teaspoon ground black pepper

1½ tablespoons minced scallion
1 tablespoon minced peeled fresh ginger
2½ tablespoons cornstarch paste
1½ cups coarse dried bread crumbs
4 cups (1 L) peanut oil
3 tablespoons onion salt

1. Mix the minced prawns, pork, and water chestnuts with 2 tablespoons water. Stirring in one direction only, gradually add the egg white, salt, sesame oil, rice wine, pepper, scallion, ginger, and cornstarch paste. Form the mixture into loose balls about ½-inch (1.25-cm) in diameter, then roll in the bread crumbs.

2. Heat the oil in a wok over an intense flame. When it is moderately hot, add the prawn balls, one by one, turning gently in the oil to cook evenly. When they begin to turn golden (60 to 90 seconds), lower the heat for 20 seconds, then turn the heat back up to an intense flame. When the balls have turned golden brown (an additional 60 to 90 seconds), remove from the oil and drain. Place on a platter and serve with a small bowl of the onion salt for dipping.

Coin-shaped Shrimp Cakes
Jinqian xiabing　金钱虾饼

2½ oz. (75 g) white bread

8 oz. (250 g) shrimp

1 scallion, finely chopped

4 teaspoons crushed peeled
  fresh ginger

1 tablespoon rice wine

1 oz. (2 tablespoons / 25 g)
  fatty pork, minced

1 teaspoon salt

(2 teaspoons Gourmet Powder)

1 tablespoon cornstarch

2 medium egg whites

3 tablespoons minced
  cooked ham

1 teaspoon black
  sesame seeds

12 coriander leaves

3 cups (750 ml) vegetable oil

Round and golden brown, with red, black, and green garnishes, these little shrimp cakes resemble exotic ancient coins. Scallions and ginger flavor the rice wine in which minced shrimp and pork are marinated. The mixture is spread onto bread rounds, then deep fried to a delicious crispness, pungent with coriander. They must be served piping hot and would make excellent hors d'oeuvres served with chilled dry white wine.

1. Cut off the bread crusts, shape into a cylinder ¼ inch (3 cm) in diameter, then slice into 20 to 24 very thin circles. Shell, devein, and mince the shrimp.

2. Combine the scallion, ginger, and rice wine and let stand for several minutes; then strain the wine to remove the scallion and ginger.

3. Combine the minced shrimp and the pork in a medium-size bowl and add the strained rice wine, salt, (the Gourmet Powder), cornstarch, and egg whites. Let the mixture stand for 15 minutes.

4. Spread the shrimp mixture on each round of bread, mounding it in the center to ⅜ inch (1 cm) thick. Smooth the surface and garnish with the minced ham, black sesame seeds, and coriander, keeping each separate (as shown in photograph).

5. Heat the oil in a wok over an intense flame. Slide in the shrimp cakes one at a time, garnished side up. Fry until they turn golden brown, about 5 minutes.

6. Remove the cakes one by one and drain. Arrange on a platter and serve.

1. Shell, devein, and mince shrimp.

2. Spread shrimp mixture on bread rounds.

3. Garnish with chopped ham, black sesame seeds, and coriander leaves.

4. Remove coin-shaped shrimp cakes to serving platter.

Tomato Shrimp Cakes
Fanqie xiabing 蕃茄虾饼

5 oz. (155 g) shrimp

4 medium egg whites

3 tablespoons cornstarch paste

¼ teaspoon salt

2 cups (500 ml) vegetable oil

3 tablespoons tomato paste

3 teaspoons rice wine

1½ tablespoons sugar

¾ teaspoon cornstarch, dissolved in ¾ teaspoon water

1½ teaspoons peanut oil

Unpeeled cucumber, thinly sliced, for garnish

This dish has a glossy red color. The tender deep-fried shrimp cakes have a slightly sweet-sour flavor.

1. Shell, devein, and mince the shrimp. In a large bowl combine the egg whites, cornstarch paste, and half the salt; stir. Add the shrimp and mix well. Let stand a few minutes, then form into balls and press lightly into round cakes 1 inch (2.5-cm) in diameter and ¼-inch (0.6-cm) thick.

2. Heat the oil in a wok over a medium flame. When it is just warm, add the shrimp cakes one by one and cook, stirring, until cakes turn pale yellow and float to the surface, about 2 minutes. Scoop out and drain.

3. Pour out the oil, clean the wok, and place over a low flame. Add the tomato paste, rice wine, sugar, and remaining salt; stir-fry until the sugar and salt have dissolved, about 30 seconds. Add 2 tablespoons water, then carefully add the shrimp cakes.

4. When the tomato paste mixture bubbles, stir in the dissolved cornstarch and sprinkle with the peanut oil. Carefully turn the cakes over to coat with the sauce. Transfer to a platter, garnish with the cucumber slices, and serve.

Crabs with "Chrysanthemums"
Juhua pangxie 菊花螃蟹

Ancient Chinese wisdom has it that one should "Never eat crabs before August." Try to obtain local river crabs—in the proper months, of course. Female crabs carry roe, which turns pink when steamed or boiled, and is made part of the stuffing in this recipe. After being partly cooked and cooled, the shell is hinged upward and the inside of the abdomen cleaned out. The meat and roe are mixed with scallion, ginger, and egg, then set by stir-frying. The cavities are stuffed with this mixture, tied shut with iris stems, and the crabs deep-fried. The "chrysanthemum" florets are formed of cucumber carved in thin spirals. The central flower is bundles of translucent noodles (made from mung bean starch) deep fried so they will hold together.

1¾ oz. (50 g) translucent mung-bean noodles

1 maraschino cherry

¾ cup (200 ml) + 6 tablespoons vegetable oil

10 live female river crabs

½ scallion, minced

1 teaspoon minced peeled fresh ginger

1 egg, beaten

Dash of vinegar

5 teaspoons rice wine

Pinch of salt

(Pinch of MSG)

10 stems of small Chinese irises

1 unpeeled cucumber cut into 3 flower shapes, for garnish

1. Cut the noodles into 3-inch (7.5-cm) sections and divide into five equal piles. Heat ¾ cup (200 ml) oil in a wok over a medium flame until hot. Hold one pile of noodles in the middle with chopsticks and gently hold in the oil. When they expand, within 1 to 2 seconds, remove, drain, and set in the center of a serving platter. Repeat, flash-cooking the remaining noodles one pile at a time. Perch the cherry in the center of the noodles.

2. Rinse and steam the crabs until they just begin to turn pink. Lift the abdomen on the underside of each crab away from the shell on top, but do not detach them. To make a cavity inside the abdomen pull away the papery gills and membranes but keep the legs and claws attached and intact. Remove the thin bone structure down the middle of the cavity (the thoracic sternum). Scrape out the roe (pink) and the liver (greenish), and pick out the meat from the legs and claws. Again, do not detach them. Rinse out the cavity in the abdomen and replace the shell on top of it. Drain and pat dry.

3. Reheat the oil in the wok over a medium flame until hot. Hold the shell and abdomen together with long chopsticks or tongs and lower each crab into the oil. Fry them until they are evenly bright red. Lift them out with a strainer-spoon, one by one, and let them drain.

4. In a bowl, combine the scallion, ginger, egg, crabmeat and roe. Stir in the vinegar, rice wine, salt, (and MSG) and mix well. Heat the 6 tablespoons oil over a medium flame until hot. Gently stir-fry the mixture until the egg is set.

5. Divide the mixture into ten equal parts and stuff the crab shells with it. Replace the abdomens. Bind the crabs carefully, making a slipknot, with the stems of small Chinese irises. Steam the stuffed crabs for 5 minutes, then arrange them around the noodles. Tuck three thinly-sliced florets carved from unpeeled cucumber around the central bed of noodles. Serve with a fine rice wine. (In China, the most prized comes from the area around the city of Shaohsing.) After the host places a crab on each guest's plate, each diner unties the iris stem binding the top of the shell and lifts it away from the stuffing in the cavity beneath. The claws and legs may be cracked open to reach the succulent meat within.

Stuffed Crabs
Rang pangxie 瓤螃蟹

The sweet, succulent meat is scooped out of steamed hard-shell crabs, mixed with ham, fish, and seasonings, then stuffed back into the shells, steamed and served with a stock-based sauce.

7 large live hardshell crabs

5 teaspoons rice wine

(1½ teaspoons MSG)

1½ teaspoons chopped peeled fresh ginger

Pinch of salt

¼ lb. (125 g) fillet of mandarin fish or black carp, mashed

1¾ oz. (50 g) pork fat, mashed

1 medium egg white

2 tablespoons cornstarch

Dash of vegetable oil

3 tablespoons minced cooked ham

¼ cup (60 ml) clear stock

2 teaspoons cornstarch, dissolved in 2 teaspoons water

3 tablespoons melted lard

1. Clean the crabs and remove the legs. Steam over an intense flame for 10 minutes. Scoop out the crabmeat and roe, being careful to leave the shells intact. Rinse out the shells, drain, and set aside. Chop the crabmeat. In a medium-size bowl, combine the crab roe, crabmeat, 2 teaspoons rice wine, (½ teaspoon MSG), the ginger, and a pinch of salt.

2. In a separate bowl, combine the fish, pork fat, egg white, 2 teaspoons rice wine, (½ teaspoon MSG), and 2 tablespoons cornstarch; mix thoroughly.

3. Brush vegetable oil over the inside of each crab shell. Make a mixture of 2 parts of the crabmeat to 1 part fish batter and stuff into the crab shells. Sprinkle each with minced ham. Steam the crabs

over an intense flame for 10 minutes. Place on a serving platter.

4. Heat the clear stock in a wok over an intense flame. Add the remaining rice wine, (MSG), and a pinch of salt. Stir in the dissolved cornstarch and simmer until sauce thickens. Sprinkle the lard over the sauce, pour over the stuffed crabs and serve piping hot.

Delicately Fried Crab Legs
Songzha hengshuangdie　松炸横双蝶

Crab meat is flavored with rice wine, scallion, and sesame oil before being dipped into a thin batter, decorated with sesame seeds and ham, and then fried until crisp and golden.

½ lb. (250 g) of the whole meat
　　from crab legs cut into
　　1-inch (2.5 cm) pieces
1 tablespoon rice wine
1 scallion, minced
(½ teaspoon MSG)
　　Pinch of sugar
1 tablespoon sesame oil
4 egg whites
2 tablespoons cornstarch
1½ tablespoons flour
2 teaspoons black sesame
　　seeds
1½ tablespoons minced ham
½ cup (125 ml) peanut oil

1. In a small bowl, mix together the pieces of crab, rice wine, scallion, (MSG), sugar, and sesame oil.
2. In another bowl beat the egg whites until very frothy but not stiff. Stir in the cornstarch and flour to make a batter. Dip firmly packed spoonfuls of the crabmeat mixture into the batter and turn to coat thoroughly. Decorate the top of each spoonful of crab meat with a line of sesame seeds and bits of minced ham as shown in the photograph.
3. Heat the oil in a wok over a low flame until hot. Gently slip the pieces of decorated crab meat, one by one, into the heated oil. Fry until seeds and ham are set, about 15 seconds. Drain, arrange in a circle on a platter, and serve.

Crabs　183

Stir-Fried Abalone
Qingchao baoyu 清炒鲍鱼

In this famous traditional Shandong dish, canned abalone is scored and parboiled, then stir-fried with bamboo shoots, cucumber, and other ingredients.

11 oz. (345 g) canned abalone

1 teaspoon chopped peeled fresh ginger

2-inch (5-cm) section unpeeled cucumber, sliced

3 tablespoons sliced bamboo shoots

1 tablespoon sliced carrot

2 teaspoons rice wine

¼ teaspoon salt

(½ teaspoon MSG)

1½ tablespoons shredded scallion

2½ tablespoons peanut oil

1 tablespoon melted chicken fat

1. Cut off and discard the curly edges of the abalone. Score one side of each abalone, making diagonal cuts ½ inch (1 cm) apart, cutting just halfway through the thickness of the abalone. On the other side of the abalone, make cuts ½ inch (1 cm) apart, perpendicular to the diagonal cuts. Crush the ginger to yield ¼ teaspoon juice.

2. In a bowl, mix together the cucumber, bamboo shoots, carrot, rice wine, ginger juice, salt, (MSG), and half of the scallion.

3. Dip the abalone briefly into boiling water; remove, drain, and squeeze dry.

4. Heat the oil in a wok over an intense flame. When hot, add the remaining scallion, the abalone, and the bamboo shoot mixture and stir-fry for about 15 seconds. Sprinkle the mixture with chicken fat, transfer to a platter, and serve.

Scallops and Egg Whites
Furong ganbei　芙蓉干贝

Dried scallops are steamed until they can be crumbled. Then they are prepared in a soup and poured over a bowl of flavored steamed egg whites.

3 tablespoons chopped peeled fresh ginger

¼ lb. (125 g) steamed dried scallops

6 egg whites

1½ cups (375 ml) clear duck and chicken stock

2 teaspoons rice wine

¼ teaspoon salt

(½ teaspoon MSG)

4 teaspoons cornstarch paste

1 tablespoon melted chicken fat

1. Crush the ginger to yield 2 teaspoons juice. After steaming the dried scallops in a bowl with 1 cup (250 ml) water for 1½ hours over an intense flame, remove the scallops and reserve the water in the bowl. Using your fingers, crumble the scallops into small pieces. Return the crumbled pieces to the water in the bowl.

2. In a serving bowl combine the egg whites with 1 cup (250 ml) duck and chicken stock, 1 teaspoon rice wine, 1 teaspoon ginger juice, and half of the salt. Steam over a low flame for 10 minutes.

3. Meanwhile, heat the remaining duck and chicken stock in a wok over a medium flame until hot. Remove the scallops from the water and add to the stock, along with the remaining salt, rice wine, ginger juice, (and the MSG). Bring the stock to boiling, and skim off the froth. Add the cornstarch paste and stir until thickened; sprinkle with the melted chicken fat. Pour over the bowl of prepared egg whites and serve.

Scallops with Two-Colored Eggs
Ganbei yuanyangdan 干贝鸳鸯蛋

This picturesque dish combines two-toned eggs and pancake rolls stuffed with a savory prawn, chicken, and pork mixture; it is served with a scallop-flavored sauce. The green and white eggs are made by steaming egg whites (half dyed green, half undyed) in egg shells; after the eggs have become firm the shells are removed. The cooked eggs are especially light since they consist of the whites alone.

2 oz. (50 g) steamed dried scallops

2 oz. (2 tablespoons/50 g) chicken breast

2 oz. (2 tablespoons/50 g) pork fat

2 shelled prawns (¾ oz./ 25 g each)

8 to 10 rape leaves

3 soaked dried black mushrooms, stemmed

12 eggs

1 cup (250 ml) cold consommé

¾ teaspoon salt

(¾ teaspoon MSG)

2½ cups (500 g) rice, cooked

5 teaspoons peanut oil

1 sweet red pepper, sliced

¼ teaspoon ground black pepper

1 tablespoon cornstarch paste

1 tablespoon melted chicken fat

1. After steaming the dried scallops for 30 minutes, drain and shred them. Mince the chicken breast and pork fat. Shell, devein, and mince the prawns. Chop the rape leaves. Slice the soaked mushrooms.

2. Carefully poke a small hole in the large end of each egg. Trim the edge with a scissors to make the eggshell look like a cup. Separate the yolk from the white and place in two bowls. Wash the shells and dry them.

3. Pour ½ cup of the cold consommé into the egg whites. Add half the salt (and half the MSG). Divide the egg white mixture between 2 bowls. Wrap the chopped

rape leaves in a piece of cheesecloth or gauze and squeeze the green juice into one of the bowls of egg white; mix well.

4. Mound the cooked rice over a plate and set the eggshells upright in it. Spoon the white egg whites into the shells, filling them halfway. Reserve a small amount of the whites. Place the plate in a steamer and steam over a low flame for 30 minutes.

5. Fill the upper half of each eggshell with the green egg-white mixture. Steam for 20 minutes. Remove eggs and cool in cold water; then remove the shells and place the two-colored eggs in a

bowl. Discard the rice.

6. Beat the egg yolks until well mixed and pour into a lightly oiled, heated wok; swirl the mixture in the wok to make a thin pancake, about 8 to 10 inches in diameter. In a bowl, mix the minced chicken, pork fat, and prawns with ⅛ teaspoon salt, (⅛ teaspoon MSG), and a little of the reserved white egg white. Spread this paste onto the egg pancake and roll up. Cut the roll into ½-inch-wide (1.25-cm) sections.

7. Rub a little peanut oil on the inside of a bowl to coat lightly. Place the pancake rolls in the middle of the bowl with the mushroom slices

around them. Steam over high heat for 5 minutes. Invert the bowl on a plate. Arrange slices of red pepper over the rolls as a garnish. Place the two-colored eggs around the rolls. Steam again until the eggs are hot.

8. Place the wok over an intense flame. Pour the remaining cup of consommé into it and add the remaining ¼ teaspoon salt, (¼ teaspoon MSG), and the shredded scallops. Bring the soup to boiling and sprinkle the ground pepper over it. Stir in the cornstarch paste; sprinkle with the chicken fat. Pour over the rolls and eggs and serve.

1. Crack small hole in larger end of egg; trim edge; pour out yolk and white.

2. Set eggshells in bed of cooked rice.

3. Fill shells halfway with white egg whites, then to top with green egg whites.

4. Carefully remove shells from cooked eggs.

Scallop Balls Hydrangea
Xiuqiu ganbei 绣球干贝

This dish is named after the showy white or pastel flowers of the hydrangea bush. Here, the "flowers" are formed from a fish and egg-white mixture rolled in finely shredded scallops and decorated with chopped rape leaves and ham.

The scallop balls are served with hearts of rape and a white sauce. The fish mixture may not make compact balls at first, but the shredded scallops will help them hold their shape, and steaming firms them up.

7 oz. (200 g) soaked dried scallops

1 oz. (30 g) soaked dried black mushrooms (about 2 mushrooms)

½ lb. (250 g) white-fleshed fish fillets

2 medium egg whites

1½ teaspoons salt

(½ teaspoon MSG)

5 teaspoons melted lard

1½ teaspoons rice wine

2 tablespoons chopped rape leaves

1½ teaspoons rice wine

2 tablespoons chopped rape leaves

1½ teaspoons minced cooked ham

8 hearts of rape

1 cup (250 ml) clear chicken stock

2 teaspoons cornstarch, dissolved in 1 tablespoon water

3 teaspoons melted chicken fat

1. After soaking the dried scallops in cold water for 1 hour, steam them in a steamer over an intense flame for 1 hour. Remove the scallops from the steamer and let cool, then shred into fine threads. Slice the soaked mushrooms into thin strips. Mash the fish fillets thoroughly.

2. Beat the egg whites until frothy, then beat in half the salt, (one third the MSG), the melted lard, 1 teaspoon rice wine, and the mashed fish.

3. Reserve 2 tablespoons of this mixture. Form the rest into small balls, about ¾ inch (2 cm) in diameter. Roll the balls evenly in the shredded scallops. Place mushroom strips in crosses on each ball, then spread some of the reserved fish batter on each ball to hold the mushroom strips in place. Sprinkle with the chopped rape leaves and the minced ham. Steam the balls over an intense flame for 5 minutes.

4. Boil the hearts of rape until tender. Place the rape hearts in the center of a platter and arrange the fish balls around them.

5. Bring the stock to boiling in a wok or pot, then add the remaining salt, (MSG), and rice wine. Add the dissolved cornstarch and stir to combine. Pour this sauce over the fish balls, sprinkle with the chicken fat, and serve.

Squid With Sizzling Rice
Guoba youyu　锅巴鱿鱼

The dried squid and dried bamboo shoots have very distinctive flavors and textures. After soaking, they are combined in a peppery-hot, ginger-spicy sauce, which is poured over crisp rice crusts as soon as the crusts are fried. This produces a characteristic—and justifiably famous—sizzling sound, indicating that the dish has attained the proper texture. Glutinous rice should be used to make the rice crusts; other kinds will not properly form crusts or hold together when fried.

Raw squid, rice crusts, scallions, and other ingredients.

2½ cups (1⅛ lb./550 g) cooked glutinous rice (short grain rice)

8 oz. (250 g) soaked dried squid

1 teaspoon baking soda

⅓ cup (75 ml) melted lard

10 dried chili peppers, soaked and sliced

1¾ oz. (50 g) soaked dried bamboo shoots, sliced

2 scallions, sliced

1½ tablespoons sliced peeled fresh ginger

2 cloves garlic, sliced

2½ cups (625 ml) clear stock

1 tablespoon sugar

2 teaspoons salt

5 teaspoons vinegar

1 tablespoon soy sauce

2 teaspoons rice wine

Pinch of ground black pepper

(Pinch of Gourmet Powder)

⅓ cup (75 g) cornstarch, dissolved in ⅓ cup water

2½ cups (625 ml) vegetable oil

1. Stir ½ cup water into the cooked rice until it becomes sticky. Spread the rice in a baking dish and press it into a layer ¾-inch (1.75-cm) deep. Bake in a moderate oven (300 F / 150 C degrees) for 10 hours. Remove and break the layer into small pieces.

2. Cut the soaked dried squid into 1¼-inch (3-cm) slices. In a bowl, cover the slices with water and stir in the baking soda; let stand 3 hours.

3. Drain the squid and fill the bowl with boiling water. Tightly cover the bowl and let stand for 1 hour. Pour out the water. Rinse the squid twice with boiling water, drain, and set aside.

4. Heat the lard in a wok over an intense flame. Add the chili peppers, bamboo shoot slices, scallions, ginger, and garlic, and stir-fry for 15 seconds. Stir in the clear stock, sugar, salt, vinegar, soy sauce, rice wine, pepper, (and Gourmet Powder). Heat to boiling and add the squid slices. Stir in the dissolved cornstarch until the stock thickens; keep warm over a low flame.

5. Heat the vegetable oil in a separate wok over an intense flame until it smokes. Add the pieces of rice crust and stir until they turn golden brown, about 1 minute, then quickly scoop them out onto a platter. Pour the squid sauce over the hot rice crusts, at the table, and serve immediately.

Litchi Squid
Lizhi youyu 荔枝鱿鱼

This exquisite dish combines pieces of squid, pork, black mushrooms, and red and green peppers, all cut into the same shape and served in a full-flavored sauce.

The squid pieces are scored in a close crisscross pattern so that when they are fried, they curl up into round pieces that resemble litchi nuts.

7 oz. (200 g) soaked dried squid

2 tablespoons baking soda

1¾ oz. (50 g) lean pork

½ cup (2½ oz. / 75 g) winter bamboo shoots

4 dried black mushrooms, 1 inch (2.5 cm) in diameter, soaked and stems removed

¼ large sweet green pepper (¾ oz. / 25 g)

¼ large sweet red pepper (¾ oz. / 25 g)

2 cups (500 ml) peanut oil

4 cloves garlic, sliced

1 tablespoon chopped scallion

1 tablespoon rice wine

1 tablespoon soy sauce

(⅓ teaspoon MSG)

½ teaspoon ground black pepper

2 teaspoons cornstarch paste

¼ cup (50 ml) clear stock

1. Soak the squid in water for 30 minutes; drain and cut into 1¼-inch (3-cm) wide strips. Score the strips ¼ inch (0.5 cm) apart, and two thirds of the way through, in a crisscross pattern. Then cut the strips into 1⅜-inch (3.5-cm) long pieces in a diamond shape as shown in the photograph.

2. In a medium-size bowl, dissolve the baking soda in enough water to cover the squid. Add the squid pieces and let stand 1 hour. Drain the pieces, then rinse them; set aside.

3. Cut the pork, bamboo shoots, mushrooms, and peppers into diamond pieces a little smaller than the squid pieces.

4. Heat all but 2½ tablespoons of the peanut oil in a wok over an intense flame until it is moderately hot. Fry the pork for 30 seconds; scoop out, drain, and set aside. Fry the bamboo shoots, mushrooms, and green and red peppers for 30 seconds, then scoop out and drain. Heat the oil until it is quite hot, then stir-fry the squid pieces. When each piece rolls up into a small ball resembling a litchi nut, remove it from the oil

with a strainer and drain. Drain off all but 2½ tablespoons of the oil.

5. Heat the oil in the wok over an intense flame. First stir-fry the garlic and scallions. Add the squid, peppers, mushrooms, and bamboo shoots; stir. Add the rice wine, soy sauce, (MSG), and ground black pepper and stir for 10 seconds. Mix the cornstarch paste with the clear stock and pour it into the wok; stir until the sauce thickens. Remove to a platter and serve.

Fried Squid Rolls
Youbao youyujuan 油爆鱿鱼卷

This Shandong dish of squid cut to resemble barley ears is served with a flavorful and richly aromatic sauce. Scoring, then boiling makes the squid curl into the desired shape; deep frying, followed by stir-frying tenderizes the squid. Sichuan peppercorns and garlic give the dish a tantalizing aroma.

10 oz. (300 g) soaked dried squid

3 medium (about 1 inch in diameter) dried black mushrooms, soaked

4 cups (1 L) vegetable oil

1 teaspoon Sichuan peppercorns

2 scallions, sliced

6 medium cloves garlic, sliced

1 -inch section of unpeeled cucumber, sliced

1 teaspoon salt

(1 teaspoon MSG)

½ teaspoon sugar

¼ cup (60 ml) clear chicken stock

2 tablespoons cornstarch paste

4 teaspoons rice wine

½ teaspoon rice wine vinegar

1. After soaking them for at least 30 minutes, drain the squid. Score in a crisscross pattern, making cuts ¼ inch apart, almost, but not quite, through the squid. Then cut the squid into 2-by-1¼-inch pieces. Remove and discard the stems from the mushrooms; slice the mushrooms.

2. Heat 1 tablespoon vegetable oil in a wok over an intense flame until very hot. Add the peppercorns and cook for about 15 seconds. Set aside.

3. Combine the scallions, garlic, cucumber, black mushrooms, salt, (MSG), sugar, chicken stock, cornstarch paste, rice wine, and vinegar in a bowl; set aside.

4. Heat 4 cups (1 L) water to boiling in a pot. Drop the squid into the boiling water and remove when the strips curl up and the scored patterns become distinct, about 5 seconds.

5. Heat the remaining vegetable oil in a wok over a medium flame. When the oil is very hot, add the squid strips and stir-fry them for 3 to 4 minutes, then scoop out.

6. Empty the wok of all but 2½ tablespoons of oil, return it to a medium flame, and add the peppercorn sauce. When the sauce is very hot, return the squid to the wok and toss the wok several times. Add the seasoning mixture, toss the wok several times, then transfer mixture to a platter and serve.

Braised Soft-Shelled Turtle
Hongshao qunzhao 红烧裙爪

This variation is prepared Hunan-style, which accounts for the ham and the use of lard rather than oil. The famous smoked hams of Hunan are similar to smoked Smithfield hams. In China, food freshness is so important that the price of vegetables drops even one day after they are harvested. Since turtles are no exception to this freshness rule, they must be butchered just before cooking. Follow the instructions in the recipe for "Steamed Turtle with Chicken Feet" or have your Chinese butcher do the job for you.

1 soft-shelled turtle
(4 lb./2 kg)

2½ tablespoons rice wine

2 sections scallion
(each 2 inches/5 cm)

2 tablespoons sliced
ginger root

2 peeled cloves of garlic (one chopped)

½ cup (1¾ oz./50 gm) dried soaked black mushroom caps

¼ cup cooked sliced ham

½ tablespoon ground pepper

(½ tablespoon MSG)

Pinch of salt

2½ tablespoons melted lard

2½ tablespoons peanut oil

2 tablespoons soy sauce

½ cup (125 ml) clear stock (see recipe following Ingredients Guide)

1 tablespoon cornstarch paste

2½ tablespoons sesame oil

2 carved red radishes, for garnish

1. After the turtle has been butchered and the blood drained, immerse it in boiling water. Bring the water back to boiling and remove the turtle from the water. Scrape away the coarse skin and black mucous membrane on the muscle along the edges.
2. Replace the turtle into the boiling water and cook it for 5 minutes. Remove the shell and viscera, and cut off its muscle meat, slicing it into 1½-inch (3.5-cm) squares. Cut off the feet, and cut each into two pieces. Plunge them in boiling water briefly to eliminate any remaining odor.
3. Remove the bones and put them, together with the meat, into a big bowl. Mix in the rice wine, scallion, ginger root, one whole garlic, black mushroom, ham, half the pepper, (half the MSG), salt, and melted lard. Steam over high heat until the meat and feet are very tender, about 30 minutes. Discard the scallion pieces, ginger root, and garlic.
4. Heat the peanut oil in a wok. Add the chopped garlic, soy sauce, (remaining MSG), and pepper. Then add the steamed turtle's meat and feet, ham, black mushroom, and consommé. Bring them all to a boil over a low flame. Add the cornstarch solution and stir. Sprinkle with sesame oil and serve with carved radish garnish.

Stir-Fried Shredded Chicken and Jellyfish
Chao jisi zhepi 炒鸡丝蜇皮

The drama of this unusual dish is the soft and tender-textured chicken contrasted with the chewy, crunchy texture of the jellyfish. The jellyfish has almost no taste of its own and requires spirited, vigorous chewing. Even so, it is a great favorite because it is thought to help keep the bones of the elderly from becoming brittle.

- ½ lb. (250 g) dried jellyfish
- 7 oz. (200 g) chicken breast meat
- 1 egg white
- 1½ tablespoons cornstarch paste
- 3 cups (750 ml) peanut oil
- 1 scallion, shredded
- 1 teaspoon rice wine
- Pinch of salt
- 1-inch (2.5 cm) section peeled fresh ginger, minced
- (5 teaspoons MSG)
- 1 tablespoon sesame oil

In the Chinese restaurant kitchen the volume is larger and the action hotter. Here a master chef in Beijing drops the chicken, scallions and jellyfish into a little oil in a very hot wok for the final, fast stir-fry before serving. Note the single-handled wok and the large stock pot.

1. Soak the dried jellyfish in water for 3 to 4 hours and rinse. Plunge into boiling water, remove immediately and drain. Cut the jellyfish and the chicken breast into very thin slivers. Squeeze the ginger in a twist of fine-mesh cheesecloth, or a garlic press, into a bowl. Pour two teaspoons of water into the squeezed pulp and squeeze it again.

2. Beat the egg white and combine with the cornstarch paste to make a batter. Dip the chicken strips in the batter and turn to coat well.

3. Heat the peanut oil in a wok over an intense flame. When the oil is moderately hot, add the chicken, stirring gently with chopsticks to prevent chicken strips from sticking together. When the chicken threads begin to separate from each other in the oil, lift them out gently with a strainer-spoon and set aside to drain.

4. Ladle all but 2 to 3 tablespoons of the oil from the wok. Heat the remaining oil over an intense flame and add the scallions, jellyfish, and chicken. Add the rice wine, salt, ginger juice, (MSG), and stir quickly 2 or 3 times. Sprinkle with the sesame oil, transfer to a platter, and serve.

"Cross-the-Bridge" Noodles
Guoqiao mian   过 桥 面

This delicious Yunnan soup has a story behind its name. In ancient times, a rich man's son repeatedly failed to pass his imperial examinations. The father became anxious and ordered his son to stay in the back garden and study. The garden cottage and backyard were surrounded by water and connected to the house by a small bridge. The rich man prohibited his son from crossing the bridge to the main house and told the cook to bring the son his meals.

Since the cottage was far from the kitchen, the cook came up with a clever idea to keep the soup hot in cold weather. He carried cold noodles and thinly sliced chicken, fish, and prawns on a platter, along with a bowl of hot chicken broth covered with a layer of chicken fat that insulated it. Before the cook served the young student he would pour the broth over the noodles and other ingredients, cooking the chicken, fish, and prawns instantly.

Both the rich man and his son were satisfied, and soup prepared in this way came to be known as "Cross-the-Bridge" Noodles. (If you prefer the ingredients more thoroughly cooked, place the soup over a high flame for 10 seconds after you have assembled the dish.)

2 cups (220 g) flour
3 eggs, beaten
2 oz. (60 g) chicken, sliced very thin
2 oz. (60 g) white-fleshed fish, sliced very thin
2 oz. (60 g) prawns, sliced very thin

½ teaspoon rice wine
½ teaspoon minced peeled fresh ginger
Dash of soy sauce
(¼ teaspoon MSG)
1 oz. (30 g) rape leaves, parboiled

7½ cups (1.9 L) clear chicken stock
¼ teaspoon salt
⅓ cup (85 ml) melted chicken fat

1. Add the eggs to the flour in a large bowl and mix just to combine. Turn out onto a lightly floured surface and knead for several minutes to make a dough. Let rest for 15 minutes. Roll the dough out into a very thin sheet, then cut into fine noodles.

2. Combine the chicken, fish, and prawn slices in a medium-size bowl; add the rice wine, ginger, soy sauce, (and a pinch of the MSG). Set aside.

3. Cook the noodles in boiling water for 15 seconds. Drain thoroughly and put in a large bowl; garnish with the parboiled rape leaves. Set aside.

4. Heat the chicken stock to boiling. Add the salt, (remaining MSG), and chicken fat, and stir quickly. Pour the mixture into a soup bowl. The thin layer of fat retains the heat; if the surrounding temperature were cold, the fat would harden, keeping the soup hot, as in the story.

5. Add the chicken and seafood mixture to the soup while the soup is still *very* hot. Add the noodles and rape leaves, stir with chopsticks, and serve.

Sizzling Rice
Taohuafan 桃花泛

This famous Zhejiang dish is crisp and has a sweet and sour flavor.

It is said that about one hundred years ago, a high court official would spend all of his evenings watching operas and feasting. He demanded that he never be served the same dish twice. One evening he dozed off while watching a performance. The cook meanwhile was frantically trying to think of something new to serve the official. In desperation he took the leftover rice crust at the bottom of the pan and deep fried it; he then made a bowl of shrimp sauce. The cook brought this to the official and quickly poured the sauce over the rice. The official was awakened by the sizzling sound. He started to eat, then praised the cook for the delicious new dish.

Glutinous rice (short grain rice) should be used in this dish; other kinds of rice won't form rice cakes when baked, and will not hold together when deep fried.

5 cups (1½ lb./750 g) cooked glutinous rice (short grain rice)

8 oz. (250 g) shrimp, shelled and deveined

1 teaspoon cornstarch

4 cups (1 L) vegetable oil

¼ cup (2 oz./60 g) diced pineapple

2 teaspoons minced peeled fresh ginger

2 to 3 (1 oz./30 g) litchi nuts, diced

¼ cup (50 ml) tomato sauce

3 tablespoons sugar

⅓ teaspoon salt

(⅓ teaspoon MSG)

1½ teaspoons rice wine

¾ cup (150 ml) clear chicken stock

1 teaspoon cornstarch, dissolved in 1 teaspoon water

1. Stir ¾ cup (200 ml) water into the cooked rice until it becomes sticky. Spread the rice in a baking dish and press it into a layer ¾ inch (2 cm) deep. Bake in a moderate oven (300 F/150 C degrees) for 10 hours. Remove and break the crust into small pieces.

2. Roll the shrimp in the dry cornstarch to coat. Heat 2½ tablespoons oil in a wok over an intense flame. Add the shrimp and stir-fry until the shrimp turn opaque, about 4 minutes; remove and drain.

3. In the same wok over a medium flame fry the pineapple, ginger, and litchi nuts together, then stir in the tomato sauce, sugar, salt, (MSG), rice wine, and chicken stock; heat to boiling. Stir in the shrimp and the dissolved cornstarch and lower the heat to keep the mixture warm.

4. Pour the remaining oil into a separate wok and place over an intense flame. When very hot, add the rice pieces and deep fry until they swell and turn a light yellow, about 30 seconds. Remove from oil and drain.

5. Transfer the rice pieces to a platter and arrange them in a mound. At the table, quickly pour the shrimp sauce over the hot rice. It will sizzle and steam.

1. Break baked rice into pieces.

2. Ladle pieces of rice into wok.

3. Pour shrimp sauce over rice pieces.

Fried Five-Shred Rolls
Zha wusitong 炸五丝筒

1 teaspoon yeast

1¼ cups (140 g) flour

3 cups (750 g) peanut oil

2½ teaspoons minced scallion

1 teaspoon minced peeled fresh ginger

1¾ oz. (50 g) bamboo shoots, shredded

¾ oz. (25 g) soaked dried black fungus, shredded

1 small carrot (¾ oz./25 g), shredded

¾ oz. (25 g) pork, shredded

2 teaspoons soy sauce

2 teaspoons rice wine

½ teaspoon salt

(2 teaspoons MSG)

1 -inch section (¾ oz./25 g) cucumber, shredded

2 teaspoons sesame oil

5 egg wrappers (see recipe that follows)

½ teaspoon baking soda

2 teaspoons prickly ash (see recipe following Ingredients Guide)

Egg Wrappers

4 eggs

2½ tablespoons cornstarch paste

Egg wrappers (pancakes) are cut into triangles and stuffed with five shredded ingredients—bamboo shoots, black fungus, carrot, cucumber, and pork. The triangles are then rolled up, dipped in a yeast batter, and deep fried. The yeast batter seals the rolled triangles so the stuffing doesn't come out during frying (from which they emerge crisp and tender). They are delicious with wine.

Editor's Note:
To make the egg wrappers, first beat the eggs with the cornstarch paste. Heat a wok over a medium flame until hot. Spoon one fifth of the egg mixture into the wok while tilting it, to form a thin, even layer about 8 inches (20 cm) in diameter. (This thin layer will stick to the pan). Turn the wok over and cook the pancake on the other side for about 10 seconds, drying it so it will come out easily. Remove the pancake from the wok. Repeat with the remaining egg mixture to make five pancakes in all.

1. Dissolve the yeast in ½ cup (125 ml) very warm water, then stir in ¼ cup (30 g) flour until smooth. Let this batter rise for 30 minutes, then stir in ¾ cup (185 ml) water until smooth. Add the remaining flour and mix thoroughly. Cover the dough and set aside in a warm spot to let the yeast work.

2. Heat 2½ tablespoons peanut oil in a wok over an intense flame. Add the scallion and ginger; stir for a few seconds. Add the bamboo shoots, black fungus, carrot, pork, soy sauce, rice wine, salt, (and MSG). Stir briefly, then remove to a bowl. Stir in the cucumber and sesame oil.

3. Cut each egg wrapper into a triangle. Place one fifth of this mixture in the center of each triangle; roll up from the wide end to the point.

4. Heat the remaining peanut oil in a wok over a medium flame until hot. Stir the baking soda into the raised yeast dough to eliminate the sour taste. Dip the stuffed rolls into the dough, then lower into the hot oil with a strainer. Deep fry, turning several times, until golden, (about 3 minutes). Remove and drain. Serve along with a bowl of prickly ash for dipping.

1. Place five-shred mixture on pancake triangle; roll up.

2. Deep fry rolls in hot oil until golden.

Fried Toast
Zha tusi 炸土司

A mixture of prawns, fish, and pork fat is spread onto pieces of bread and deep-fried. Serve these plump, golden nuggets with two dips. One is prickly ash (crushed peppercorns dry-heated until brown and mixed with an equal amount of salt). The other is plain tomato sauce.

7 oz. (200 g) white bread, 1½ inches (3.5 cm) in diameter and ¼ inch (0.7 cm) thick

3¼ oz. (100 g) prawns

3¼ oz. (100 g) white-fleshed fish fillets

3¼ oz. (100 g) pork fat

4 egg whites

5 teaspoons cornstarch paste

3 teaspoons salt

(Pinch of MSG)

Pinch of ground black pepper

1 scallion, chopped

4 cups (1 L) peanut oil

5 teaspoons sesame oil

¼ cup (60 ml) tomato sauce

2 tablespoons prickly ash (See recipe following Ingredients Guide)

1. Cut the bread into rounds 1½ inch (3.5 cm) across and ¼ inch (0.7 cm) thick. Shell the prawns and mash with the back of a cleaver. Mash the fish fillets and pork fat. In a large bowl, combine the egg whites with the cornstarch paste. Mix in the salt, (MSG), ground pepper, and scallion; stir in the mashed prawns, fish, and pork fat. Form this mixture into balls 1¼ inch (3 cm) in diameter; place one ball on each round of bread and press down lightly.
2. Heat the peanut oil in a wok over a medium flame. When the oil is moderately hot, adjust heat to a low flame and gently slide the mixture-laden bread slices into the wok, garnished side up. (Keep the oil just moderately hot; if it gets hotter, remove the bread rounds from the flame for a moment.)
3. Fry until the balls of seafood mixture plump up and turn golden, about 5 minutes. Drain, remove to a serving platter, and sprinkle with sesame oil. Serve accompanied by small bowls of tomato sauce and prickly ash.

1. Some of the ingredients: prawns, fish, pork fat, bread, eggs.

2. Form fish batter into balls; place on bread rounds.

3. Fry them in moderately hot oil until they plump up.

196　Starches

Pork Tenderloin Dumplings
Hebao liji　荷包里脊

This dish must be prepared with care; it is a very decorative and tasty pouch-shaped delight. The pancakes should be stuffed as they are made, while they are still warm. They are very fragile, so they must be handled gently. Substitute romaine lettuce if rape leaves are not available.

8 oz. (250 g) rape leaves

1¾ oz. (50 g) pork tenderloin, minced

1⅓ oz. (40 g) soaked dried black mushrooms (about 5, each 1 inch / 2.5 cm in diameter), minced

2 tablespoons minced soaked dried bamboo shoots

1 teaspoon rice wine

½ teaspoon salt

(Pinch of MSG)

1½ teaspoons cornstarch, dissolved in 1 tablespoon water

4 eggs

2 cups (500 ml) peanut oil

5 teaspoons flour, mixed to a paste with 1 tablespoon water

1 tablespoon minced ham

½ cucumber, for garnish

1. Mince enough rape or romaine lettuce leaves to fill 1 tablespoon; shred the remaining leaves and set aside for garnish.

2. In a bowl mix the pork with the mushrooms, bamboo shoots, rice wine, half the salt, (and the MSG). In a separate bowl, beat the eggs.

Combine the remaining salt with the dissolved cornstarch and stir into the eggs.

3. Brush a little of the oil on the inside of a wok and heat over a low flame. Pour a tablespoonful of the egg mixture into the wok; then tilt the wok to make a round, thin crepe about 3 inches (8 cm) in diameter. Make 30 crepes in this way. Make a pouch with each crepe by placing a little of the pork mixture in the center of each one, then fold the edges over the mixture. Press the stuffing toward the middle with chopsticks, crimping together the outer

edges; spread some of the flour paste over the crimped edges of each pouch and some in the middle of the plumped-up surface. Sprinkle the minced ham and minced rape or lettuce leaves on the paste. Repeat to make about 30 dumplings.

4. Heat the remaining oil in the wok over a medium flame until warm. Fry the dumplings in the oil for 3 minutes. Arrange on a platter, garnish with thinly-cut spirals of unpeeled cucumber, the reserved shredded rape or romaine lettuce leaves, and serve.

Fried Rolls in the Shape of Buddha's Hand
Zha foshoujuan   炸佛手卷

This is a delightful, delicate appetizer of crêpe-thin egg pancakes made in a wok. Before frying they are cut in half and moistened along one side with a flour-paste. Then they are stuffed with a mixture of minced pork, scallions and ginger, then rolled up, sealed and sliced part-way in to make fingers. When deep-fried these stuffed rolls puff up with steam and look like little pudgy hands.

½ lb. (250 g) lean pork, minced

1½ scallions, minced

4 teaspoons minced peeled fresh ginger

(Pinch of MSG)

Pinch of salt

1½ teaspoons sesame oil

1 teaspoon rice wine

2½ teaspoons cornstarch dissolved in 4 teaspoons water

3 eggs, beaten

1½ teaspoons cornstarch

2 cups (500 ml) peanut oil

1 tablespoon flour

1. In a medium-size bowl, combine the pork, scallions, ginger, (pinch of MSG), pinch of salt, sesame oil, and rice wine. Add to this mixture the dissolved cornstarch, mix well, and set aside.

2. In a large bowl, mix the beaten eggs with 2 teaspoons water, the dry cornstarch, and another pinch of salt. Brush a small amount of the peanut oil over the bottom and sides of the wok to coat and heat over a medium flame. When the oil is hot, pour in half the egg mixture and quickly swirl the wok so that the egg coats the bottom and sides, form-ing a round, thin layer about 9 inches (22.5 cm) in diameter. Cook just until the egg is set, about 10 seconds. Invert the wok for just a few seconds, so that the flame can lightly toast the top of the egg pancake. Gently loosen the pancake from the sides and bottom of the wok and turn out onto a plate. Repeat the process with the second half of the egg mix-ture. Cut each pancake in half.

3. Mix the flour with enough water to make a thin paste. Spread the paste around the rounded edge of each pan-cake half, then spread a small amount of the pork mixture over each. Starting with the straight edge, roll up each pancake half into a cylinder about 1½ inches (3.5 cm) in diameter. Make four slits, crosswise, on each cylinder (being careful not to cut through), creating five sec-tions that resemble five stubby fingers.

4. Heat the remaining peanut oil in a wok over a medium flame until hot. Fry the egg rolls until they puff up and turn a golden brown. Scoop out, drain, and serve on a platter.

Braised "Shark's Fin" in White Sauce
Baipa yuchi　　　　　白扒鱼翅

For this vegetarian dish, bamboo shoots and red and green peppers are cut to resemble sharks' fins and teeth. They are steamed with a rich mixture of three different kinds of mushrooms and served with a white sauce. As with all vegetarian dishes developed to enliven the meatless cuisine of Buddhist monks, there is no flesh of a living creature in this dish.

3¼ oz. (100 g) soaked dried black mushrooms

1½ oz. (50 g) soaked dried mushrooms

1½ oz. (50 g) soaked dried morels

12 oz. (375 g) whole bamboo shoots

½ (2 oz./50 g) sweet red pepper

½ (2 oz./50 g) sweet green pepper

2 cups (500 ml) peanut oil

⅓ cup (85 ml) sesame oil

1 teaspoon minced peeled fresh ginger

1¼ cups (315 ml) White Soup (see recipe following Ingredients Guide)

1 tablespoon soy sauce

1½ teaspoons sugar

2 teaspoons rice wine

(1 tablespoon MSG)

Pinch of salt

1 tablespoon cornstarch paste

1. After soaking the black mushrooms, mushrooms, and morels, rinse them with cold water; remove and discard stems. Cut each mushroom in half.

2. Cut all but one bamboo shoot into pieces 2½ inches (6.5 cm) long, 1½ inches (3 cm) wide, and ¼ inch (0.5 cm) thick. Make 20 horizontal slashes one third of the way up each bamboo shoot, producing a feathery effect (as shown in the photographs). These are the "sharks' fins." Take the remaining bamboo shoot and cut it vertically into three 3-inch-long (7-cm), ¾-inch-wide (2-cm) strips.

Using the same method, cut horizontal slashes on both sides of each of the 3 strips, forming the sharks' "teeth."

3. Cut the red and green pepper into strips the size of the bamboo shoot "teeth."

4. Heat the peanut oil in a wok over a medium flame until warm. Add the bamboo shoot "sharks' fins" and deep fry until they have turned pale yellow, about 30 seconds. Drain the fins; arrange alternately with the green and red peppers and the bamboo shoot sharks' teeth in a heatproof bowl coated with a little sesame oil.

5. Heat ¼ cup (60 ml) sesame oil in a wok over an intense flame until hot. Add the ginger and stir-fry. When you can smell the gingery aroma add the black mushrooms, mushrooms, and morels and stir-fry for a few seconds. Reduce heat to a low flame; pour in ½ cup (125 ml) White Soup, the soy sauce, 1 teaspoon sugar, (a pinch of MSG), and 1 teaspoon rice wine. Simmer until most of the liquid has evaporated, about 4 minutes.

6. Transfer the mushroom mixture to the center of the bowl of sharks' fins. Put the bowl in a steamer and steam over an intense flame for 15 minutes. Remove the bowl from the steamer and flip it over into a shallow serving platter.

7. Heat a wok over a medium flame. Add the remaining White Soup, sugar, rice wine, (the remaining MSG), and the salt. When this mixture comes to a boil, add the cornstarch paste. Sprinkle with the remaining sesame oil, pour over the "sharks' fins," and serve.

1. Cut bamboo shoots into long pieces, then make slashes for a feathering effect.

2. Arrange deep fried "sharks' fins" around bowl.

3. Place mushrooms and morel mixture in center of bowl.

4. Steam "sharks' fins" and mushrooms for 15 minutes.

5. Flip bowl over onto serving platter.

Eight Treasure "Whole Duck"
Babao zhengya   八宝整鸭

As with other vegetarian dishes, this one is made to look like a very non-vegetarian entrée. Bean curd sheet is softened and wrapped around a hearty stuffing and molded to resemble a duck. The "duck's" head is formed from a piece of yam, a mushroom, and a pea; its tongue from a sliver of carrot.

2 cups (500 ml) peanut oil

1 dried bean curd sheet

½ cup (3¼ oz. / 100 g) glutinous rice

½ cup (3¼ oz. / 100 g) lotus seeds, shelled and washed

5 oz. (150 g) Chinese yam

1¾ oz. (50 g) soaked dried bamboo shoots

5 soaked dried black mushrooms (each 1 inch / 2.5 cm in diameter)

1¾ oz. (50 g) deep-fried gluten with seasonings added

5 fresh mushrooms

½ cup (125 ml) sesame oil

3 tablespoons minced ginger

¼ cup (¾ oz. / 25 g) fresh peas

1 cup (250 ml) White Soup (see recipe following Ingredients Guide)

3 tablespoons soy sauce

Pinch of salt

(2 teaspoons MSG)

3 tablespoons cornstarch paste

Sliver of carrot

½ teaspoon sugar

1. Heat the peanut oil in a wok over an intense flame until hot. Add the bean curd sheet and deep-fry for 30 seconds, being careful not to tear it. Remove to a bowl of warm water and soak until it is soft, about 3 minutes. Using chopsticks, transfer to a plate.
2. Wash the rice and place in a bowl; add ⅔ cup water. Place the bowl in a steamer. Put lotus seeds in a separate bowl and place in the steamer. Place the yam in the steamer. Steam these ingredients over high heat for 30 minutes. (Use a two-tier steamer, or steam one ingredient after another.) Peel the steamed yam; set aside a piece big enough for the "duck's" head; mash the rest.
3. Cut the bamboo shoots, black mushrooms, deep-fried gluten, and four of the mushrooms into cubes. Heat ⅓ cup (85 ml) sesame oil in a wok over a high flame. Add these cubes, half the minced ginger, and all but one of the peas. Stir-fry for a few seconds. Pour in ⅓ cup (85 ml) White Soup, 5 teaspoons soy sauce, the salt, (and 1 teaspoon MSG), and cook over an intense flame for 2 minutes. Add 1 tablespoon cornstarch paste, toss, and transfer to a plate. Mix the rice, lotus seeds, and the mashed yam.
4. On the plate, form this mixture into the shape of a duck, using the piece of yam reserved for the head. Wrap it carefully with the bean curd sheet. Make a slit in the "duck's bill" and insert the carrot sliver, making the "tongue." Use the remaining mushroom and pea to make the eye. Steam this "duck" over an intense flame for 10 minutes.
5. Heat half of the remaining sesame oil in a wok over an intense flame. Add the remaining ginger, and stir-fry for a few seconds. Pour in the remaining White Soup, soy sauce, (MSG), and the sugar, and heat to boiling. Add the remaining cornstarch paste and stir until thickened. Pour this sauce over the "duck," sprinkle with the remaining sesame oil, and serve.

"Chicken Liver" Rolls
Liu jiganjuan 熘鸡肝卷

3¼ oz. (100 g) soaked dried black mushrooms (about 10, each 1 inch (2.5 cm) in diameter)

3¼ oz. (100 g) soaked dried mushrooms

3¼ oz. (100 g) canned mushrooms

5 sheets dried bean curd

¾ cup (250 ml) sesame oil

½ teaspoon minced peeled fresh ginger

1 cup (200 ml) White Soup (see recipe following Ingredients Guide)

⅓ cup (85 ml) soy sauce

4 teaspoons sugar

2 teaspoons rice wine

(1 tablespoon MSG)

2 tablespoons cornstarch paste

2 eggs

2½ tablespoons flour

2 cups (500 ml) peanut oil

½ sweet green pepper, cut into thin strips

½ sweet red pepper, cut into thin strips

These "chicken liver" rolls are stuffed with three different kinds of mushrooms and served in a sauce flavored with sesame oil, red and green peppers, and fresh ginger. This tasty vegetarian dish is fun to make and eat.

1. After soaking both kinds of dried mushrooms, rinse with cold water; remove stems. Set aside 2 whole black mushrooms; finely chop the remaining soaked mushrooms. Finely chop the canned mushrooms. Mix the dried and canned mushrooms; set aside.

2. Cover the dried bean curd sheets with a very wet towel for 15 minutes; cut them into twenty 3-inch (8-cm) squares.

3. Heat ½ cup (125 ml) sesame oil in a wok over an intense flame. Add ¼ teaspoon minced ginger and stir-fry for a few seconds. Pour in ¾ cup (200 ml) White Soup, ¼ cup (60 ml) soy sauce, 1 tablespoon sugar, 1 teaspoon rice wine (and 2 teaspoons MSG); cook for

5 minutes. When the mixture thickens, add 2 teaspoons cornstarch paste, stir, and pour into a bowl.

4. Place a little of the mushroom mixture on each piece of bean curd sheet. Fold each square, pinching the edges, and form a roll 1¾ inches (4 cm) long and ⅓ inch (1 cm) in diameter.

5. Break the eggs into a bowl, add the flour and 1 tablespoon cornstarch paste, and mix.

6. Heat the peanut oil in the wok over a medium flame until hot. Dip the bean curd "chicken liver" rolls into the egg batter, one by one, holding with chopsticks to keep them from unrolling. Gently lower them into the oil

and deep fry until golden brown, about 2 minutes. Scoop out, drain, and place on a platter. Pour out the peanut oil.

7. Cut the remaining black mushrooms into thin strips. Heat ⅓ cup (85 ml) sesame oil in the wok over an intense flame until hot. Add the remaining ginger and stir. Add the mushroom and pepper strips and stir-fry for a few seconds. Then pour in the remaining White Soup, soy sauce, sugar, rice wine, (and MSG). When this mixture boils, add the remaining cornstarch paste. Drop in the rolls and immediately toss the wok. Sprinkle the rolls with the remaining sesame oil and serve.

"Croaker" in Hot Sauce
Ganshao huangyu 干烧黄鱼

This fishless, vegetarian creation is shaped to resemble a croaker, a yellowish, saltwater fish that makes a kind of grunting noise. The skin is a sheet of dried soybean milk. This yellowish, almost translucent material is soaked to soften it, then wrapped around a mixture of mashed potato, mushrooms, peas, and bamboo shoots. A flour and cornstarch batter helps hold the "fish" together when it is deep fried in very hot oil. If the bean curd sculpture does not emerge from the wok looking like a fish, cut it into pieces and arrange them on the serving platter in the proper shape before pouring the sweet and hot sauce over it.

1 medium potato
(3¼ oz./100 g)

2½ oz. (75 g) bamboo shoots

1¾ oz. (50 g) soaked dried mushrooms

2½ oz. (75 g) soaked dried black mushrooms

5 oz. (150 ml) sesame oil

1 teaspoon minced peeled fresh ginger

¼ cup (¾ oz./25 g) fresh peas

5 oz. (150 ml) White Soup

½ cup (110 g) sugar

5 teaspoons soy sauce

(5 teaspoons MSG)

5 teaspoons cornstarch paste

3½ tablespoons flour

5 teaspoons cornstarch

1 sheet dried bean curd

2 cups (500 ml) peanut oil

1 tablespoon hot thick broad bean sauce

1 teaspoon rice wine

¾ oz. (25 g) cubed sweet red pepper

¾ oz. (25 g) cubed sweet green pepper

1. Peel the potato, cut in quarters, and steam until almost cooked. Mash in a large bowl. Mince two thirds of the bamboo shoots, mushrooms, and black mushrooms; cut the rest into cubes.

2. Heat one third of the sesame oil in a wok over an intense flame. Add ½ teaspoon ginger and stir for a few seconds. Add the minced bamboo shoots, mushrooms, black mushrooms, and the peas and stir-fry for a few seconds.

3. Pour in ½ cup (125 ml) White Soup, ⅓ cup (75 g) sugar, 3 teaspoons soy sauce, (and a pinch of MSG); stir to combine and cook for 2 minutes. Add the cornstarch paste and toss the wok; transfer the mixture to the bowl with the mashed potato and mix well.

4. In another bowl, mix together the flour and dry cornstarch with enough cold water to form a batter. Cover the bean curd with a very wet towel until the curd is soft, 10 to 15 minutes. Spread on a board, spoon the potato and mushroom stuffing in the center, and fold it up into the shape of a fish. Make a little flour paste to secure the edges.

5. Heat the peanut oil in a wok over an intense flame until very hot. Brush the "fish" with the batter, gently lower into the wok, and deep fry until golden brown, 3 to 4 minutes. Remove the "fish" and drain. Place on a serving platter whole, or cut into pieces and arrange in the shape of a fish.

6. Heat one half of the remaining sesame oil in a wok over an intense flame. Add the remaining ginger and the broad bean sauce and stir-fry for a few seconds. Add the cubed bamboo shoots, mushrooms, and black mushrooms, the remaining sugar and soy sauce, the rice wine, (and remaining MSG) and stir for a few seconds. Lower the heat to a low flame, pour in the remaining White Soup, and simmer until thickened, 2 to 3 minutes. Add the red and green peppers and stir-fry for a few seconds more. Sprinkle with the remaining sesame oil, pour the sauce over the "fish," and serve.

Dry-Fried Bamboo Shoots
Ganshao dongsun 干烧冬笋

This is a good recipe on which to practice proper timing and gauging levels of heat in deep frying and stir frying. Watch the color and crisp texture closely. Lowering the flame allows the bamboo shoots to cook through; raising it again turns them golden. Pickled mustard greens are a cabbage-like vegetable sold in bulk, soaked in brine, in Chinese shops; or in one pint (500 ml) jars and cans. Substitute sauerkraut if the Chinese pickled greens are not available.

¼ lb. (125 g) pickled mustard greens

1½ lb. (750 g) bamboo shoots

3 cups (750 ml) peanut oil

¼ teaspoon salt

(½ teaspoon MSG)

1. Soak the mustard greens in water for 5 minutes to remove the salty taste. Drain, rinse, squeeze dry in a towel, and cut into 1-inch (2.5-cm) pieces. Dice the bamboo shoots.

2. Heat the oil in a wok over an intense flame. When hot, add the greens and fry for 30 seconds. Scoop them from the wok, drain, and set aside.

3. Add the bamboo shoots and fry for 2 minutes. Lower the heat to a low flame and fry for 3 minutes, then increase to an intense flame and fry the bamboo shoots until they turn golden, about 3 minutes more. Add the mustard greens and fry with the bamboo shoots for 5 minutes, stirring two or three times.

4. Drain the bamboo shoots and greens in a strainer. Ladle the hot oil from the wok. Return the bamboo and greens to the empty, but still oily wok, and place it over an intense flame. Add the salt (and MSG) while you toss the wok for about 10 seconds. Transfer to a platter and serve. This is a perfect dish to make and serve in cold weather.

Assorted Vegetables Ji
Sushijin 素什锦

A variety of vegetables and stir-fried nuts make up this glossy and theatrical vegetable dish. Its taste is fresh and a touch sweet. Its texture must be crisp. Prepare all ingredients and put them in containers you can reach easily from the stove before you start step 3. Lightning-fast stir-frying over very high flame is the secret to retaining the fresh, crisp texture of the ingredients.

We (the Chinese) eat food for its texture, the elastic or crisp effect it has on our teeth, as well as for fragrance, flavor and color.
Lin Yutang

⅓ cup (1¾ cup / 50 g) shelled walnuts

1¾ oz. (50 g) soaked dried black mushrooms
(6 each 1-inch / 2.5 cm in diameter)

1 soaked bean curd roll (1¾ oz. / 50 g)

1¾ oz. (50 g) cucumber

1¾ oz. (50 g) canned mushrooms, drained

1¾ oz. (50 g) canned water chestnuts, drained

1¾ oz. (50 g) shelled hyacinth beans

½ cup coarsely chopped red and green peppers (1¾ oz. / 50 g)

1¾ oz. (50 g) bamboo shoots, thinly sliced

¼ cup plus 1 tablespoon (75 g) vegetable oil

⅓ cup (1¾ oz. / 50 g) shelled peanuts

2 teaspoons rice wine

½ teaspoon salt

(Pinch of MSG)

Pinch of powdered ginger

2 teaspoons sesame oil

1. Soak the walnuts in hot water for 20 minutes; remove skins. Remove and discard black mushroom stems; cut the mushrooms into sections. Cut the bean curd roll into 1¼-inch (3-cm) sections (about 10 sections). Slice the cucumber and cut into rhomboid shapes. Cut each canned mushroom and water chestnut in half. Pull the string on the hyacinth bean pod and discard.

2. Add the peppers, black mushrooms, bamboo shoots, bean curd roll pieces, and hyacinth beans to a pot of boiling water; scoop out after 30 seconds and drain.

3. Add the vegetable oil to a wok placed over an intense flame. When the oil is hot, add the peanuts and all of the prepared ingredients. You will hear a loud crackle. Immediately add the wine, salt, (MSG), and ginger powder and stir-fry for 30 seconds. Sprinkle on the sesame oil and toss the wok a few times to mix. Slide the mixture onto a platter and serve.

Fried Bamboo Shoots
Ganbian dongsun 干煸冬笋

This easy-to-prepare dish is made with bamboo shoots and pork. Scallions add a bright color and lively flavor. Stir-frying in lard gives this dish its distinction. Substituting vegetable oil will change both the flavor and texture.

3 cups (750 ml) vegetable oil

1 lb. (500 g) bamboo shoots, cut into 2½-inch slices

½ cup (125 ml) melted lard

4½ oz. (140 g) lean pork, chopped into small pieces

Pinch of salt

1 tablespoon soy sauce

2 teaspoons rice wine

½ teaspoon sugar
(Pinch of Gourmet Powder)

2 tablespoons chopped preserved cabbage

2 scallions, chopped

1½ teaspoons sesame oil

There is a popular saying that a woman and her husband should be compatible. The 'Book of Etiquette' by Li Chi, also said that one is judged by the company one keeps. Cookery is no different. Food cooked must need something to go along with it. Clear should go with clear, thick with thick, hard with hard, and soft with soft. Only then would there be a perfect blending.

Yüan Mei

Some of the ingredients: scallions, bamboo shoots, preserved cabbage, and pork.

1. Heat the vegetable oil in a wok over an intense flame until hot. Add the bamboo shoots and stir-fry until they turn golden brown, about 5 minutes. Remove from the oil; drain and set aside.

2. Heat ⅓ cup (85 ml) lard in a wok over an intense flame until hot. Add the pork and stir-fry for 15 seconds. Add the salt, soy sauce, rice wine, sugar, (and Gourmet Powder) and continue to stir-fry for 15 seconds more.

3. Stir in the fried bamboo shoots and preserved cabbage. Add the scallions, sprinkle with the sesame oil and remaining lard and toss the wok. Remove to a platter and serve piping hot.

Braised Asparagus
Pa caixin longxu 扒菜心龙须

This colorful and delicious dish is made with asparagus and rape hearts braised in a sauce flavored with ginger, scallion, chicken and duck stock, and chicken fat.

1 lb. (500 g) rape hearts
(about 2½ lb. / 1.25 kg rape)

3 tablespoons peanut oil

1 scallion, minced

1 teaspoon minced peeled
fresh ginger

2 teaspoons rice wine

(½ teaspoon MSG)

¼ teaspoon salt

¾ cup (200 ml) clear chicken
and duck stock

6 asparagus spears
(5 oz. / 150 g)

2 teaspoons cornstarch paste

3 tablespoons melted chicken
fat

1. After removing the roots and tough outside ribs of the rape, dip the rape hearts into boiling water, remove, and transfer immediately to cold water. Remove from cold water, drain, and pat dry, squeezing out any excess water.

2. Heat the peanut oil in a wok over an intense flame. When hot, add the scallion and ginger and stir-fry for about 5 seconds. Add the rice wine, (MSG), salt, and chicken and duck stock. When the stock is hot, add the asparagus and rape hearts and continue to heat over an intense flame to boiling.

3. Reduce the flame and let simmer until the asparagus is tender, but still crisp, about 3 minutes. Stir in the cornstarch paste until the sauce thickens. Sprinkle with the chicken fat, transfer to a platter, and serve.

Mrs. Pockmark's Bean Curd
Mapo doufu　麻婆豆腐

This popular and delicious Sichuan homestyle dish is named for the woman who originated it. It is made with two complementary peppers: hot pepper and Sichuan peppercorn powder. The first makes the dish quite "hot," the second cools it down; the bean curd helps to absorb some of the bite. The thick broad-bean sauce which is sold in bottles is the kind made in Sichuan's Pi County. Careful control of the cooking temperature is important to the success of this dish.

1 lb. (500 g) bean curd

⅔ cup (170 g) vegetable oil

5 oz. (150 g) lean beef, chopped

2 teaspoons rice wine

2 teaspoons chopped peeled fresh ginger

2½ tablespoons thick broad-bean sauce

2¾ tablespoons hot pepper powder

2 teaspoons salt

5 teaspoons soy sauce

(Pinch of Gourmet Powder)

1¼ cup (315 ml) clear chicken stock

4 scallions, coarsely chopped

5 teaspoons cornstarch, dissolved in 5 teaspoons water

½ teaspoon Sichuan peppercorn powder

1. Cut the bean curd into ½-inch (1.25-cm) cubes, plunge them into boiling water, remove immediately and drain.
2. Heat the oil in a wok over an intense flame. Add the beef and stir-fry for about 30 seconds. Add the rice wine, ginger, and bean sauce and stir-fry until the oil turns a reddish-brown color, about 1 minute. Add the hot pepper powder and stir-fry until beef gives off a pungent aroma.
3. Add the bean curd, salt, soy sauce, (Gourmet Powder), and chicken stock and bring to a boil. Reduce flame to low and simmer until most of the liquid has been absorbed by the bean curd, about 4 minutes. (Be careful not to let curd dry out too much.) Add the scallion and dissolved cornstarch and continue to simmer briefly, just until sauce has thickened. Sprinkle with the Sichuan peppercorn powder, transfer to a platter, and serve.

1. Cut bean curd into ½-inch (1.25-cm) cubes.

2. Add dissolved cornstarch; stir until sauce is thickened.

Silkworm Cocoon Bean Curd
Canjian doufu 蚕茧豆腐

A stuffing of shrimp is enclosed in a "cocoon" of bean curd. The cocoons are deep fried and served with a simple sauce made with clear stock.

8 oz. (250 g) shrimp
1 lb. (500 g) bean curd, mashed and drained
1 egg
¼ teaspoon salt
(¼ teaspoon Gourmet Powder)

2½ tablespoons sesame oil
Pinch of shredded peeled fresh ginger
4 cups (1 L) peanut oil
1½ tablespoons clear stock
½ teaspoon rice wine
1 teaspoon cornstarch paste

A man should not eat so much that his breath smells more of meat than of rice.   Confucius

1. Shell the shrimp; remove the heads and tails. Devein and chop.

2. Mix the bean curd with the egg, a pinch of salt, (and a pinch of Gourmet Powder). Form into patties 1½ inches (4 cm) in diameter and ⅓ inch (1 cm) thick.

3. Mix the shrimp with 1 tablespoon sesame oil, the ginger, a pinch of salt, (and a pinch of Gourmet Powder). Place a bit of this mixture into the center of each bean curd patty. Folding the patty around the mixture, shape it into the form of a silkworm cocoon.

4. Heat the peanut oil in a wok over a medium flame. When hot, deep fry the "cocoons" until brown, about 5 minutes. Drain and place on a serving platter.

5. Pour the clear stock and rice wine into a wok with the remaining sesame oil. Add the remaining salt (and Gourmet Powder); stir to mix. Heat over a medium flame to boiling. Add the cornstarch paste and stir until thickened. Pour over the "cocoons" and serve.

1. *Some of the ingredients: bean curd and chopped shrimp.*

2. *Place shrimp mixture in centers of bean curd patties.*

3. *Deep fry "cocoons" until brown.*

Fried Bamboo Shoots, Mushrooms and Preserved Cabbage

Shao sandong 烧 三 冬

This vegetable dish offers the contrast of three distinct flavors and textures. The bamboo shoots are pale and slightly crunchy; the mushrooms are soft, dark, and earthy-tasting; and the preserved cabbage is green, tender, and pleasantly acidic.

½ lb. (250 g) bamboo shoots

10 soaked dried black mushrooms (each 1 inch / 2.5 cm in diameter)

2 oz. (60 g) preserved cabbage

2 cups (500 ml) vegetable oil

Pinch of minced peeled fresh ginger

¼ cup (60 ml) clear chicken stock

1 tablespoon soy sauce

1 tablespoon rice wine

5 teaspoons sugar

(1 teaspoon Gourmet Powder)

2 teaspoons cornstarch, dissolved in 2 teaspoons water

4 teaspoons sesame oil

1. Cut the bamboo shoots into 2-inch (5-cm) "rolling knife" pieces. Remove and discard the mushroom stems and cut caps into ½-inch (1-cm) slices. Wash and drain the preserved cabbage; cut into ¾-inch (2-cm) slices.

2. Heat the vegetable oil in a wok over a medium flame. Add the bamboo shoots and mushroom slices and stir-fry for 1 minute. Remove the vegetables from the oil and drain.

3. Empty the wok of all but 3 tablespoons oil and heat over a medium flame. Add the cabbage, ginger, bamboo shoots, mushrooms, chicken stock, soy sauce, rice wine, sugar, (and Gourmet Powder) and stir to combine.

4. Cook until most of the liquid has evaporated, then stir in the dissolved cornstarch to make a thin sauce. Transfer to a serving platter, sprinkle with the sesame oil, and serve.

Golden Coin Black Mushrooms
Jinqian xianggu 金钱香菇

Soaked dried black mushrooms are simmered in chicken stock and filled with a mixture of chicken and water chestnuts. They are decorated with egg, mushroom strips, ham, and threadlike moss, then steamed and served with a sauce made from chicken stock.

24 (10 oz./315 g) soaked dried black mushrooms

2½ cups (625 ml) clear chicken stock

2 tablespoons rice wine

2 teaspoons salt

1 tablespoon cornstarch

7 oz. (220 g) chicken breast, chopped and mashed

(½ teaspoon MSG)

1 tablespoon melted chicken fat

1 egg white, beaten

3 water chestnuts, mashed

1 egg, beaten

Dash of vegetable oil

3 tablespoons minced ham

2 tablespoons threadlike moss, soaked and cleaned

14 cooked fresh green peas

1½ teaspoons cornstarch, dissolved in 1 tablespoon water

1. Plunge the soaked mushrooms into boiling water; remove immediately. Repeat the process; drain and squeeze out excess water from the mushrooms by pressing them gently with the flat side of a cleaver. Slice 10 of the mushrooms into 1½-by-¼-inch (4 x 0.5-cm) strips. Set aside. Trim the edges of the remaining 14 mushrooms to form rounds 1¾ inches (4 cm) in diameter.

2. In a wok, combine 1¼ cups (315 ml) of the clear stock, 2 teaspoons rice wine, ¾ teaspoon salt, and the mushroom rounds. Simmer over a low flame for 5 min-

utes. Pour off the liquid and discard; remove the mushrooms, drain, and squeeze out excess liquid. Place the mushroom rounds on a plate and dust with the dry cornstarch.

3. In a medium-size bowl, combine the mashed chicken, a few tablespoons of the chicken stock, 2 teaspoons of the rice wine, ¾ teaspoon salt, (pinch of MSG), and 2 teaspoons of the chicken fat. Add the egg white and the water chestnuts and mix well.

4. In a separate bowl, combine the whole beaten egg, 1 teaspoon rice wine, and ¼ teaspoon salt. Brush the

bottom and sides of the wok with vegetable oil and heat over a medium flame. When hot, add the egg mixture, quickly swirling the wok so that the egg coats the bottom and sides of the wok forming a round thin pancake about 9 inches (22.5 cm) in diameter. Cook just until egg is set, about 10 seconds. Turn the pancake out onto a plate and cut into 28 (1½ x ¼-inch/ 3.5 x 0.3-cm) strips.

5. Form the chicken mixture into small balls. Place one ball on top of each of the mushroom rounds. Arrange the egg and mushroom strips, parallel to each other, on top of the chicken mixture, mak-

ing each one look like an ancient coin. Sprinkle each "coin" with a small amount of ham and threadlike moss. Place a pea in the center of each. Steam over an intense flame for 2 minutes, then transfer coins to a serving platter.

6. In a small saucepan, heat the remaining chicken stock to boiling. Add the remaining rice wine, salt, (MSG), and the dissolved cornstarch and stir. Sprinkle the remaining chicken fat over the sauce, pour over the "golden coins," and serve.

Stewed Mushrooms in White Sauce
Pa baimo 扒白蘑

This vegetarian dish is very easy to prepare. The mushrooms are fried with ginger and briefly stewed in White Soup with bamboo shoots, red pepper, and cucumber.

1 lb. (500 g) soaked dried black mushrooms

½ cup (125 ml) sesame oil

1 teaspoon sliced peeled fresh ginger

1¼ cup (315 ml) White Soup (see recipe following Ingredients Guide)

2 teaspoons salt

1 teaspoon sugar

(Pinch of MSG)

3¼ oz. (100 g) bamboo shoots, cut into thin rectangular slices

3 -inch (7.5-cm) section (3¼ oz./100 g) unpeeled cucumber, cut into thin rectangular slices

½ sweet red pepper (1¾ oz./50 g), sliced

1 tablespoon cornstarch paste

1. After soaking the black mushrooms, rinse with cold water; remove stems.

2. Heat ⅓ cup (85 ml) sesame oil in a wok over an intense flame. Add the ginger and stir-fry for a few seconds. Reduce heat to a low flame; add the White Soup, mushrooms, salt, sugar, (and MSG) and simmer for 4 minutes. Add the bamboo shoots, cucumber, and red pepper and cook for 2 minutes. Add the cornstarch paste and toss the wok until the ingredients are well mixed. Sprinkle with the remaining sesame oil and serve.

Stuffed Mushrooms
Xianggu roubing 香菇肉饼

Mushrooms stuffed with pork, ginger, and dried shrimp are deep fried briefly and then stewed in a seasoned chicken stock.

1 bamboo shoot tip, about 4 inches long (2½ oz./75 g)

4 oz./100 g (about 10, each 1½ inches in diameter) soaked dried black mushrooms

1 tablespoon dried shrimp

6½ oz. (200 g) pork tenderloin, minced

2 medium egg whites

5 teaspoons soy sauce

¼ teaspoon salt

¼ teaspoon minced peeled fresh ginger

(½ teaspoon MSG)

½ teaspoon sugar

2 teaspoons rice wine

½ teaspoon cornstarch, dissolved in 1 teaspoon water

2 cups (500 ml) vegetable oil

1½ cups (375 ml) clear chicken stock

Cuisine is technique, art, culture, life, knowledge, and philosophy.

1. Cut the bamboo shoot tip in quarters lengthwise. Then slice each quarter lengthwise into thin slices.

2. After soaking the black mushrooms in hot water for 30 minutes, remove stems and squeeze out excess water. Soak the shrimp in hot water for 30 minutes; drain and chop.

3. Combine the pork, shrimp, egg whites, 2 teaspoons soy sauce, salt, ginger, (¼ teaspoon MSG), a pinch of sugar, 1 teaspoon rice wine, and ½ teaspoon dissolved cornstarch. Stuff the mushroom caps with this mixture.

4. Reserve ½ teaspoon oil; heat the remaining oil in a wok over an intense flame. Before the oil is quite hot, add the mushrooms, stuffed side up, several at a time. Fry for 1 minute, then remove the mushrooms carefully from the oil. (Do not fry for longer than 1 minute; the batter may come off.)

5. Arrange the stuffed mushrooms in a wok, placing the bamboo slices on top. Add the remaining soy sauce, rice wine, (MSG), sugar, and the chicken stock. Simmer, uncovered, over a low flame for 30 minutes. Increase the heat and cook until most of the sauce has evaporated, about 10 minutes more. Combine the reserved oil and the remaining dissolved cornstarch, dribble over the mushrooms, and serve.

Stuffed Black Mushrooms
Guota xiangguhe 锅熅香菇盒

Black mushrooms are stuffed with a chicken mixture, dipped in an egg batter, and deep fried. They are simmered in a clear, flavorful chicken stock, then served sprinkled with sesame oil.

3¼ oz. (100 g) chicken breast meat

12 soaked dried black mushrooms (5 oz. / 150 g)

1⅔ cups (400 ml) clear chicken stock

5 teaspoons rice wine

(½ teaspoon MSG)

2 eggs, separated

1¼ teaspoons salt

3 tablespoons cornstarch

4 cups (1 L) peanut oil

1 tablespoon peeled fresh ginger cut in strips

1 scallion, cut in strips

5 teaspoons sesame oil

1. Finely mince the chicken and pound with the back of a cleaver to mash well. Remove and discard the mushroom stems; place the caps in a large shallow bowl with 1 cup chicken stock, 2 teaspoons rice wine, (and a pinch of MSG). Steam for 1 hour. Drain the mushrooms, carefully squeezing out excess liquid; discard cooking liquid.

2. In a separate bowl, combine the chicken, egg whites, 2 teaspoons rice wine, (pinch of MSG), and 1 teaspoon salt; mix thoroughly. Stuff *each* mushroom cap with this mixture. Then put two filled mushroom caps together to form six "sandwiches" from the 12 caps.

3. Beat the egg yolks and stir in the cornstarch. Heat the peanut oil in a wok over an in-tense flame. Meanwhile, dip each mushroom sandwich into the egg batter. When the oil is hot, gently lower each sandwich, separately, into the wok and deep-fry until they puff up, about 3 minutes. Remove mushroom sandwiches and drain.

4. Empty the wok of all but 3 tablespoons of the oil. Reheat the oil over an intense flame until hot. Add the ginger and scallion and stir for 2 to 3 minutes. Add the fried mushrooms and the remaining chicken stock, rice wine, salt, (and MSG). Simmer over a low flame for 3 minutes. When most of the liquid has evaporated, transfer the mushrooms to a serving platter, sprinkle them with the sesame oil, and serve.

Braised Mushrooms
Xianmo suhui 鲜蘑素烩

Carrots and bamboo shoots are carved to look like mush-rooms and cooked with black and white mushrooms and threadlike moss in clear chicken stock. The ingredients are cooked and steamed individually, then combined to create a colorful, mild-flavored vegetable dish.

The principle of Chinese medicine is "harmonization" — a proper mixture of ingredients. The essence of Chinese cuisine is synthesis—the artistic view of the Chinese nation and its philosophy.

- 4 medium carrots (½ lb./250 g)
- 1 lb. (500 g) bamboo shoots
- 12 pieces (¾ oz./25 g) soaked white fungus
- 2 tablespoons (½ oz./15 g) threadlike moss
- 1 cup (250 ml) clear chicken stock
- 1 tablespoon salt
- (2 teaspoons MSG)
- 6½ oz. (200 g) canned mushrooms
- 1 tablespoon sugar
- 2½ tablespoons melted chicken fat
- 1 tablespoon cornstarch paste

1. Peel the carrots and cut into 4-inch lengths, then carve each piece to resemble a mushroom. Cut and carve the bamboo shoots into the same shape. Drain the soaked white fungus pieces. Soak the threadlike moss and rinse.

2. Dip the carrots and bam-boo shoots briefly into boiling water, then dip directly into cold water and drain.

3. Place the white fungus pieces in a small bowl, white side up. Add 5 teaspoons chicken stock and steam for 10 minutes.

4. Shape the threadlike moss into small balls and place on a plate. Sprinkle with ½ tea-spoon salt (and ½ teaspoon MSG) and steam for 10 minutes. Dip the mushrooms into boiling water, remove, and drain.

5. Heat the remaining chicken stock in a wok over a medium flame to boiling. Add the carrots, bamboo shoots, 1 teaspoon salt, 2 teaspoons sugar, (1 teaspoon MSG); and heat to boiling again; boil for 2 to 3 minutes.

6. Drain the steamed white fungus pieces and place in the center of a serving plat-ter. Remove the carrots and bamboo shoots from the chicken stock and arrange with the threadlike moss and mushrooms around the white fungus. Set the chicken stock aside.

7. Heat the chicken fat in a wok over a medium flame. Add the reserved chicken stock, remaining salt, (MSG), and sugar. Stir in the corn-starch paste and cook until the mixture thickens. Pour evenly over the vegetables, threadlike moss, and white fungus and serve.

White Fungi Peony Flowers
Mudan yiner　牡丹银耳

This dish is beautiful, exotic, and fairly easy to prepare. Peony flowers are formed from pieces of white fungus surrounding a chicken batter. They are sprinkled with a shredded egg pancake, steamed, and served with a chicken and duck sauce. The flowers are too large for most bamboo steamers, but you can improvise a steamer by placing a plate on top of a heatproof glass inside a large covered pot with enough water not to evaporate during the steaming process.

3½ oz. (110 g) soaked white fungus pieces (40 to 50 pieces)

1 small tomato

5 oz. (150 g) chicken breast

3 medium egg whites

⅓ cup (85 ml) plus 1 teaspoon peanut oil

1 egg, beaten

1½ cups (375 ml) clear chicken and duck stock

3 teaspoons salt

(2 teaspoons Gourmet Powder)

2 teaspoons cornstarch paste

¾ teaspoon chicken fat

½ unpeeled cucumber cut into decorative shapes, for garnish

1. After soaking the white fungus pieces for at least 15 minutes, drain well. Clean and remove the discolored portions. Divide the pieces into 6 equal parts and arrange them in a circle on a large plate to resemble 6 white peonies.

2. Cut out the stem end of the tomato. Without cutting all the way through, cut the tomato vertically (stem end up) in half. Scoop out and discard the pulp. Still being careful not to cut through the base of the tomato, make two more vertical cuts to make 6 equal petal-shape wedges.

Spread the wedges apart to resemble an open flower. Set aside.

3. Mince the chicken breast and mash with the flat side of a cleaver. Mix with the egg whites and ⅓ cup peanut oil. Spoon a little of this mixture into the center of each white fungus "flower."

4. Heat the remaining oil in a wok over a medium flame. Pour in the beaten egg and quickly swirl it over the bottom and sides of the wok to make a thin pancake. Cook just until dry, about 15 seconds, remove, and cut into fine shreds. Sprinkle the

shreds over the flowers.

5. Steam the flowers over an intense flame for 5 minutes. Remove from the steamer and place the tomato in the center of the plate.

6. Heat the chicken and duck stock in a wok and add the salt, (Gourmet Powder), and the cornstarch paste and stir until thickened. Pour the sauce over the "flowers" and the tomato, sprinkle with the chicken fat, garnish with the cucumber, and serve.

Stuffed White Fungi
Rang yiner 瓤银耳

Black mushrooms are stuffed with a mixture of prawns, fish, and pork fat; then topped with white fungi and steamed. They are served with a sauce made with clear chicken stock, and garnished with shredded rape leaves. Also known as *tremella*, white fungi (and mushrooms) hold the popular imagination because they are believed to enhance vitality and longevity.

1¾ oz. (50 g) soaked white fungi

3¼ oz. (100 g) shelled prawns

3¼ oz. (100 g) white-fleshed fish fillet

3¼ oz. (100 g) pork fat

2 egg whites

1½ teaspoons salt

(½ teaspoon MSG)

3 tablespoons sesame oil

1 teaspoon chopped peeled fresh ginger

1 teaspoon chopped scallion

5 oz. (150 g) soaked black mushrooms
(18 mushrooms, each 1 inch / 2.5 cm in diameter), stemmed

1⅔ cups (400 ml) clear chicken stock

Pinch of ground black pepper

4 teaspoons cornstarch paste, diluted with 4 teaspoons water

5 teaspoons melted chicken fat

Shredded rape leaves, for garnish

1. After soaking the white fungi in warm water for 2 hours, remove stems and discolored parts. Mash the prawns, fish, and pork fat with the back of a cleaver. Place in a large bowl with egg whites, 1 teaspoon salt, (¼ teaspoon MSG), 2 teaspoons sesame oil, the ginger, and the scallion.
2. In a pot over a medium flame, heat the black mushrooms, the remaining salt, (MSG), 4 teaspoons sesame oil, and ½ cup (125 ml) clear stock to boiling. Boil for 2 minutes to allow the mushrooms to absorb the flavors. Remove the mushrooms from the pot; pat dry. Squeeze the white fungi dry. Lay the black mushroom caps, open side up, on a heat-proof plate, stuff them with the fish mixture, and cover them with the white fungi. Steam over an intense flame for 10 minutes.
3. Heat a wok over an intense flame until hot; add the remaining sesame oil and stir-fry the rape leaves; remove and set aside for garnish. Clean the wok and add the remaining clear stock to the wok, over an intense flame. Add the ground pepper; heat to boiling. Stir in the diluted cornstarch paste until the sauce thickens; sprinkle with chicken fat, then pour over the stuffed white fungi. Garnish with the fried shredded rape leaves and serve.

Almond Float
Xingren doufu 杏仁豆腐

This sweet, light dessert is made with a soup of sugar-water in which float almond-flavored gelatin squares garnished with candied plums and hawthorne jelly. You can grind the almonds with a mortar and pestle or a nut grinder. The dessert soup is refreshing after a rich meal. It is also often served as an "intermission" course to clear the palate at banquets.

When the mouth is cleared, it tastes well. When the mind is clear, it thinks well.

Chuang-Tse

8 shelled almonds
  (½ oz. / 15 g)
1 bar (⅟₂₀ oz. / 1.5 g) agar-agar
1 teaspoon milk
¾ cup (150 g) sugar

⅓ oz. (10 g) hawthorne jelly (or crabapple jelly), cut into ½-inch (1-cm) rounds
6 (⅓ oz. / 10 g) candied plums, cut into ½-inch (1-cm) rounds

1. Soak the almonds in hot water for 10 minutes; remove the skins. Grind the almonds to a smooth, milky consistency. Add a few teaspoons of water, wrap tightly in fine-mesh cheesecloth, and squeeze out the juice; discard the almond pulp.
2. Heat the agar-agar in ¾ cup (200 ml) water until dissolved. Add the milk and almond juice, stir to blend well, and pour into a square pan. Chill until set. Cut the gelatin into ¾-inch (2-cm) squares.
3. Add the sugar to 2½ cups (625 ml) water and heat until the sugar dissolves. Chill in a bowl.
4. Add the almond gelatin squares, jelly, and candied plums to the chilled sugar water and serve.

Peanut Cream
Niunai huasheng lao 牛奶花生酪

This is a thick, sweet, cream-of-peanut soup. Unroasted, unsalted peanuts should be used. If raw peanuts are not available, use roasted, unsalted ones, and remove the skins before soaking the peanuts in the hot water. After frying, the peanuts can be ground with water, using a mortar and pestle or a blender.

9½ oz. (300 g) peanuts

1 tablespoon peanut oil

2 cups (500) milk

1 cup minus 1 tablespoon (6½ oz. / 200 g) sugar

3 tablespoons cornstarch, dissolved in 6 tablespoons water

1. Shell the peanuts. Cover the nuts with boiling water and let stand 3 to 5 minutes. Drain; remove the skins.

2. In a wok, fry the soaked peanuts in peanut oil for 1 to 2 minutes, then crush them. Measure the peanuts; add water to equal twice the measurement of the peanuts, a little bit at a time, and grind the mixture until smooth.

3. Heat the milk over a medium flame to boiling; remove from heat.

4. Wash the wok to remove the oil. Place over a medium flame and add the milk and the ground peanuts. Heat to a boil and stir in the sugar.

5. Add the dissolved cornstarch. When the mixture boils again, pour into bowls and serve.

Snow-White Walnut Dessert
Xuehua taoni   雪花桃泥

This delectable sweet is made from walnuts and a variety of candied fruits, all topped with egg white. Although its presentation is elaborate, it is simple to prepare, and well worth the effort. The Chinese olive has a sour taste that's piquant with the sweets. Use a new olive that has not been pickled.

8 oz. (250 g) leftover bread, cut into cubes

4 egg whites

¾ cup (200 ml) vegetable oil

1¾ oz. (50 g) coarsely chopped walnuts

¾ cup (200 ml) melted lard

1 cup (220 g) sugar

¾ oz. (25 g) candied squash, finely chopped

¾ oz. (25 g) candied tangerines, finely chopped

¾ oz. (25 g) candied dates, finely chopped

½ oz. (15 g) fresh Chinese green olive, finely chopped

½ oz. (15 g) crystallized rose petals, finely chopped

Some of the ingredients: bread; candied tangerines, squash, dates, and Chinese green olives; walnuts; and eggs.

1. Soak the bread cubes in cold water for 1 minute, squeeze out the water, and mash the bread. In a bowl, beat two egg whites until frothy; mix well with the mashed bread crumbs.

2. Heat the vegetable oil in a wok over a low flame until just warm, then add the walnuts. Stir-fry for 1 minute, drain, and chop fine. Beat the remaining egg whites until stiff but not dry.

3. Heat the lard in a wok over a medium flame until hot. Add the bread mixture and stir-fry until crisp, 3 to 5 minutes. Add the sugar, nuts, candied fruits, and rose petals, and stir-fry for 15 seconds. Drain off excess lard and slide the mixture onto a plate. Spoon the beaten egg whites over the mixture, garnish with candied fruits and serve immediately.

Hot Candied Apples
Basi pingguo 拔丝苹果

Candied apples are one of the most famous Chinese dessert dishes. Apple wedges (or wedges of any other firm fresh fruit) are coated with a cornstarch batter and deep fried. They are then coated with a sesame oil-based caramel and dipped in cold water, which results in a wickedly delicious confection that is crispy on the outside yet soft on the inside. The trick to achieving this contrast of textures is to make sure that the oil for deep frying is very hot and that you drain it off well afterward. Also, the sugar for the caramel must be well dissolved in bubbling hot sesame oil so that the mixture forms "strings" when drawn up with chopsticks. This recipe calls for three medium-size hard green apples; you can simply adjust the quantity of cornstarch paste for larger or smaller apples.

3 medium green apples (20 oz./625 g) of a crisp and slightly sour variety, peeled, cored, and wedged

½ cup (110 g) cornstarch

½ cup (110 g) cornstarch dissolved in ¼ cup (60 ml) water, plus more, as needed

3 tablespoons sesame oil, plus 1 teaspoon for brushing on platter

5 cups (1.25 L) vegetable oil

¼ cup (100 g) sugar

1. Roll the apple wedges in the dry cornstarch, then place in a bowl of the cornstarch paste; stir to coat them evenly.

2. Brush 1 teaspoon of the sesame oil on a large serving platter and warm the oiled platter. The oil will keep the apples from sticking when they are ready to serve.

3. Heat the vegetable oil in a wok. When the oil is *very* hot and smoking, drop the apple pieces in, one by one. When they crackle (indicating that the cornstarch coating is well fried and crisp), scoop them out with a strainer and drain them thoroughly.

4. Clean the wok and heat the remaining sesame oil over a medium flame. Add the sugar and stir, slowly at first and then quickly, until the mixture turns golden and bubbles. Lower the heat; when the bubbling has *completely* subsided, add the apples to the syrup. Toss the wok repeatedly, gripping both handles with pot holders and bouncing the sections around inside so that they pick up the syrup evenly on all sides, until each piece is thoroughly coated.

The hot candied fruit is served on a warmed oiled platter, along with bowls of cold water with ice cubes in it. The host will first explain how to eat the fruit, then will demonstrate by dipping a piece in the water and placing it on a guest plate.

To eat the candied apple wedges, first dip the tips of your chopsticks into the bowl of iced water. Then dip an apple wedge into the water; hold it under for at least five seconds if the apple is still very hot. The sugar coating will be brittle and will not stick to your teeth, and the steamy apple inside will be cool enough so that it will not burn your tongue. Eat all you want quickly, before the candied apples cool down.

Deep-Fried "Sparrow Heads"
Zha maquetou 炸麻雀头

To make this delectable dessert called "sparrow heads," bean curd sheets must first be soaked by covering with a wet towel since they are very brittle when dry. They are then cut into rhomboid shapes, filled with a sesame and candied osmanthus flower mixture, and rolled up. (If these flowers are unavailable, crystallized rose or violet petals may be substituted.) They are deep-fried in moderately hot oil; placing them individually in the oil with chopsticks and holding the rolls closed for a couple of seconds ensures that they hold their shape and remain closed.

3¼ oz. (100 g) sesame seeds

2 teaspoons candied, sweet-scented osmanthus flower

7 tablespoons sugar

2 sheets dried bean curd (round sheets about 13½ inches / 34 cm in diameter)

2 cups (500 ml) peanut oil

1. Heat a wok over a medium flame and add the sesame seeds; stir-fry until golden brown. Spread seeds on a wooden board; when they are cool, crush with a rolling pin and transfer to a bowl. Add the candied flowers and 5 tablespoons sugar and mix thoroughly.

2. Cover the bean curd sheets with a very wet towel until they become soft, 10 to 15 minutes. Cut into rhomboid pieces about 3½ inches (8.5 cm) on a side. Place a bit of the sweet sesame filling in the center of each piece, roll it up, and pinch together at the ends to make the "sparrow heads."

3. Heat the oil in the wok over a medium flame. When it is only moderately hot, slip in the "sparrow heads," one by one, holding them closed for several seconds with chopsticks. Deep-fry until golden brown, about 2 minutes. Scoop out and drain. Sprinkle with the remaining sugar and serve.

1. Some of the ingredients: dried bean curd sheets, sesame seeds, sugar, candied osmanthus flowers.

2. Crush stir-fried and cooled sesame seeds with rolling pin.

3. Roll up sesame and ginger filling in pieces of bean curd sheets to make "sparrow heads."

Honeyed "Gourds"
Mizhi hulu 密汁葫芦

Small balls of batter are deep fried until browned, then glazed in a mixture of sugar-water, honey, and fried sesame seeds. This dessert is said to have been made more than a hundred years ago by a Henan cook for the Empress Dowager Ci Xi, who had a sweet tooth. The key to its success is keeping the oil the right temperature during the deep frying process. Test-fry one dough-ball first. If it browns and rises to the surface in under five minutes, the oil is too hot; if it takes longer, it's not hot enough. Remember that as you add more dough-balls to the hot oil it will cool.

5 teaspoons sesame seeds
½ teaspoon yeast
5 oz. (150 g) flour
1 medium egg
3 tablespoons melted lard
6 cups (1.5 L) peanut oil
5 tablespoons sugar
5 teaspoons honey
  Sugar, for sprinkling

1. Some of the ingredients: eggs, honey, flour.

2. Add boiling water to flour; stir to form batter.

1. Heat a wok over a medium flame. When it is hot, add the sesame seeds, stirring constantly until golden. Remove seeds to a plate.

2. Dissolve the yeast in 2 tablespoons warm water. Stir in 1 tablespoon flour; cover and allow to rise.

3. Mix the remaining flour with 2 teaspoons of the risen dough. Stir in 1 cup (250 ml) boiling water, then the egg and lard; mix well. Shape the

3. Add egg and lard to batter; mix well.

4. Form batter into balls; deep fry in hot oil until they turn golden and rise to surface.

dough into small balls about 1 inch (2.5 cm) in diameter.

4. Heat the oil in a wok over an intense flame. When it is hot, drop in the balls of dough and deep fry them until they turn golden brown and rise, about five minutes; they should resemble gourds. Scoop the balls out with a slotted spoon and drain.

5. Pour off the oil and place the wok over a medium flame; add the sugar and 4 teaspoons water and stir slowly with a spatula until the sugar is dissolved. Stir in honey. Cook, stirring, until the syrup bubbles. Drop in the fried "gourds"; then, using the spatula, roll them in the syrup to coat well and sprinkle with the toasted sesame seeds. Transfer "gourds" to a serving plate, sprinkle with sugar, and serve piping hot.

Almond Tea

Guiyuan xingren cha 桂元杏仁茶

This hot, sweet infusion is made from almonds and rice ground fine then flavored with the juice of the longan fruit. Longan is a close relative of the litchi nut but the taste is not the same; and it looks different from its sibling litchi because it is dusted all over with a fine reddish-tan powder. Longan juice is sold in cans. Like most Chinese infusions, including teas, almond tea is considered a health-sustaining tonic.

1 cup (7 oz./200 g) whole shelled almonds

½ cup (1¾ oz./50 g) uncooked rice

1¾ cups (14 oz./400 g) sugar

¼ cup (60 ml) longan juice

1. Soak the almonds in hot, boiled water to cover. Remove the brown skins. Chop them up and soak them again in cold water for about five minutes. Scoop them out with a strainer and discard the liquid. Rinse the rice and let it soak in cold water for about five minutes. Scoop it out with a strainer and discard the water.

2. Pour 2⅓ cups (600 ml) water in a mortar or blender. Add the rice and almonds. Grind or blend until puréed. Strain through a fine-mesh cheesecloth into a bowl, reserve the liquid and discard the residue.

3. Heat 1¾ cups (450 ml) water in a wok over a weak flame. As it warms, add the sugar and stir until it dissolves. Slowly pour in the liquid from the almond and rice mixture, stirring constantly to prevent it from burning. When it starts to simmer, keep the flame low enough so a froth does not form. Simmer very gently for a minute then pour it into a serving bowl. Pour the longan juice in two lines across the surface as shown in the photograph. Ladle it into a bowl for each guest.

Jade-Like Soup
Feicui geng 翡翠羹

For the Chinese, *yin* and *yang* represent the mutual complementarity of all forces in the universe. The *yin* is the dark, the moon, the quiescent, the female; *yang* is the light, the sun, the active, the male. The schematic picture of *yin* and *yang* is a circle with two interlocking, light and dark halves. Because the Chinese also believe that there is a little *yang* in all *yin* forces and vice versa, there·is a dot of egg in the dark, and a dot of cherry in the white.

Cornstarch helps the yin and yang sections of this soup remain separated when you bring it to the table. The green part has a fresh spinach base, the white part is made with chicken. When you stir it all together before eating, the soup will glisten like a bowl of jewels.

1 oz. (30 g) skinned and boned chicken breast meat

¼ lb. (125 g) fresh spinach leaves, washed, drained, and chopped

1 teaspoon rice wine

Pinch of sugar

Pinch of salt

(Pinch of MSG)

5 tablespoons (75 ml) vegetable oil

1¼ cups (300 ml) clear chicken stock

2 teaspoons cornstarch, dissolved in 2 tablespoons water

6 medium egg whites

¼ teaspoon minced peeled fresh ginger

½ red cherry, pitted

1 end slice of the white of a hard-boiled egg

1. Place an S-shaped piece of metal in the center of a serving bowl. (Such a flexible strip can be made easily by cutting a section out of a disposable aluminum foil pan.)

2. Mash the chicken meat with the flat side of a cleaver. Squeeze all excess water out of the spinach; the spinach should be as dry as possible. In a mixing bowl, combine the spinach with ½ teaspoon rice wine, a pinch each of sugar, salt, (and MSG); stir.

3. Heat 2 tablespoons oil in a wok over an intense flame. When it is moderately hot, add the spinach mixture and stir for 1 minute. Add ½ cup of the chicken stock and continue to stir until it comes to boiling. Stir in half of the dissolved cornstarch and cook, stirring, until the soup thickens. Pour the soup into one side of the divided serving bowl and cover to keep warm while the other half is being prepared.

4. In a bowl, combine the egg whites with the chicken, remaining rice wine, a pinch each of sugar, salt, (and MSG), the remaining cornstarch, and the ginger. Beat until the mixture is frothy. Stir in the remaining chicken stock.

5. Heat the remaining oil in a wok over an intense flame until moderately hot. Stir in the chicken mixture and continue to stir until the mixture becomes a thick white soup. Pour into the other side of the serving bowl and remove the metal strip. The two soups will retain their shapes because they are so thick. Garnish with the cherry half and the slice of egg, placing each as an eye on the "head" of the white and the green soups respectively. Stir the two soups together at the table just before serving, so that the glistening green soup mixes with the white.

Snow-White Chicken, Prawn, and Bamboo Shoot Soup

Sanxian ji douhua 三鲜鸡豆花

This famous Chinese soup—a combination of chicken, prawns, and bamboo shoots in a savory broth—has a topping of cooked egg whites that gives it the appearance of a snow-capped mountain. The thick egg-white layer also keeps the soup hot. You won't know it's a soup until you stir it! A sprinkling of minced ham and bits of rape leaf adds contrasting colors and makes the dish even more flavorful.

1 oz. (30 g) cooked chicken

1 oz. (30 g) prawns

1 oz. (30 g) winter bamboo shoots

5 medium egg whites

3 cups (750 ml) clear chicken stock

(2 teaspoons MSG)

2 teaspoons rice wine

½ teaspoon salt

1½ tablespoons chopped rape leaves

1 tablespoon minced cooked ham

1 tablespoon melted chicken fat

1. Chop the chicken into small cubes. Shell and devein the prawns, cut each in half lengthwise, and cut the halves into ½-inch (1-cm.) pieces. Cut the bamboo shoots into 1¼-by-½-by-⅛-inch (3-cm-by-1-cm-by-2-mm) pieces. Beat the egg whites until stiff.

2. Heat 2 cups (500 ml) water to boiling in a wok. Add the chicken, prawns, and bamboo shoots and cook for 1 minute. Scoop out, drain, and transfer to a soup tureen; discard the water.

3. Heat the chicken stock in a pot to boiling. Add the (MSG), rice wine, and salt.

4. Pour the egg whites into the hot stock and gently ladle the stock over the egg whites, which will be cooked instantly by the heat of the stock and will remain floating on top.

5. Pour the stock into the tureen with the chicken, prawns, and bamboo shoots. Sprinkle the chopped rape leaves, minced ham, and chicken fat over the top of the soup and serve.

"Do not try to gulp down soup with vegetables in it, nor add condiments to it. Do not keep picking the teeth, nor swill down the sauces. If a guest add condiments, the host will apologize for not having had the soup prepared better. If he swill down the sauces the host will apologize for his poverty."

Li Chi

Winter Melon Balls With Mushrooms
Pa xianmo dongguaqiu　　扒鲜蘑冬瓜球

This attractive and colorful dish is made with balls of green winter melon and white mushroom caps. They are braised together in a savory chicken and duck stock and served surrounded by halved cherry tomatoes.

½ teaspoon minced peeled fresh ginger

9½ oz. (300 g) winter melon, peeled

1⅔ cups (400 ml) chicken and duck stock

3 cherry tomatoes

7 oz. (200 g) fresh mushrooms (each 1 inch / 2.5 cm in diameter), washed and stemmed

Pinch of salt

(½ teaspoon Gourmet Powder)

½ teaspoon cornstarch, dissolved in 1 teaspoon water

1 teaspoon melted chicken fat

1. Mash the ginger and combine with ¼ teaspoon water. Scoop the winter melon into balls about 1 inch (2.5 cm) in diameter. Heat 1¼ cups (315 ml) stock to boiling. Add the winter melon balls and boil gently until they are a little more than half cooked, about 5 minutes. With a slotted spoon, remove the melon balls; discard the stock.

2. Peel the tomatoes and cut each in half. Arrange the halves around the edges of a shallow serving bowl.

3. Heat the remaining stock to boiling in a wok or pot. Add the mushroom caps and winter melon balls and simmer over a low flame for 3 minutes, stirring occasionally. Skim off froth from surface and stir in the ginger mixture, salt, (and Gourmet Powder). Add the cornstarch paste and stir until the liquid thickens. Sprinkle the chicken fat over the melon balls and mushrooms. Arrange in a pattern in the bowl (as shown in the photograph), pour the sauce over them, and serve.

White Fungi Wolfberry Soup
Gouqi yiner 枸杞银耳

White fungus, also called tremella and jelly fungus, is sold in dried form but has a jellylike consistency and appearance when cooked. Greenish-white wolfberries (related to the honeysuckle) turn red when cooked and make an attractive contrast to the glossy, cream-colored white fungus.

This soup is an imperial delicacy and is considered a tonic for the lungs and kidneys. During the Han Dynasty (206 B.C.–220 A.D.) it was made without wolfberries; these were added to the recipe during the Tang Dynasty (618–907 A.D.).

Chinese cuisine is unique in the world for its complicated technique and great variety.

Professor Wu Enyu

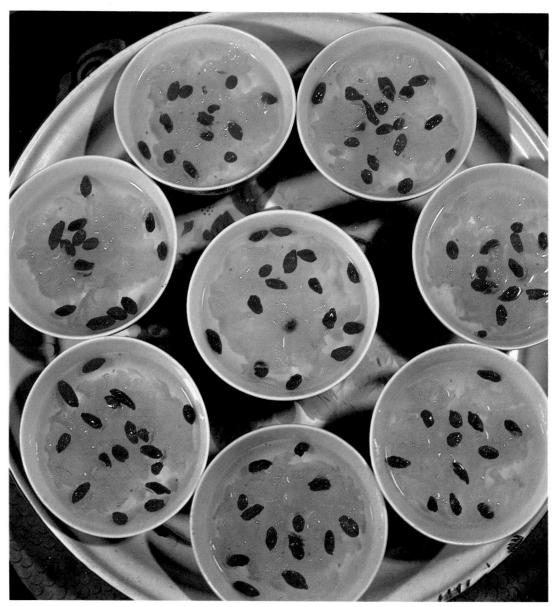

2 cups (½ oz. / 15 g) dried white fungus

⅙ oz. (5 g) wolfberries

5 oz. (150 g) crystal sugar

3 tablespoons granulated sugar

1 egg white, lightly beaten

1. Soak the dried fungus in warm water until softened, 30 to 60 minutes. Drain, then cover with cold water. Remove any hard parts and drain again. Rinse the wolfberries in cold water.
2. Boil 4 cups (1 L) water over a weak flame in a clay pot. Add the crystal sugar, granulated sugar, and egg white; stir to combine, then skim off the froth. When the liquid is clear, add the white fungus and wolfberries. Simmer, covered, over a weak flame for 1 to 1½ hours. Ladle into bowls and serve.

Dragon Well Bamboo Fungus Soup
Longjing zhusun tang 龙井竹荪汤

Bamboo or staghorn fungus is rare and extremely expensive, even in China. It is used in Buddhist vegetarian dishes made for special occasions. The fungus, delicately branched like the antlers of a deer, is gathered from bamboo plants in Sichuan Province. It is sold in small bags or in bulk. Substitute another light-colored fungus, such as white fungus, if necessary, but the taste of the dish will be quite different.

16 dried staghorn (bamboo) fungus

7 oz. (200 g) white-fleshed fish fillets

2 teaspoons salt

(1 teaspoon MSG)

2 teaspoons rice wine

2 teaspoons melted lard

2 egg whites

10 canned cherries

Threadlike moss and rape slices for garnish

1 tablespoon minced ham

5 cups (1.25 L) clear chicken stock

1. Soak the fungi for 48 hours until it is white. Cut off the bases and cut the large fungi in half.

2. Mash the fish fillets. In a bowl mix ½ teaspoon salt (½ teaspoon MSG), 1½ teaspoons rice wine, lard, and the egg whites. Mix in the mashed fish. Place the fungus on a plate and cover it with this batter, shaping each to resemble a fish. Form the eyes of the fish with the cherries, and their mouths with pieces of threadlike moss. Arrange the rape slices and minced ham in lines along the back of the "fish" (as shown in the photograph). Place the plate in a steamer and steam the "fish" for 4 minutes.

3. Place the steamed "fish" in a tureen. Heat the chicken stock to boiling in another pot. Add the remaining rice wine, (MSG), and salt. Pour this soup over the "fish" and serve.

White Fungi With Light Sauce
Qingtang yiner　清汤银耳

This flavorful dish is easy to prepare. The tender soaked and cooked white fungi contrast with the crisp, crunchy bean sprouts. Red cherries add another contrast in color and taste. The portions are very small, as this soup is meant to supplement several other dishes.

2-inch (5-cm) section un-peeled cucumber

4 (¾ oz. / 25 g) soaked large whole white fungi

¾ oz. (25 g) bean sprouts (about ⅓ cup)

4 canned cherries

½ cup (125 ml) clear chicken stock

2 teaspoons rice wine
Pinch of salt
(Pinch of MSG)

1. Cut the cucumber section into quarters lengthwise, then cut each quarter into a fan shape.

2. After soaking the white fungi in lukewarm water for 3 hours, drain, then cut off and discard the stems and discolored parts. Place the fungi in a medium-size pot, add enough water to cover, heat, and boil for about 3 minutes. Remove from the water, drain, and place in a serving tureen..Arrange the bean sprouts over the fungi, then place a cherry on top of each fungus.

3. In a wok over a medium flame, heat the chicken stock, rice wine, and salt. When the stock boils, skim off the foam (and stir in the MSG). Pour this light broth over the fungi and bean sprouts, garnish with the cucumber "fans," and serve.

Steamed Turtle With Chicken Feet
Qingzheng yuanyu　　　清蒸元鱼

1 live soft-shell turtle,
(2 lb. / 1 kg)

10 chicken feet (13 oz. / 400 g)

1 tablespoon rice wine

3 cups (750 ml) clear
chicken stock

½ teaspoon salt
(Pinch of MSG)

1 tablespoon vegetable oil

2 tablespoons minced scallion

2 teaspoons minced peeled
fresh ginger

1 clove garlic, minced

10 dried black mushrooms,
soaked and stemmed

1¾ oz. (50 g) ham

1¾ oz. (50 g) bamboo shoots,
cut into thin slices

5 oz. (150 g) chicken breast,
minced

Pinch of ground black
pepper

This nutritious dish is from Jiangsu province on the North-eastern seacoast. Soft-shelled turtles are sold live in China's markets and some Chinese believe the flesh has curative properties. There are many ways to prepare the live turtle for the pot—one of which is described in step 1 of this recipe. Another technique is to treat it like a lobster by putting it into a pot of boiling water before cleaning it as described in step 1. Another, easier, solution would be to have a fishmonger clean it.

The second main ingredient in this dish, chicken feet, gives the soup a gelatinous consistency. The tendons become succulent and tender. The chicken feet are removed from the dish before it is served (but be sure to save them for another meal). Chicken feet can be bought from specialty stores or from Chinese poultry shops. They are delicious, entertaining to eat, and well worth the search.

1. To prepare the turtle, turn it upside down on the chopping board. Chop off the head at the base of the neck. Hold it up by the tail to drain the blood; rinse the turtle. Drop it first into boiling water, for 2 minutes, and then immerse in cold water. Press at the edge of the shell until the 16 bone ends pop up. Lift the shell and remove the fat and internal organs. Cut off the claws and tip of the tail. Rinse the turtle once more, then cut the meat into 1¼-inch (3-cm) squares. Place the squares in boiling water just long enough to scald them, getting rid of blood clots and odor. Put the turtle squares into a deep bowl or clay pot. Place this container in a steamer, with several inches of water at the bottom. Set aside.
2. Cook the chicken feet in boiling water to cover for 2 minutes. Drain and cool. Cut in two at the ankle joint.
3. Mix the rice wine, chicken stock, salt, (and MSG). Heat vegetable oil in a wok. Add the scallions, ginger, and garlic, and stir-fry briefly. Add the chicken stock mixture. Heat to boiling and skim off the froth. Strain to remove the scallion, ginger, and garlic.
4. Cut the mushrooms in half, and the ham into ¾-inch (2-cm) slices. Place mushrooms, ham, bamboo shoots, and chicken feet on top of the turtle squares. Pour the chicken stock mixture over the turtle. Cover the pot and steam for 2 hours or longer, until the turtle and chicken feet are tender, adding water to the steamer as needed. Remove the chicken feet. Place the turtle, mushrooms, ham, and bamboo shoots in a large soup bowl. Reserve the turtle soup.
5. Add 3 tablespoons water to the minced chicken and stir. Bring the reserved turtle soup to a boil in a wok. Add the minced chicken and stir. When the mixture is about to boil again, skim off the oil, froth, and residue of chicken meat; strain. Pour the remaining clear soup onto the turtle, sprinkle the black pepper, and serve.

Four Treasure Soup
Huiya sibao 烩鸭四宝

Although some of the main ingredients may be unfamiliar in the West and difficult to obtain without planning ahead and making special arrangements with a butcher, preparation is not difficult. Make the chicken and duck stock according to the recipe following the Ingredients Guide, but substitute duck for the pork bones.

Ginger root juice is made by peeling and mincing about two tablespoons of fresh root; squeeze it in a twist of fine-mesh cheesecloth, or a garlic press, into a bowl. Pour two teaspoons of water into the squeezed pulp and squeeze it again.

3¼ oz. (100 g) duck breast meat

1¾ oz. (50 g) duck tongue

1 duck's foot, with the web intact

5 oz. (150 g) duck pancreas

5 cups (1.25 L) clear chicken and duck stock

2 teaspoons soy sauce

½ teaspoon salt

Pinch of chopped coriander leaves

Pinch of minced peeled fresh ginger

5 teaspoons rice wine

(½ teaspoon Gourmet Powder)

1 tablespoon cornstarch paste

2 teaspoons vinegar

Pinch of ground black pepper

1 scallion, minced

2 teaspoons ginger juice

1 teaspoon sesame oil

1. Cook the duck breast meat, tongues, and foot in boiling water until each is tender. (The web on the foot will be the last to become tender.) Scald the pancreas with boiling water until soft. Cut the duck breast meat into 1-by-⅝-by-⅛-inch (2.5 x 1.5 x 0.3-cm) slices. Cut the tongues into ⅛-inch (0.3-cm) thick slices. Cut the pancreas into ¾-inch (2-cm) lengths. Remove the bones from the duck foot and cut the web into 3 pieces. Plunge all the duck pieces into boiling water, scald for a few seconds, then scoop them out.

2. In a wok over an intense flame, bring the duck pieces, the chicken and duck stock, 1 teaspoon soy sauce, and ¼ teaspoon salt to boiling. Scoop out all the pieces of duck and place them in a serving bowl. Sprinkle with the chopped coriander leaves and minced ginger, and set aside in a warm place.

3. Reheat the chicken and duck stock. Add the remaining soy sauce, salt, and the rice wine. Bring to boiling, then skim off the surface froth. Stir in the cornstarch paste (and the Gourmet Powder), then stir in the vinegar, pepper, scallion, ginger root juice, and sesame oil. Pour the thickened broth into the bowl containing the pieces of duck and serve.

Golden Fish Soup
Jinyu tang 金鱼汤

Pieces of fish fillet are decorated with cucumber and red pepper to look like live fish swimming in an aquarium. The fish are delicious, and the soup has a delicate flavor.

4 oz. (250 g) fish fillet

1/6 oz. (5 g) sweet red pepper

2 -inch (5-cm) section of cucumber

1/2 teaspoon salt

(Pinch of MSG)

1/4 teaspoon rice wine

4 egg whites

1/4 teaspoon cornstarch paste

3 cups (750 ml) chicken broth

3/4 teaspoon melted chicken fat

1. Cut fish fillet into 2-by-1-by-1/2-inch (5 × 2.5 × 1.5 cm) strips; trim corners of each strip to resemble a fish. Cut red pepper into circles, each about 1/4 inch (0.5 cm) in diameter (these will be fish "eyes"). Cut cucumber into thin slices and cut slashes in each, like a fan, to resemble a fish tail.

2. In a bowl, combine a pinch of salt (and MSG) with the rice wine and brush the fish strips with this mixture. Let stand for 5 minutes.

3. Make a batter by mixing the egg whites with the corn-starch paste and beat until frothy. Coat the fish pieces with this batter. Now assem-ble the pieces to resemble fish, using the red pepper pieces as eyes and the

cucumber slices as tails. Drop each "fish" into 140-158 F (60-70 C) degrees water to set. Continue to heat the water until the fish are cooked, about 1 minute; scoop out and chill in cold water.

4. Clean the wok and heat over an intense flame. Add the chicken broth, the re-maining salt, (and the MSG). Add the "golden fish," heat to boiling, skim off the froth, add the chicken fat and stir gently. Pour soup in a tureen and serve.

Recipe Listing by Beijing Restaurant and Regional Cuisine

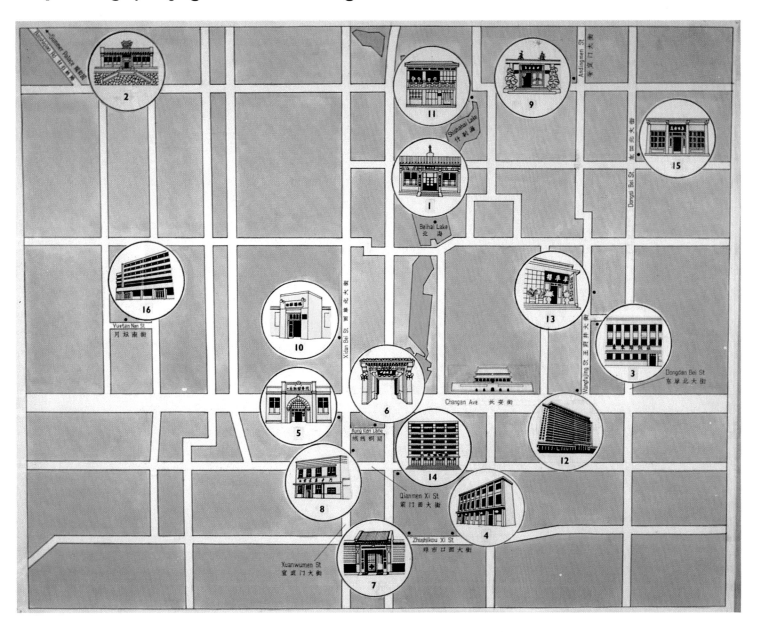

The master chefs who contributed recipes for this book preside over the sixteen restaurants on the following page. The names of their recipes are listed below the name, address and telephone number of each restaurant. Note the regional specialty of each.

For visitors to Beijing, the pictographic map of Beijing (above) shows where to find each restaurant. It pictures the facade and gives the name and approximate location of each. The number inside the circle, with the drawing of the facade, corresponds to the number given each restaurant in the listing. The street names on the map are given in both Chinese characters and romanized spellings to help the non-Chinese visitor find his or her way. (A guide to pronunciation of the romanized spellings is given for English speaking peoples on page 57).

When going to an eating house, go to one which is full of customers (because there everything is fresh, and you can always get what you want).
Chinese Proverb

1. Fangshan Restaurant
(Qing Court Cuisine)
Fangshan Fanzhuang
Bei Hai Park, Tel. 442573

Golden Coin Black Mushrooms
Stir-Fried Fish Fillets
Pork Tenderloin-Filled Dumplings
Fried Rolls in the Shape of
 Buddha's Hand
Scallop Balls Hydrangea
Pigeon Eggs in White Sauce
Sauteed Chicken Breasts in White
 Sauce
Stuffed Mandarin Fish
Buddhist Prawns
Red Shark's Fin
Venison with Black Mushrooms
 and Ham
Golden Fish Duck Webs
Consomme of White Fungi
Dragon Well Soup with Staghorn
 Fungus

2. Tingliguan Restaurant
(Court Cuisine)
Tingliguan
Summer Palace, Tel. 281926

Dragon and Phoenix Cold Dish
Shark's Fin in the Shape of a
 Citron
Longevity Quail
Delicately Fried Crab Legs
Dragon With Pearls
Palace Gate Fish
Maid Marrying Herself Off
White Fungi Wolfberry Soup
Beautiful Lady Marries Gifted
 Scholar
Moon and Flowers

3. Donglaishun Restaurant
(Beijing and Inner Mongolian
 Cuisine)
Donglaishun Fanzhuang
Dong Feng Market,
off Wang Fu Jing, Tel. 550069

Mongolian Hot Pot
Steamed Mandarin Fish
Velvet Chicken With White Fungi
Shashlik
Braised Lamb Slices

4. Fengzeyuan Restaurant
(Shandong Cuisine)
Fengzeyuan Fanzhuang
Zhushikou Xi St., Tel. 332828

Shark's Fin Casserole
Fried Five-Shred Roll
Jellyfish with Shredded Chicken
Swallow's Nest Soup
Scallops and Egg White
Shandong Roast Chicken Legs
Stir-Fried Abalone

Fish Hot Pot
Fried Prawn Balls
Dry Fried Bamboo Shoots
Braised Asparagus
Fried Quail

5. Tongchunyuan Restaurant
(Jiangsu and Shanghai Cuisine)
Tongchunyuan Fanzhuang
Xuan Wu Men St., Tel. 662115

Stuffed Crucian Carp
Deep-Fried Mandarin Fish
Stuffed Crabs
Walnut Pigeon Eggs
Fried Eels with Sauce
Green and White Fish Balls

6. Sichuan Restaurant
(Sichuan Cuisine)
Sichuan Fandian
Rong Xian Lane, Tel. 336356

Fish-Flavored Shredded Pork
Mrs. Pockmark's Bean Curd
Fried Bamboo Shoots
Home-Style Beef Tendon
Braised Prawns with Shell
Squid with Sizzling Rice
Duck Smoked with Camphor
 Leaves and Tea
Snow-White Walnut Dessert

7. Jinyang Restaurant
(Shanxi Cuisine)
Jinyang Fanzhuang
Zhushikou Xi St., Tel. 331669

Succulent Duck
Silkworm Cocoon Bean Curd
Butterfly Sea Cucumbers
White Fungi Peony Flowers
Winter Melon Balls With
 Mushrooms
Golden Fish Prawns
Deep-Fried Meats
Three Delicacies Hot Pot
Taiyuan-Style Braised Beef

8. Vegetarian Restaurant
(Absolutely meatless recipes)
Sucai Canting
Xuan Wu Men St., Tel. 334296

Deep-Fried "Sparrow Heads"
Stewed Mushrooms in White
 Sauce
"Chicken Liver" Rolls
Braised "Shark's Fin" in White
 Sauce
"Croaker" in Hot Sauce
Eight Treasure "Whole Duck"

9. Kangle Restaurant
(Fujian, Zhejiang,
 Jiangxi and Anhui Cuisine)
Kangle Canguan
An Ding Men St., Tel. 443884

Orchid Prawns
Sizzling Rice
Pickled Chicken Cubes
Crabs with "Chrysanthemum"
Phoenix-Tail Prawns
Stuffed Mushrooms
Grape-Cluster Fish
Steamed Turtle Soup
Jade-Like Soup
Peacock Spreads Its Tail
"Cross-the-Bridge" Noodles
Steam Pot Chicken
Fried Fish Slices

10. Quyuan Restaurant
(Hunnan Cuisine)
Quyuan Jiulou
Xi Dan Bei St., Tel. 661414

Litchi Squid
Dongan Chicken
Braised Soft-Shelled Turtle
Scallops with Two-Colored Eggs
Stuffed White Fungi
Fried Toast

11. Ji—Roast Meat Restaurant
(Beijing Cuisine)
Kaorou Ji
Shi Sha Hai Lake, Tel. 445921

Grilled lamb
Ruyi Prawns
Gansu Duck
Beef Steak
Sweeter Than Honey
Tomato Shrimp Cakes
Fried Chicken Shisk Kabob
Assorted Vegetables
Almond Float
Golden Fish Soup
Assorted Cold Dishes

12. Beijing Hotel (Beijing Tan
 Family/Guangdong Cuisine)
Beijing Fandian
Chang An Ave., Tel. 552231

Chicken with Straw Mushrooms
Bundled Duck
Sunflower Pork
Braised Mushrooms
Almond Tea
Chicken in Oyster Sauce
Curry Chicken
Fish Balls in Fruit Sauce
Stir-Fried Fish
Slab Bacon with Fermented
 Bean Curd
Peanut Cream

13. Cuihualou Restaurant
(Eastern Shandong Cuisine)
Cuihualou Fanzhuang
Wang Fu Jing St., Tel. 554581

Sauteed Chicken with Walnuts
Grilled Chicken Legs with
 Romaine Lettuce
Fried Squid Rolls
Jade-Like Velvet Chicken with
 Water Chestnuts
Pigeon Egg "Elephant Eyes"
Stir-Fried Pork Tenderloins with
 Coriander
Crispy Prawns
Hot Candied Apple
Snow-White Chicken, Prawn, and
 Bamboo Shoot Soup
"Goldfish and Lotus"
 —An Assorted Cold Dish

**14. Quanjude Beijing Duck
 Restaurant** (Beijing Cuisine)
Quanjude Kaoyadian
Qian Men Xi St., Tel. 338031

Beijing Roast Duck
Bejing Duck—Western Style
Thin Pancakes for Duck
Sweet Bean Paste Sauce
Beijing Duck Rolls
Duck Hearts Maotai
Four Treasure Soup
Fried Duck Gizzard and Liver

15. Senlong Restaurant
(Jiangsu and Shanghai Cuisine)
Senlong Fanzhuang
Dongsi Bei St., Tel. 442610

Frog-Shaped Chicken
Braised Shrimp
Braised Fish Maw with Ham and
 Bamboo Shoots
Coin-Shaped Shrimp Cakes
Fried Eel Strips
Fried Bamboo Shoots

16. Henan Restaurant
(Henan Cuisine)
Henan Fanzhuang
Yue Tan Nan St., Tel. 866313

Pine Cone Carp
Stuffed Black Mushrooms
Two-In-One Shrimp
Sweet and Sour Fish "Tiles"
 and Baked Noodles
Bird's Nest Rolls
Skillet-Baked Souffle
Tian Dan Recovering the
 Qi Territory
Daokou Fried Chicken
Honeyed Gourds

The Index

Men eat the flesh of grass-fed and grain-fed animals, deer eat grass, centipedes find snakes tasty, and hawks and falcons relish mice. Of these four, which knows how food ought to taste?

Wang Ni

To make the best rice, Li Yu (Ching dynasty cooking writer) would send his maid to gather the dew from the flowers of the wild rose, the cassia, or the citron and would add this to the water at the last minute; dew from garden roses, however, was too strong in flavor, felt Li, and could not be recommended.

Yüan Mei

240